Make Your Movie

What You Need to Know About the Business and Politics of Filmmaking

Make Your Movie

What You Need to Know About the Business and Politics of Filmmaking

Barbara Freedman Doyle

Focal Press
Taylor & Francis Group
NEW YORK AND LONDON

First published 2012

This edition published 2015 by Focal Press
70 Blanchard Road, Suite 402, Burlington, MA 01803

and by Focal Press
2 Park Square, Milton Park, Abingdon, Oxon OX14 4RN

Focal Press is an imprint of the Taylor & Francis Group, an informa business

Library of Congress Cataloging-in-Publication Data
Application submitted

British Library Cataloguing-in-Publication Data
A catalogue record for this book is available from the British Library.

ISBN-13: 978-0-240-82155-9 (pbk)

Acknowledgements

Thanks to all the friends and colleagues at Chapman and the cheerleaders who helped to make this happen.

And for their patience and invaluable contributions, in order of appearance:

Andy Horwitz
Allison Ewart
Priscilla Elliott
Cornelius Uliano
Bryan Schulz
Harry Ufland
Brent Lilley
Robert Kaplan
Michael Shoob
Walter Coblenz
Travis Knox
Jawal Nga
Shana Feste
Jacob Chase
Christopher Cronyn
Linda Montanti
Paul Seydor
Dawn Taubin
Russell Schwartz
Pat Quinn
Ted Mundorff
Derek Horne

Special thanks to Jeff Lancaster and to all my students, past, present, and future.

Extra special thanks to Ray, who listened and continues to listen to it all. And of course to Seamus and Murphy.

Contents

Section II
Production: No Such Thing as a Free Lunch

Introduction

What You Should Know . . . and Why You Need to Know It

Make Your Movie is a practical guide to navigating the complex and confusing business and politics of the film industry. You may be a film school grad or someone who's known what you wanted to do since you got that video camera for Christmas or since you saw *Star Wars*. You've read the books, attended the workshops, made the 20-minute short, maybe submitted it and been accepted into a festival, and you're ready to make a feature. You have confidence in your skill. You've written or found a story. You have a script. The characters are original. The setup is unique. All you need is the money, the cast, and the opportunity. You've made it your business to understand how to make a movie. The question you now have to ask yourself is, do you understand the business of how to get a movie made?

The creative process is challenging—the stuff of sleepless nights, shaping an outline or pieces of dialogue to make your script sharper, funnier, more real. You wrestle over a plot point or a motivation, you develop a character, and you sweat to perfect a scene until you're sure it's playing just right. It's a struggle, but it's exciting and invigorating and often—let's face it—it's fun, because it's a job that you want to do. You are dedicated to the idea of getting your movie made.

OR . . . You're a creative problem-solver, a people person, someone who wants to find a great story and get it out there. You aren't a writer or director, but your strength is organization, and leading a team. You've always been able to mediate between your friends, your family, and everyone looks to you to help make things happen. You are a filmmaker, but rather than being hands-on and making your own film, your talent and acumen for putting people and projects together might lead you to help a film—or several films—get cast, financed, distributed, and promoted. Maybe you'll end up at a production company, a management company, or a studio. You want to make a career of working in a pivotal position in the Industry, to be someone who in some way influences the life of a movie.

No matter your exact goal, the problem is this: you want to make movies that will be seen outside of your living room and appreciated by an audience beyond your friends and family. You would like your work to be seen at art houses or multiplexes or on TV, not just online. You need the resources to make the kind of film that made you want to make films. That usually means money. You the filmmaker must be not only a creative person in a world of business people, but you must be the kind of artist that a business person—an industry person—will want to trust with his or her investment of time, effort, and money. You must find a way to convince the people with the money and the experience to hop onto your bandwagon and not someone else's.

The process of getting a movie made—searching out and assembling the best cast, the best team, the best distribution, getting those butts in the seats, and coming up with the way to make the best film possible with the resources available—can be prolonged and convoluted. The fundraising, the pitches, the meetings—so many meetings! meetings with development executives, creative executives, production executives, managers, agents, lawyers, union reps, completion guarantors, meetings with all the people who have the power to help you or to stop you from moving ahead—that process can be manageable, or heartbreaking, exciting or brutal, your personal black hole. Usually it's all those things at once.

And the business is changing. Many of the old rules don't apply. Digital technology, new audience expectations, and the economic climate have changed everything. The people with the money and the power—the studios, production companies, and agencies—are all asking the question "what's next?" You want the chance to give them the answer.

This book is not about the artistic or technical aspects of filmmaking, it's an overview, a guide to understanding the business part of the film industry for people who are not businessmen. *Make Your Movie* is about how to work with people in the film industry—about who they are, what they do, and what they want. It's about how to become one of them, if that's the road you'd like to take. They are the people who finance, invest, produce, package, market, and distribute movies. They can green-light a project, tell you how long it's going to take to shoot, how much it's going to cost, whether or not you should go union, and if you do, how that will change the way you make the movie. They can sometimes tell you in advance how much money your film will make. They are the vendors, the bond guys, the insurance companies, the attorneys, the exhibitors, and even your production crew. You know what you're worried about—getting your first chance. You know you'll succeed as long as you get up to bat. But unless you have a feel for why they worry and for what all those meetings are about, you probably won't have the opportunity. You must acquire the soft skills involved in getting started and gain a sense of the etiquette of the Industry, so when you do get your chance you don't blow it.

Here is a list of some of the positions I've held: line producer, unit manager, and production supervisor on feature films (studio and independent), made-for-television movies, documentaries, commercials, and industrials. I've also been a production associate, production coordinator, reader, and consultant. I've been associate dean of production at the American Film Institute, a chair in the Film Department of Brooks Institute of Photography, a guest lecturer at various college and university film programs, a panelist at film festivals, and now I'm a chair and professor at Chapman University's Dodge College of Film and Media Arts. In one way or another, my career has been spent making movies or helping people to get their movies made.

For the past twenty years I have been fortunate enough to work with filmmakers at all levels of success, from Academy Award nominees and winners to interns. Listening to them, working on films, and working with students has taught me that you have to pay as much attention to what is going on beneath the surface as to what is going on in front of you.

It's important to focus on your craft with all your energy and talent, but it is also imperative that you realize that in a high-stakes, personality-driven, high-visibility business, you have to watch and listen, ask the right people the right questions, know when it's personal and when it's not, and develop an instinct about the dance that goes on between the two.

Section I

First Steps (Before You Even *Think* of Shooting)

Chapter 1

About You

Filmmakers, by nature, are dreamers and communicators. More than the need to have a stable income, health insurance, or a pension, a filmmaker feels compelled to tell stories, to use a camera to find a new universe, or to explore the old universe in a new way. Whether you are an aspiring screenwriter, producer, director, cinematographer, editor, production designer, story editor, development person, or production executive, there is a reason you have decided that you want to work on movies more than you want security. Your friends and family may support your ambition—or not. You may care what they think in an abstract way, but you're not about to be shifted off course from doing what you want to do. You don't want to be difficult, but you're sure you've found the thing you need, the thing you care about doing more than anything else. You've found your passion.

Passion is a word you'll hear used over and over to explain and describe what it takes to work in the film industry. Passion is determination, and guts, and love. Any one of the three is not enough. You MUST feel passion in order to want to stick with a process that can be demeaning and demoralizing.

Filmmakers often pass through a series of stages:

First there is The Dream—I Love Film, I Will Make Films.
Then The Pep Talk—I'm Talented; Everyone Agrees that I'm Talented

After a while . . .

Loss of Confidence—Maybe It's *Not* Just About Talent.
And Anger—Who Do These People Think They Are Anyway?

This is the stage when many people decide that they'd better do something less random and more pleasant for a living. If that feels OK to you, you should stop reading right here and figure out what else you'd like to do. You will save yourself uncertainty and pain. Every producer, director, and screenwriter I know has stated about making a film, "If you can imagine being happy doing something else, do it!"

If you can't imagine being happy doing something else, stay with me for the final stage: the Realization. By the time a filmmaker has reached Realization, he or she is usually a little beat up and a lot less idealistic. The realization is, there's no secret handshake, there's just figuring out the way things work.

Make Your Movie: What You Need to Know About the Business and Politics of Filmmaking.

It's about art, but it's also about money and politics. The filmmaker who has no sense of the politics of the industry is a soldier marching into battle with no armor. The cause may be noble, but he or she is going to get hurt.

Understanding the business will not get you the keys to the kingdom. Success in the film business is about talent, perseverance, timing, and luck. A sense of the way the business works will not make you a better filmmaker—a lot of it *is* about talent. But talent alone will probably not get you where you want to go. Understanding the way things work can give you a road map, a way to remain sane in the midst of a seemingly insane world.

Thanks to new technology, these days it is possible to make a film anywhere in the world. You can rent a camera (film or digital), gather up some actors, and mount a production without ever leaving home. That's probably not quite what you had in mind, though. If you want to make a feature that gets distributed, and that will be the breakout project that paves your path to making more features, you will most likely have to relocate to a film center—in the U.S. that means Los Angeles or New York. Unlike writing a book or composing music, the making of a film is not a solitary experience. You must work with other people at every stage. You will have to learn to effectively present yourself and your ideas, to instill confidence in those who have far more know-how than you do, to rely on other people (some of whom you would never in a million years choose as friends), and to compete with established filmmakers. All of this just to have your work viewed, hopefully admired, and definitely critiqued by strangers.

Making a film is a commitment. It takes a special sort of discipline to resolve to do something very difficult with the possibility that there may never be a reward. In other types of work, if you hang in there long enough there is usually some promise of success. But there is no guarantee that you will ever make your movie. You must be the kind of person who can get out of bed every morning knowing that you will face indifference and rejection and still be ready to make the calls, shake the hands, and pitch your story again and again. Skillfully. With enthusiasm.

The actual shooting of a movie can take from just three weeks to several months, with several months after that spent in postproduction. But it can take *years* to find material, develop or write a script, raise funds, get people on board, and cast actors who will add something to the *distribut-ability* (not a word, but an extremely important concept) of your project. It can take even longer to make people aware of the project once it's completed, and to get the finished project in front of people. It's an endurance test with lots of talking and pushing while trying not to seem as if you're pushing.

If you have a hard time dealing with difficult people, or you're someone who does not work well with others, you will have an especially tough time with the process. Despite the stories of filmmakers who finance their projects via their own credit cards, most people in the industry believe that you should not invest in your own movie. Your investment will be time—not only the time spent putting together your project, persuading, and cajoling, but the time spent finding a way to earn an income that won't keep you from doing your primary job,which is getting the movie made. You will likely be spending time doing work you don't enjoy to support your basic needs of food and rent. If this is something you don't think you can do and you're not independently wealthy, then we're back to the Passion thing. It's not that you aren't talented, and it's not that you don't care about your film, it may simply be that you won't last.

As this book moves through the stages and people involved in the business of filmmaking, I'll be addressing the changing politics of the people and the language—*politics* meaning the way things work between people in the industry, who needs who in order to move ahead and survive, the pecking order, and the management of those relationships to your advantage. It's crucial that you know who has the power and that you gain a sense of how and if you can fit in. As for the language, understanding the language of the industry is important for the same reason you hire a guide or translator or buy a phrase book when you travel to a foreign country. You don't want to sound as if you studied issues of *Variety*. In fact, you probably shouldn't use any industry buzzwords at all at this stage—you may sound like a poseur. But you should understand what people are talking about before you're in a meeting and they're talking about *you*.

Chapter 2

Who Are These People, and What Do They Do?

IT'S EASIER TO SAY NO

Every job in the movie business is about finding and securing material and talent (***creative elements***) for a project; securing funding, and supervising the creative, logistical, and financial execution of the project; finding a way to get the finished project in front of an audience *or* finding a way to get an audience in front of the project. Depending upon the exact title of the executive, the responsibilities vary but in general all the jobs are there to support or lead the process of development, funding, preproduction, production, postproduction, sales, distribution, marketing, or publicity.

The Players

Studios are publicly owned entities. Almost anyone can call a stockbroker, put down some cash, and buy a very tiny share of the corporation that owns Universal or Fox. As a stockholder, you want your investment to make money. The Board of Directors of the corporations that own the studios know that if a film costs $100 million to make, it must show a profit of two and a half to three times the investment, otherwise the studio and the stockholders won't make money. (This two and half to three times the production budget formula is in part because the cost of effectively marketing and distributing a film is so high). If the studio doesn't make money, the shareholders don't make money. The president of production loses his or her position and sometimes the other executives are out of a job when the new president arrives, because that person wants to be surrounded by his or her own people. The "business" of the parent corporations is not only movies: Universal is NBC Universal, Warner Bros. is part of Time Warner, Disney is Disney/ABC, Paramount is part of Viacom, 20th Century Fox is owned by News Corporation, and Sony Pictures Entertainment is owned by Sony, the electronics corporation. For some of the stockholders in these entertainment conglomerates, movies are just a single aspect of a complex web of media investment and no one invests their money intending to lose it. Critical acclaim is nice but the dollar is king.

The dilemma of the studio executive is that the shelf life of his or her position is extremely limited. A few bad calls and he or she is out of the game. The probability of maintaining an executive position at the same studio or major production company for several years is so low that experienced executives have their lawyers negotiate their "exit packages" as part of their arrival signing and bonus contracts. The job is fraught with peril. No matter how much the production executive might love your project, if it's going to be a hard sell it will be an uphill battle. Nobody wants to spend the time and energy it takes to shepherd a project that won't get made, or worse, to get a project made that no one wants to see. The easiest response to a project is a *Pass,* which means No. Executive compensation (paychecks and bonuses) is lavish by ordinary standards, and so is the lifestyle that kind of compensation affords. Why risk it to make a movie just because you think it *might* be good? Then there are the ***perks*** (short for *perquisites*). These are the bonus benefits, like tickets to playoff games, traveling first class, the right tables at the best restaurants. Why give them up if you can avoid it? Few films are profitable. An entire career can be built by someone who consistently rejects almost all pitches, scripts, or acquisitions. Pass, and the risk is minimal.

Of course there is always the possibility that the project will be picked up by another company and become a smash hit. That's another kind of risk, and it's happened. *Home Alone* was passed on by Warner Bros., made by Fox, and ended up with ticket sales topping $534 million and a series of sequels. *My Big Fat Greek Wedding* was an independent film that struggled to find financing for a $5 million budget and eventually earned $369 million. *Slumdog Millionaire* almost didn't get made at all. But $362 million later, the film was a runaway hit and won eight Oscars, including Best Picture.

HOW IT WAS

In general, when people refer to a studio, they're speaking of *the majors,* or the big six: Universal, Warner Bros., Paramount, Fox, Sony, Disney. As recently as ten years ago, many studios did it all—developed projects (generated ideas, optioned material, closely supervised the script drafts), packaged them (put together the talent that would make the project viable), produced them (sometimes on their own back lots, so there was even money to be made as the cash simply moved from one area of the studio to another), then marketed and distributed them.

To supplement this internal development and production of material, they also contracted out. Studios had ongoing deals with producers and production companies who took on some of the responsibilities listed above, so that although the studios funded and distributed the films, not all the work was done directly by studio personnel. There were companies with *housekeeping deals.* A producer was given an office on the studio lot, the studio covered some or all of the producer's expenses, and the producer was expected to find, develop, and produce the product—the movies. The studio would finance part or all of the budget, would market and distribute the film, and would profit from the investment. An executive from the studio would work with the producers so there would be an "inside" representative watching out for the studio's interests.

Additionally, studio executives met with producers and agents with whom they did not have deals but "relationships" and who consistently brought them projects for consideration. When industry money was difficult to find, the studios found outside investment and venture capital groups who raised production money. Finally, on rare occasions, the studios partnered. *Titanic* was financed and distributed by both 20th Century Fox and Paramount. The two competitors shared the risks and the rewards.

The bottom-line intention of all of these machinations was to acquire the best, most commercial material; to gain access to the most talented and commercial creative elements (stars, directors); and to offset costs and minimize loss.

After several very tough years, the people who ran the studios and who answered to the board of directors and the stockholders looked at the direction the business was headed. They made changes that had an immense impact on the way the studios now do business.

Great reviews are nice. Thumbs up and good word of mouth used to sell tickets, and occasionally word of mouth can still send a movie's earnings skyrocketing. But now if moviegoers don't buy tickets the first weekend that the film is released, it is unlikely that the film will be a big moneymaker. These days as audiences leave the theatre, they are posting and tweeting. We are a wired society, and word of a bad—or a great—movie makes its way around the world at warp speed. There isn't time to build word of mouth. Now usually word of mouth is there early—the results of previews, festival success, or industry buzz—or not at all. In general, if the audience isn't in line the first weekend, it's not coming. Audience power is now instantaneous. It's difficult to save a film from a bad opening weekend. Occasionally a film will be rescued from certain death, but it's unusual.

It's necessary to have a strong first weekend in order for a film to succeed at the box office.

The studio overhead—the cost of keeping the studio running with personnel, facilities, and equipment—was extremely high.

There is more investment in the physical real estate of the lots now, in facilities that can be rented out to outside productions at a premium, and in general there is more emphasis on ways to offset expenses. If you're Universal Studios and the Universal Tour is a bigger moneymaker than most of your films, then you're going to take a hard look at your priorities. Those sound stages? When they're not being used for shooting, they're rental spaces for parties and events.

When producers develop their own projects *then* bring the projects to studios for financing and distribution, the studio doesn't have to foot the bill for the development stage. The result of the development process for a project might be a notable script or it might not. Rather than the studio putting money behind something at the idea stage, an actual script is tangible and easier to evaluate. The more the studio knows about a project, the less chance of an unpleasant surprise. In other words, the less risk involved.

In-house production and development deals were expensive. There were usually at least three sets of salaries and benefits to be paid—one to the producer, one to a development person, and a small salary for an assistant. Plus there were offices and expenses. But there was no evidence that housekeeping deals yielded scripts or films that were more successful than the already completed scripts that were brought to the studios. In-house deals often ran two or three years and yielded no projects at all. Sometimes there were *first look deals*, which meant that the studio would cover the producers' expenses and get first dibs on whatever resulted. But if the "sponsoring" studio didn't like the project, the producer was free to bring it elsewhere. Imagine supporting a producer and his or her staff for three years to the tune of more than a couple of hundred thousand dollars a year, only to have that same producer bring the picture to a competing company—and imagine if it becomes a hit. Not only a loss of the investment but embarrassing too.

Studios now develop few projects in house and spend more on outside projects that are further along than the idea stage. Most housekeeping deals have been discarded. There is a heavy reliance on relationships with filmmakers outside the studio who have ongoing deals with individual studios to create and then submit a steady stream of potential material.

The expectation of a studio used to be that a film would make money in several ways (***revenue streams***). One stream was ticket sales (box office). Another was domestic (U.S.) cable and network television sales. A film could be sold to foreign territories (international distribution) for screening in theatres and television sales. Some films that weren't hits in the United States found audiences elsewhere. It was also very possible that a film could not do well at the box office but could do well in the home video and DVD rental market. Another revenue stream was merchandising—soundtracks, book spin-offs, T-shirts, the toy, cereal, and tie-in deals. The targeted consumers for merchandising products and tie-ins are young kids and teenagers.

Now cable and network television are still around, but there is less demand as other entertainment options (the internet, gaming, etc.) have shrunk the size of the TV viewing audience. The development of digital downloads and streaming video has reduced the DVD sales and rental revenue stream and it is expected to dwindle further. But merchandising is still a major source of profit. After the merchandising mega successes for big action/fantasy films, the studios view merchandising possibilities as a fairly essential component in moving ahead with bigger budget films.

Cut to 2012. The ways that studios look at recouping investments has changed, so the type and number of films the studios invest in have changed.

Rather than spread resources thin by covering the production of several films per year, studios are making fewer films. The demographic (the age, sex, ethnicity, education level) of the movie viewer has changed. It is increasingly difficult to get people out of their apartments and houses.

We're watching films in different ways.

Who hasn't watched a movie on their laptop? Who hasn't at least thought of ordering a movie through Pay Per View (PPV) or Video On Demand (VOD)? Remember trying to decide whether to see a movie in the theatre or wait until it was available on DVD? Or when the thought of seeing a movie on a cell phone was pretty funny? Now there is the shrinking ***release window***—the time between when a film is released in the theatres and when it is released on PPV or VOD and even DVD. Normally, a studio film would have a theatrical release, then a few months later it would be released for DVD sales and rentals, and finally to network television. The market and enthusiasm for the theatrical release would feed the DVD and network audience. But it's expensive to release a film theatrically. In order to justify theatrical distribution, there had to be the sense that a theatrical distribution would be worth it. When films were judged to be lacking the potential to do well at the box office, they often did not receive theatrical distribution. Instead they went ***direct to video***. These films could still earn a profit. Audiences began to feel that their home theatres were more comfortable and convenient and sometimes more economical than finding a babysitter, driving to the multiplex, and having to schedule their movie viewing.

Studios aren't making many original character-driven dramas for the thirty and older crowd. They may do well on the East and West Coast, but they don't often make the profits that big, plot-driven action films make, either domestically or internationally. Older audiences don't run to see a film the first weekend it's out. This audience is staying home with the kids, or working long hours to finance their more expensive lifestyle. They see films but not in the crowds that the 18-to-25-year-olds do—they are not crucial to the theatrical run of a movie.

Eighteen-to-twenty-five-year-olds and kids see the most movies, so studios are making films for them.

These are expensive fantasy and action films derived from already established material—comic books, graphic novels, bestsellers, even games. Individual ticket prices are up, which helps to make up for the older audiences who are staying home more. Studios are placing their bets on ***tent pole*** films—these are event movies, buoyed by extremely high-dollar marketing campaigns. It is expected that audience awareness will push profits high enough to support the rest of the year's films. These types of films (*Spiderman*, *Men in Black*, etc.) become ***franchises***. They can be spun off into at least one and in some cases several sequels. IMAX and 3D have also helped this kind of movie. As newer technology becomes part of selling the idea of a special experience that audiences want and are willing to pay extra to see on the big screen, 3D and IMAX have magnified the excitement.

At the other end of the spectrum, studios are desperately trying to find a way to make money using the Web, through downloads and Web programs. As most of the studios are in some way tied in to television, and television depends upon sponsorship (ads) or subscription (premium cable), they are concerned about the development of Web TV and other new platforms. When you can DVR your way through commercials, then ad revenue decreases. When sponsors are not sure when the program is really airing (as opposed to a scheduled air time), they aren't certain of their demographic and tend to be more cautious in terms of spending money for commercial time. When a chunk of prime consumers (18-to-35-year-olds) are watching programming on their computer, and even on their phones, the traditional models of how to make a profit don't quite work.

Traditionally, the movie business thrives during economic depressions and recessions. During the recent recession, though, that didn't happen.

The industry was hit almost as hard as other business. There were massive layoffs and contracts were not renewed. Agencies trimmed their client lists and concentrated on the superstars and the potential superstars. This resulted in the production of fewer films but with more of the proven (less risky) elements that tend to ensure commercial success—remakes and adaptations, and established producers, directors, and stars.

With all this, there continue to be real concerns about the changing technologies available and the changing moods of the movie-going public.

Films made by major directors with major stars are failing (*State of Play*). Studio executives are surprised when a film they expected to do good business becomes a massive hit (*The Blind Side*). They rush to second-guess and explain these unprecedented successes and failures to each other, and to the press—"People are tired of politics and war"; "People want hope and inspiration." But why didn't they know that ahead of time?

The truth is that our tastes morph faster than ever, and we have a shorter attention span. For studios, the ability to predict what will resonate two years down the line is all important.

It can easily take a full two years from the moment production on a movie is *green lit* to when it comes out in the theatres. If the audience is going to be full of surprises, how can strategic decisions be made? Studios can't turn on a dime. Even when a studio acquires a finished independently made film, there is insecurity about how to market and distribute it.

And there is yet more competition.

There are the *mini-majors,* for example: DreamWorks, Summit Entertainment, Relativity Media. These companies are run like studios, but they do not have the overhead costs of the big six because they have no physical lot and not as many employees. They are smaller, and they can react and make decisions more quickly. They can take on just a little more risk.

And what about independent films?

Many of the films we think of as independent were actually financed and produced by the studios or by companies collaborating very closely with the studios. Until fairly recently, most studios even had a ***specialty*** (independent) division, and they acquired festival films looking for distribution. Executives flocked to the Sundance Film Festival. There were bidding wars. It was an exciting avenue for young up-and-coming filmmakers. After a while studios began producing their own independent-style films. But now most of those independent divisions have closed, in part because producing small, personal, character-driven films is not what the corporate-run studios of today do best. Studios are not set up to devote the time to develop or produce lower-budget, edgy productions, and there is not usually enough profit to warrant the manpower involved. Many of the independent divisions failed because of too many incorrect choices and not enough income. Now studios have taken a step back from actually financing and producing independent films, although they do acquire, market, and distribute them.

The studios are not happy. The executives are scared. No one feels that they really have a handle on where the money is to be made. They aren't sure where to place their bets because the game is constantly changing.

HOW IT IS NOW

The production of fewer films but with more of the "proven" elements that tend to ensure commercial success.

The studios are making the kind of films that justify higher ticket prices to make up for diminishing theatre-going audiences, the more spectacular the better, in order to capture first weekend box office. Studios may distribute a smaller, more niche film, but the film will probably be developed and financed in part outside of the studio system.

In an attempt to maximize profit the window for a film's theatrical release has been shortened—sometimes by months. This year the discussion is about distributing films by the "Day and Date" route—Day and Date means that a film is released for a premium price the same day it's released in the theatres. And all the big guys are worrying about "monetization"—finding a way to make money and protect investments in a digital world.

Social developments and innovations—the changing expectations and interests of audiences and the costs of failure have caused upheavals for a business that was comfortable sticking to a formula.

WHAT DOES THIS ALL MEAN FOR YOU?

The good news is that all the changes in the industry have created an exciting climate for people like you. Bad news for the established players and the way things were means great news for people who are young, have original ideas and creative voices, and aren't afraid to take chances. The studio executives and the investors and the old-school Industry veterans are smart enough to know that they *don't* know, and they're out looking for creative solutions. For you, this time of upheaval can be an opportunity. You just have to learn the rules, learn how to work with them and around them, and then figure out which of them can be broken.

Chapter 3

It's a Small World After All

IF IT'S ABOUT WHO YOU KNOW AND YOU DON'T KNOW ANYBODY, WHAT DO YOU DO?

You have probably studied film and seen as many significant films as possible. You have also gone to the library or bookstore and read the books and plays and history upon which some of those films are based. (If you haven't, now is the time to do that.) If you see an interview with a filmmaker whose work you admire and he or she mentions a book, a film, or a piece of art, you should check it out. Most filmmakers—directors and writers especially—feel that in addition to knowing about film you must also know about art, history, philosophy, psychology, literature, politics. The days of someone making a film that is purely an *homage* to other films she has seen are over. You must have a broad base of life and knowledge in order to bring something new to the cinematic table.

More practically speaking, if you are a well-rounded albeit focused person rather than a one-track obsessed one, you will be happier. You don't have to search out isolation and pain to make films. It will find you soon enough. Don't lock yourself in; don't close yourself off from people and shun things that are not involved with film. First, your life will be lonely and miserable. Second, the more perspective you have, the more you will be able to cope with the struggle ahead. It will smooth away the rough edges of desperation. Desperation is death in the film industry, and people can smell it a mile away. So get a life. And realize that most first films that do well these days are quirky and reflective of the filmmaker's uniquely personal take on life. That's what makes them interesting.

WHY CONTACTS ARE SUCH A BIG DEAL

How many times have you heard it said that he (or she) is *connected*? You should know that being connected only means only that he knows people, or knows people who know people, who can help them. It doesn't mean that the person is any more important than you are. The connection may just mean that she is the niece or cousin of a bigwig, or that there is some vague business or school or hometown relationship. Being connected is a shortcut. It makes things easier. It's helpful when there's a buddy or an Aunt Jen who is savvy in the ways of whatever road you're about to go down and they're looking out for you. Before you disdain or discount the concept of connections or that much repeated term "networking," take a minute and think about how important these may be and why.

If you want to be a lawyer, you go to law school. Once you graduate, you study for and presumably pass the Bar exam and ultimately you practice law. If you want to be in finance, you get your MBA, and it can be assumed by corporate recruiters that at minimum you have the basic know-how to make economically prudent decisions. If you want to teach, you get a teaching certificate; if you want to practice medicine, etc. Shifting away from the professions it's even more cut and dried. Building contractors must be licensed. Police officers and firefighters go through training and many wash out. In other words, there is an assumed basic skill set that you must have, and there is a qualifying certification required.

Every day hundreds of people arrive in Los Angeles with the intention of making movies. Film studios and production companies receive piles of script submissions and resumes. But there is no qualifying certification. It's like going on a date with someone you met through the Internet. They seem OK, but how can you really know? Anyone can say, "I'm a director/producer/screenwriter." You may be articulate, brilliant, and talented, but how can you prove you have a real and singular vision? You may be great with people, have wonderful taste and ideas, be a terrific problem-solver, but how can they (remember who "they" are) be sure you can produce? On the basis of your track record? Great, if you have one. But someone starting out doesn't. Your short film or school experience may give them a clue, but not really. In these days of layoffs and cutbacks no one wants to make an expensive mistake. They have to be certain that they're betting on the right horse.

These people are busy. They're under extreme pressure. They don't have the time to have a cup of coffee and guess at your potential. They can't give everyone just a few minutes, or there would be no time left for them to do anything else. So relationships and referrals are important. They serve as a filter. They lend you that minimum certification. And once someone does a favor for a friend by meeting you, they will be able to ask a favor in return. That's politics.

Most people starting out in film don't come conveniently equipped with connections and are pretty much on their own. So what can you do?

HOW TO BEGIN NETWORKING (MEETING PEOPLE)

Tell everyone you know your plan.

You are moving to Los Angeles to get your start in the film business. Is it possible that they know anyone you might call for advice once you get there? You'll be surprised by how many people have an old roommate working at a studio, or who is a friend of a manager, or *something*. Entertainment is a major industry in Los Angeles, and there are lots of people directly and indirectly involved. For several years, I rented an apartment in a very ordinary building in Santa Monica, California. There were eleven tenants. Eight of them worked in film, television, or music. When after several years I bought a house in a completely different neighborhood, the guy down the street was a location manager, a neighbor on one side of me worked on a TV show, and the one across the street was a freelancer working on commercials. A Director of Photography and a screenwriter shared a house around the corner. Los Angeles is like a factory town. Certain neighborhoods are overflowing with people who support the industry.

NEVER use someone's name without asking permission first. If they seem hesitant when you ask, don't do it.

They may not feel comfortable for reasons that have nothing to do with you—or maybe even reasons that *are* because of you. Either way, unless they are happy to help you make the contact, don't do it. If they agree to help, let them set it up in their own way. They are doing you a favor. If the contact is not responsive, try once more then let it go. If the contact is willing to speak with you or answer your email, don't take up too much time—don't write epic emails. In the words of a friend of mine who agreed to take a call from a friend of a friend then lived to regret it, "I said I'd talk to the kid, not adopt him."

Is there a film festival in a city near you?

Most festivals bring industry professionals in to speak. Festivals use volunteers. Usually in exchange for your unpaid assistance, you can attend as many panels and workshops as can fit around your work schedule. You will make the acquaintance of people who might be willing to give you advice. The filmmakers at smaller festivals are sometimes willing to spend time speaking with you, which is something they might not do on their home turf or at a bigger festival where they are too busy. A director on a panel at a secondary festival (more about those later) told me once that since the organizers of the event treated him so well, he felt that he should make himself accessible to the festival-goers. I saw him speaking to a bunch of students from the local junior college. Had they met him at Sundance, it wouldn't have happened. Use your local festival to practice and immerse yourself in the language and feel of the industry, so that by the time you're ready to transplant yourself to L.A. or New York you'll be more accomplished at sorting out the real guys from the fakes.

When a panelist at a festival mentions a film to watch or a book to read, do it!

If you're going to be attending a festival and you don't know the work of the panelists, familiarize yourself with their work ahead of time. What they say on the panel, or in the green room if you are able to meet them, will make more sense if you know what they've done. You don't have to have a one-on-one conversation with someone to pick up valuable information. If by chance you do end up in a conversation, it helps to understand someone's body of work.

They will expect you to know about the obvious films, and they will be pleased when you know about their more obscure work. It shows that you are thorough and that you do your homework. This kind of research—seeing the films and reading the interviews, not just stopping at the imdb.com credits list—should quickly become a valuable career-long habit. You can bet that when you are about to have any sort of important meeting with an industry figure in the future, their assistant or intern has researched you.

Where Should You Live?

Entire books could be devoted to the debate of New York vs. L.A. And even after reading them you might not know the best choice for you. Without spending a lot of time on the details . . . Think about who you are.

Get a sense of the lifestyle and cost of living in each city. Life is going to be difficult enough in your chosen profession. You should at least be content with your environment. It's a plus to have family or friends within shouting distance. You may be in for some hard times, and a shoulder to cry on and knowing that someone who is on your side is close by can make all the difference. Are you an urban or suburban type? Do you like to drive? What is your financial situation? Are you in love with or do you hate or are you indifferent to the cold or warm weather?

New York can be tough and extremely expensive. You should be at ease with crowds and fairly aggressive. To do well in New York you must have confidence. You must be flexible in dealing with the challenges that come with living in an often enervating cultural and creative hub. You can't mind being shoulder to shoulder with other people on the bus or the subway. In New York, a car can be an outrageous expense. A parking space could cost more than your monthly rent would in Los Angeles. In New York you must be able to function without being derailed by the day-to-day chaos that is a byproduct of living in the most populous city in the United States. New Yorkers can be intense, sophisticated, and attuned to the cultural and political zeitgeist. Film is only one of several creative industries there, and there seems to be more social crosspollination. (Yes, this is all a tremendous generalization, so take it with the proverbial grain of salt.)

Los Angeles appears to be more relaxed. In Los Angeles it is easy to drift along and lose momentum. It can feel as if every single person in L.A. wants to write, make, or be in a movie. There are hundreds of ancillary businesses that exist only to serve the interests of the industry—public relations firms, managers, agents, sales and distribution companies, rental houses, equipment and technical service vendors—so there is no shortage of ways to meet people. The upside is you have access to more opportunities. The downside is there are thousands of people who are doing exactly what you are doing. It's competitive and sometimes ridiculously insular. One important note: in L.A. you not only need a driver's license, you absolutely need a reliable car. No matter what you might hear, public transportation is limited and L.A. is spread out. No one is the least bit sympathetic towards someone who can't get where he or she needs to go, and absolutely no one wants to accommodate your lack of wheels.

If you make New York your base, you should research the communities outside Manhattan. Most starting out filmmakers I've met live in Brooklyn and Queens, areas that are expensive but not quite as prohibitive as Manhattan. If L.A. becomes your base, you may be determined to live in one of the beach cities, but there are much more affordable and safe rentals in Burbank and Culver City, and lots of film people gravitate towards the more urban and artsy feel of Silver Lake and Los Feliz. Walk or drive around—where do the people most look and feel like you? Start where you feel most at home. You can take your time getting your bearings. You can move later if there's a better option.

Both New York and Los Angeles are hosts to numerous film-related events, conferences, festivals, and organizations. They can be costly to attend, but almost all of them make use of volunteers, which might be your way in. The trick is to scrutinize the organizations so you can figure out which are useful, which are industry-valid, and which are scams.

Wherever you move try to create an extensive phone and email contact list in advance. This list should be comprised of friends, friends of friends, alumni groups, anyone who might possibly have advice for you about their particular city. Then call them. Some people will be wonderfully cordial, and some may leave you feeling that you shouldn't have bothered. Try not to take anything personally. It's just research. Obtain as much information as you can about where you want to be and what your first move will be when you get there, then make an educated decision. Don't stress too much. Both Angelenos and New Yorkers admire "cool." Remember, nothing is irrevocable.

Film Schools

It's better to move to a new place when something is waiting for you. It gives you structure. There is someplace you have to be, and people who are expecting you. One good strategy is to register for a film class or program. You are immediately in the company of like-minded people, many of whom are also starting out and looking to meet people with interests and goals that will complement or align with yours.

There are undergraduate programs, graduate programs, extension courses, and dozens of non-degree workshops. Don't be swayed by ads for programs or by claims of job placement. Look at schools you or people you know have heard of, that are located within an hour of production-center cities. There are schools with strong industry connections and affiliations. The faculty is often partially composed of the industry professionals who will be your first exposure to the life and politics of the film business. These people may be your first connections. Maybe you have a degree already or you don't have a lot of money. Take an extension course. Research all of this thoroughly online before you leave home. Make the calls.

You'll be amazed at how much you learn about survival in the film business simply by attending the right workshop. You'll also be surprised by how much access you have to internships and to opportunities that will be made available to you just by being part of a school program. One word of caution—at most film schools students make shorts, not feature-length films. You're taught the basics of how to make a movie, and your short may even get into festivals. Everything helps, but don't assume that even an award-winning short festival film is going to do more for you than give you a little confidence. It used to be that an impressive short film from one of the more prestigious film schools meant something in terms of the producer, director, or cinematographer's future. At least it might get them a meeting.

Now there are so many film schools and so many festivals that the value of a film program can be found much more in terms of who you meet and what you learn. You can learn a huge amount about both the creative aspects of filmmaking and the film industry by attending a good film school or program. You will be starting out at step twenty of one hundred rather than at step one. The best film programs can serve as great stepping-stones, but only if you do your part by meeting your fellow students, getting to know the faculty, taking advantage of internships and special academic privileges, and using your film to meet vendors and to go to festivals where you will add to your network.

Internships

One would think that being willing to work for free would be an asset, but hiring unpaid workers has all kinds of legal and insurance implications. Many companies do not want to deal with the problems that can occur as a result. Usually it is necessary to be enrolled in an educational program in order to work as an intern. Companies often prefer to place their requests for interns through academic channels as a way of avoiding the weird, the personality issues, the nonachievers. Also, as student interns receiving course credit, you aren't counted as an employee and the company is not responsible for you the way they would be if you were just a volunteer.

An internship can be a great experience or a waste of your time. It is your job to shop for internships and to interview whatever company or person you're meeting as carefully as they are interviewing you. Before sending your resume or letter in for an internship listing, find out as much as you can about the company and, if at all possible, about the person for whom you'd be interning. Google them and read every article. Pay no attention to the personal stuff. You're interested in the hard facts. What is this company, who is this person? What have they done? You'll feel more informed and may be able to tailor your resume more closely to the internship.

An internship usually involves a commitment of time (sixteen hours a week, three days a week, etc.) and of duration (usually a semester). It is a painless way for you to accustom yourself to the pace and the language of the Industry. It is also a way to learn the names, which simply means familiarizing yourself with who is who, where they work, what their significance is in the Industry. As you try to move ahead, you'll have a better idea of who might be interested in your abilities or your projects and why.

Sometimes interns are given scripts to read and evaluate. That's called writing *coverage*. Coverage is a little like a book report—you read a script and write a two-page *synopsis* (summary) of the plot, comment on the strong and weak points of the script, then either *Recommend* and the script goes on to be read at the next highest level of the chain of command, or *Pass*. When a script receives a Pass, it is often dropped onto a huge rejection pile and the evaluation process stops right there, so read and write carefully. Writing coverage is good experience, because you have no emotional investment in the material. You learn to look at scripts in a critical way, which helps you to cast a more objective eye when evaluating your own work. Writing coverage also gives the executives at a company the chance to gain a sense of whether you are articulate, a sharp thinker and communicator, and whether you share their taste in material. If an executive begins to respect and trust your taste, there is a good chance that you will have made a valuable long-term connection in the Industry.

If writing coverage is not your strength, use an internship to hone your efficiency. Organizational and people skills are important in making an internship work for you.

View your internship as a professional experience. Show up early, work late, and try to get a feel for asking questions when it is appropriate and not necessarily as things come up. You'll acquire a sense of when to say something and when to keep still. Look at the way the other people at the company dress and dress accordingly. Don't make personal telephone calls, don't text your friends or send personal emails, even if someone else at the company does. Be fifteen minutes early. No one cares about why you didn't show up on time, they remember only that you were late.

If a production executive or a development person or an agent takes a liking to you, they are often willing to make a call or two to help connect you with someone else who might help you, although they are under no obligation to do so. This often happens as the internship is drawing to a close and your supervisor has had the time to evaluate you, because no one is anxious to help someone who hasn't proven him or herself.

Film Organizations

In Los Angeles, there are organizations that exist to help filmmakers. A particularly useful group is Film Independent. Film Independent is a nonprofit organization that focuses on the needs and interests of independent filmmakers. As a member you receive discounts on goods and services that are important in the making of a film, and discounted rates on workshops and special events. The events are informative, and attending them is a good way to meet people.

Helping Out on Other People's Films

Many low-budget films and graduate film school thesis projects are short on crew. It's easy to find someone to direct and shoot, and usually to produce, but finding script supervisors, art department help, production assistants, office help, and other positions is not as simple. If you want to help out on projects as a way to meet people and to learn, here are some things to keep in mind:

1) These projects have no money. The hours will be long, the food is usually bad, and sometimes the people in charge don't know any more than you do. Scope out the project and the people involved before you agree to help. If you are going to work for free, and many people do this when they're starting out, make sure that the project is one that's worthwhile. Read the script. Ask yourself if you would want to see the finished film.
2) For the principal filmmakers this project may be the culmination of years of study and effort. Never think of it as just a low-budget film or just a student project. Work as if you're getting paid.
3) Don't BS about what you know. If someone wants to hire you knowing that you're just learning that's fine, but be honest.
4) Attitude is all. Work your butt off and don't become part of the complaint and gossip department. Quit only if the conditions are unsafe or unsavory, or if the production goes on so much longer than expected that it seems as if it will never be completed.
5) Don't work for free for the same person more than once unless you've really become friends with the filmmakers—and you're sure that everyone else is working for free too.
6) Keep in touch with the people you worked with.

More Volunteering

There are annual events run by *Women in Film*, *Film Independent*, and the *Producers Guild of America*. These groups all run seminars and stage large-scale industry events. Even if you are only making lists of *RSVP*s and running errands, you will meet people, learn who is who and why, and find out a little about what it takes to manage a major event, which may help you when it comes time to make a film. All of this can only help you, and you'll probably have a good time.

Temping

If you don't know anyone in the industry and you aren't yet relaxed about calling strangers, one of the easiest ways to get acclimated is to temp. If you have strong office and computer skills, you can register with one or several of the Los Angeles-area agencies that specialize in furnishing temporary help to film-related businesses. A temp job sometimes becomes a permanent one once you show people how smart, hard-working, and professional you are.

It is important to view a temp job as if it is a permanent position. Conduct yourself in a businesslike way. If the person for whom you're working seems agreeable and knows things that you don't, on one of your last days on the job ask if he would be willing to meet with you for a few minutes to give you some advice. Often if you are a long-term temp and someone at the company likes you, he will offer to help out in some way or tell you to stay in touch. Do it. Send him an email—but not a lot of emails; you don't want him to think you're desperate. Follow up with a call—*one* call, unless he tells you, as people sometimes will, to give him a call every so often to check in. Every so often means once every couple of weeks, not every other day. No one owes it to you to help you. You have to be the kind of person that people want to help.

FINDING A MENTOR

Everybody tells you this, but it's easier said than done. A mentor is someone at least a few steps ahead of you, someone who has "been there, done that" and can help steer you along. A business mentor is not a buddy, and finding someone who wants to help you can be hard. People don't have time, they don't want to feel obligated, and they don't want to be blamed if things don't work out. Some people feel that they had to find their own path and so should you. They may fear that you will expect things—contacts, access—and they aren't willing to give them. *Don't ask someone to be your mentor.* That's too formal and official, and it's too much of a commitment. Have more than one person whom *you* think of as a mentor, and from whom you can ask advice.

When you find someone with whom you have a rapport, or someone you've worked with who seems to be happy with you, ask if they have ten or fifteen minutes to meet. Some will say no, and some will tell you to call their office to set something up. If you don't get a return call within a few weeks then call again, but after that drop it. They were either just being polite or have become too busy. If the person agrees to meet with you, prepare for the meeting. You want to make the most of your few minutes. Know in advance the kind of questions you want to ask. This is a meeting for advice, not to pitch your idea or ask for a job. And if you are outside someone's office waiting to meet, and there is an assistant sitting by the door, remind yourself that an assistant in the film business is likely to be someone who is in the same position as you are, just a few steps ahead. Be polite and professional. If your meeting goes well, ask if you can contact them again. Assure them that you will not be a pest, and save that call or email for a really big question. Soon you'll figure out who to ask about other people, who to ask about technical issues, who to ask about legal issues, etc. Different people excel in different areas. It's your job to build an entire network of mentors.

Learn the Names

You can go online and research people, you can read the *trades* (*Daily Variety*, *The Hollywood Reporter*), and you can read Nikke Finke's daily newsletter *Deadline* at www.deadline.com/hollywood/. You will learn an immense amount about what is happening in the industry very quickly, including the names of people and companies, and you will begin to become aware of the rhythm of how things work.

The Etiquette of the Meeting

When you are able to get in to see someone either through a contact, or through an internship or even on a blind call, *shut off your cell.* You may say, "it's on vibrate, so that's OK." It's not. Turn it off. If you can hear or feel the buzz it's likely that the person you're meeting with can too. It's annoying. Here they are giving you some time, and you haven't decided that they are important enough to warrant a complete shut down. You will react. Your mind will wander. Who is calling or texting? You're momentarily distracted and you've broken concentration, and you've also broken the connection you are trying so hard to build.

The other side of the equation is that the person you're meeting with can answer calls/texts at any point and it's OK. Don't act irritated. Smile. You understand. Since they are doing you the favor of meeting you it's all in their court. They can get away with it, you can't.

And incidentally, if they meet with someone higher up on the chain than they are (or someone from whom they are hoping for a favor), you can bet they've turned their phone off too.

Chapter 4

Relationships and Reputations

YOUR REPUTATION AND CREDIBILITY

In a business where much of the deal-making and negotiations are verbal, your word and your reputation is EVERYTHING. The film industry is small. Everyone who is established can easily make contact with anyone else or can get the straight scoop by making a few calls. How much you are paid, your title on a project, how hard you work, how honest you are, how you treat people—there are no secrets. The business is populated by talkers. Even enemies communicate all the time. There is no place to hide. If you are seen as creative, reliable, capable, and easy to work with, you will find luck. If you are seen as difficult, a prima donna, high-strung, or irrational, you will be known that way even by people who haven't met you. No one cares that you're tired or have had a rough day. With no track record, it won't matter how talented you are. When it comes to a decision as to whether or not to work with you, the decision will be negative. They will say, "Life is too short." If you promise things and don't come through, that will follow you and you will have damaged your credibility. Delivering what you say you can deliver is key. Extenuating circumstances don't count. You're trying to break into an industry of impatient people. Rationalizations won't work. These people have seen it all and maybe done it successfully themselves.

The word *relationship* is possibly the most overused word in the film business. Someone gives someone a chance because he and the other person have a relationship. Person X always works with Person Y because there is a relationship. A producer would prefer that a director hire a particular cinematographer but won't interfere with the director's first choice because the director and the second choice have a relationship. Relationships are not about friendship, they are about history. In the industry people come and go and a shiny new flock of ambitious competitors fly and drive in every day. History—having worked together on a previous project, gone to school together, and experienced something together in the past—can feel like protection against the hostile unknown factors that arise when trying to make a film. A relationship is the sum of shared goals and the hope of mutual loyalty. Friendship might play a part, but in fact there are long-time filmmaking teams where the people involved never see each other outside of the office or off the set. Successful working relationships are often based on astute co-mingling of strengths and weaknesses that might gel creatively but not socially. People trust an unpleasant history that resulted in success more than no history at all. People in the industry often believe, "better the devil you know."

The people with the power to say yes to you are educated gamblers. They plays the odds, hedge their bets. An abundance of anxiety accompanies most decisions, and the most anxiety-provoking of all decisions are those that lead to the spending of cash. These decisions are rarely spontaneous. This philosophy extends even to something as minor as hiring someone for an assistant spot. If someone has held Industry internships, if they have some kind of pre-training with a stellar reference from someone the employer already knows or knows of, that diminishes the risk that the new hire will do or say the wrong thing, breach a confidence without even knowing it, or behave in some way that might prove embarrassing. It's stacking the deck. In a business where most people work their way up from assistant—and on set from Production Assistant (PA) to almost every other position—the decision to hire someone at the lowest rung of the ladder is about potential. If you received a good reference or if someone with influence made a call for you, you must be at least OK. It's common sense that the known is more comfortable than the unknown.

ATTITUDE

Your attitude is one of your most precious assets. Chances are given to young newcomers because they're talented, bright, and have a great attitude. If you're in a business where the tensions run high, you want to be able to count on your people to handle things well, efficiently, and with a lack of bad attitude. On a film set where the days are long and the working conditions often not ideal, the crew member with the bad attitude is the one who is complaining, finding fault with someone else's work, laying blame, and nagging about how long until wrap. It doesn't even matter if this person is correct in his judgments or if everyone else agrees that Yes, it sucks to be out all night in 20-degree weather in the mud and rain, and No, no one is making enough money for this. No one has to hear it. You must be agreeable, helpful, and in general happy that you're on the set of a film (commercial, television show, music video). The whiners and troublemakers are noticed, and they are not invited back. Even if their complaints are justified, everyone is in the same boat—who needs to hear about it? Write it in your private diary or journal if you keep one. Tell your best friend. Do not blog or post about it!

Along with the whiners are the princes and princesses, the egos: "I could do it better"; "I saved their butts"; "They couldn't have finished the movie without me." I promise you, they can always finish the movie without you. You are expendable. There are lines of people behind you, waiting for you to leave or be told to leave.

In an office, the people with an attitude are the drama kings or queens. It's all about them. They do everything. They work harder than anyone else. Everyone else is incompetent. Their ideas are the best. They don't get the credit they deserve. And of course there is the gossip. The drama king or queen is the first with the bad news, the nasty comment, the information that may or may not be true but is certainly no one's business. These people are a drain on the energy of the work environment. They are also the manipulators, the connivers, the liars who set their co-workers up for a fall. Succeeding in a hypercompetitive industry is hard. Stay away from the attitude-challenged. You'll be stunned at how a bad attitude rubs off on you and how it effects other people's perception of you. Keep your eye on the road ahead of you, smile, and be the first one anyone thinks of when they need someone they can count on to do the job with a minimum of fuss. You will do well.

Cautionary Tale: You're at the Bottom of the Food Chain Until You Aren't

Sometimes, you won't even know that you're violating the no bad attitude rule.

Note: All the stories in this book are true-only the names have been changed to protect the innocent.

Will was volunteering on an independent film. Every day he was asked to run to a specific vegan café to fetch lunch for the lead actress. He had to leave set and fight the L.A. traffic to do this, and he was quite put out about it. He felt that getting lunch for an actress he'd never heard of was demeaning, and that since he was working for free, he should at least be doing something worthwhile. On the third day of the shoot he was asked again to pick up the lunch. He rolled his eyes. The producer, who was himself doing the director a favor on this one and who usually made much more high-profile films, pulled Will aside. He told him, "No one should ever know you're unhappy or that you think you're better than this. You know why? Because when they started all these people, including me, had to do something we didn't want to do. We were all better than that. Every job on a set is the same. It's doing whatever has to be done to get the movie made. If getting the lunch helps, then that's the most important contribution you can make, and you'd better hustle and do it gladly, until it's not your job anymore. There are people waiting for you to get booted so they can snag your spot. Once you move up you'll be telling the next guy what I'm telling you. You have to suck it up and look as if you're having a good time."

Cautionary Tale #2: Just Because It's in Your Head, It Doesn't Have to Come Out Your Mouth

This is a sad one. Danny idolized a certain big-name director. Danny was charming, personable, and very smart. He spent a year digging up anyone who had a connection to his director hero. He wanted to "shadow" this director, to watch him work and to learn.

Someone who knew someone and was sympathetic to the cause arranged for Dan to meet the director. The director liked him, and finally after a prolonged process involving reference checks, phone calls, and emails that went unreturned, finally Dan was given the go-ahead. He was told when and where to show up on the first day of shooting a major film. He arrived on set early. So far, so good. As instructed, he found the director's assistant, who promptly sent him to the catering truck to get the director his espresso. He was a little surprised that he was being told what to do by an assistant, but he did it. He got the coffee and handed the cup to the director. The director took it and continued his conversation with the cinematographer. The director handed his empty cup to Dan, who returned to the catering truck, got another, and handed the full cup to the director. Over the course of the morning, this was repeated several times. It was the only interaction Dan had with the director. Towards lunch, Dan's girlfriend called him on his cell to ask how it was going. He told her, "OK, I guess. I'm the director's coffee whore."

This was overheard by the makeup person who told the director's assistant who told the director, who fired his unpaid shadow at the end of his first day. The director had enough to deal with. He didn't want anyone working close to him who was resentful and indiscrete. If Danny wanted to voice his opinion to his girlfriend, he could have waited until he was home and in private to do it. Danny thought he was being hip and funny, but the director's assistant and the director felt he was being negative and rude.

What's the point here? Neither Will or Danny did anything truly awful, they just didn't understand the politics. ***The hesitation before you agree, the rolling of your eyes, what you say over your cell phone, even if you whisper, is noticed. What you post is public.*** You are trying to convince people to invest in your talent, your skills, and your ability to navigate the often treacherous waters of the business. They must trust in you personally. You may say to yourself, "I hate politics, I can't deal with this kind of BS." But you have to learn. Some of it is common sense, some of it is courtesy, and some of it *is* BS, but it's all part of the business. You may think, there are lots of jerks out there—I've read about their bad behavior, and *they* succeeded. True. But usually the bad behavior didn't begin until after they were successful. And these bad guys or girls get work and are able to get their films financed because they bring in the big bucks. The minute a film is less than hot at the box office, they find that their calls are not returned as quickly, their scripts are not read as eagerly, and their green lights come more slowly, if they come at all. When people behave badly there is a crowd of people sitting back gleefully awaiting their failure. Human nature is such that payback often tastes sweet. Why go there at all?

Many beginning filmmakers make the mistake of thinking that industry people are casual about behavior. They are not. Most people with the power to help you make your film are sharp observers, with acute instincts. They are constantly checking you out, consciously and unconsciously. Are you a good risk? Do they believe you? Do they believe *in* you? Perhaps because so much money and ego is tied up in the decisions they make, they feel betrayed if you prove their initial impression of you was incorrect. No one expects you to be perfect, but you are expected to be credible, and they remember when you're not. Picture a neighborhood in a very small town, all the residents sitting out on the front porch, watching, noticing, and commenting. That's the film business.

Looking back from a few years out, here are a few comments from some film school grads.

Andy Horwitz

Andy Horwitz is currently Creative Executive at Atlas Entertainment, producers of *12 Monkeys, Three Kings, Batman Begins, The Bank Job, The Dark Knight, The Dark Knight Rises* (2012), and *Superman: Man of Steel* (2013). Andy's knack for producing films began at a very early age and only continues to grow as he climbs the ladder of success in Hollywood.

My path started out as a rocky one, as I'm sure most recent film school graduates experience. Like everyone out of film school, I sent out my resume—which I thought was amazing, since I produced so many short films in film school, only to find out that production companies in Hollywood couldn't give two shits what I did as a student, especially a student who only produced all of the films he worked on. What I started to realize pretty quickly after sending out 100 resumes and getting ZERO calls back was that nobody cares where you went to college or what you've accomplished as a student. Hollywood execs only care about two things when hiring an assistant or entry-level person. Who do you know, and what have you worked on recently? Unfortunately, I can honestly say that if you don't know anyone in Hollywood and have nothing to show for yourself, it's probably best you pack your stuff up and head home. Harsh, I know, but this business is every bit as harsh on the young ones with stars in their eyes.

After many unsuccessful attempts trying to get my foot in the door in Hollywood, I finally cracked and reached out to a friend I had known since childhood who was working for Peter Segal at the time. Pete had directed many great films, and I assumed that my friend Chris, who'd been working for Pete for a few years, could help me get my reso [resume] inside a door or two. His first email back to me went something like this . . . "Hey dude, Have you heard of Charles Roven? He's producing a film called *Get Smart* that we're doing right now, and I hear he's looking for a second assistant. I'll give his current assistant your resume so be prepared for a call." I'll be honest, I had no idea who Charles Roven was at the time, but as soon as I looked him up I instantly became nervous. His preproduction credits at the time were *Get Smart, The Dark Knight, The Bank Job,* and *The International.* This guy is a legend and operates successfully at the highest levels of Hollywood. It's exactly what I wanted. Low and behold, two days later the call came in, and I went in for my first interview since I graduated film school two months earlier.

I was scared SHITLESS when I went into his office to interview with his current assistants. I'll never forget looking at the city views and the office decor

Continued

Andy Horwitz—cont'd

telling myself I was on the set of *Entourage*. I was sitting next two three other guys who were also trying to get the same job that I was. I remember looking them over and noticing that not only were these guys at least five years older than I was but they were wearing suits and ties and carrying briefcases. I looked down at myself only to find a wrinkled button-down shirt and a casual pair of slacks. The only thing in my hand ... my resume, no briefcase. I almost walked out at that very moment for fear of embarrassing myself when finally sitting down in the interview. Well, I stuck it out and sat down with Charles Roven's current two assistants for my interview. At that point I quickly realized that in order to get this job I'd need to LIE MY ASS OFF. I literally said YES to every question they asked me. Can you do this? YES. Can you do that? YES. Have you rolled calls before? OF COURSE—although I didn't even know what that meant at the time! I knew that I was smart enough and knew enough people that if I got the job I'd be able to figure out what all that shit meant quickly. And if you choose to exaggerate what you are capable of and what you've done and give your experience a little industry self-promotion, you'd better be able to fake it. If you've successfully helped out at your mom or dad's busy construction company by manning the busy reception desk and answering phones, you can "roll calls" - industry speak for fielding constantly ringing phone lines, putting calls through, connecting calls to the boss's cell, and taking messages all at the same time. But if you stammer and freak when five lines are ringing at once, don't pretend - you won't be able to carry it off.

Whatever I did must have worked. Two weeks later after I had convinced myself I blew an amazing opp [opportunity] and figuring they found out I might have misrepresented myself, the call came. Chuck's in town from scouting for *The Dark Knight* and he'd like to meet you tonight ... at his house in the hills ... at 10:00 pm. It's the only time he has to see you, so if you want the job you'll be there. Of course, I was sitting in front of his house at 9:30 pm, only to see one of the guys I was sitting in the lobby with two weeks earlier walk out of his house. Great, I said, there's my competition. You know what ... "FUCK that guy," I said. I'm perfect for this job, and I'm going to march in there and tell Charles Roven that right now. Sitting down with Chuck in his home was a surreal experience, to say the least. I was barely able to get my words out for the first few minutes, let alone say to him "Fuck that other guy" like I told myself I would. This guy's a legend, I kept telling myself, so don't fuck this up. Chuck spent the next 30 minutes telling me why I DIDN'T want the job. He told me that if I worked for him my life as I knew it was over, and he'd be the most important thing in my life at that point. I ate it all up with a smile on my face because I knew, this is what I wanted. I wanted to learn from a master producer, and low and behold, I was sitting in the living room of one at the age of 23 years old, fresh out of college. This is what I wanted. I was willing and able at that point in my life to put everything on hold and make Chuck my priority over everything else.

I think he saw my passion, drive, and ambition as he called me a day later and offered me the job as his second assistant.

Two months after starting on Chuck's desk and just as we began production on *The Dark Knight* and *Get Smart* (back to back, I might add), I was starting to get the flow of

Andy Horwitz—cont'd

the office. I finally figured out what rolling calls was and how to speak to someone as intelligent and sharp as Chuck Roven. I'll never forget, it was June 13th, 2007, just two and a half months working as the second assistant and a day before my birthday, when Chuck fired his 1st assistant in the middle of the day. Things were very unsettling in the office on a daily basis because the 1st at the time had some communication issues with Chuck and didn't pay attention to detail. Either he had to go or Chuck was going to have a heart attack ... I'll never forget Chuck looking at me just after firing him and saying, "I hope you've been paying attention the past two months, because starting tomorrow, you're taking over. I've never only had one assistant before, and I've also never been this busy at one time, so we're going to have to get through this together. When we slow down, I'll hire you a second assistant."

I knew this was my time to shine ... this was my time to show him I was capable of playing with the big dogs. This was going to become my grad school ... only I was getting paid to attend. Well, I rode it out for just about a year by myself, which was unprecedented on Roven's desk at the time. There were a few people I tried to bring in to help ... three actually during my time on the desk. One lasted two months, one lasted two weeks, and one ran out of the office after just six hours. It wasn't an easy desk, to say the least. Probably without a doubt one of the hardest desks emotionally and physically for an assistant in Hollywood, but one of the most rewarding as well. The day I went solo on Chuck's desk he made me a promise ... "If you last two years from right now and you're still here, I'll promote you. Just know that I've been making movies for 30 years, and only five or so people have ever lasted two full years, and NONE of them have ever done it alone." Long story short, I lasted two years and Chuck, true to his word as he always is, promoted me. I didn't have to ask him nor did I have to remind him. He remembered and, like very few people in Hollywood, went above and beyond to make me an executive at this company where I've been serving as creative executive for the last two years. I've been at Atlas for almost five years now and wouldn't take a single thing back. I got lucky, was presented with a great opp, took it, gave up my life and everything else important to me for two years, and it worked out in the end ...

Describe what you do, and if you are in production, how you got your first few opportunities.

As a creative executive at Atlas I read and develop all of our material at the company. I'm the first line of defense in terms of new projects at Atlas. I guess you could say I'm the creative gatekeeper. If you want us to produce your movie, you've got to get through me first. If a script is great, I'll run it up the flagpole. If it's terrible, my bosses never knew it came in and I pass on behalf of Atlas to the agent or manager that sent it. I read a lot, give notes to writers, make creative lists [lists of potential projects, writers, directors, and actors] for directors and actors for our development, and generally assist in all creative elements of Atlas projects. I'm also responsible for keeping my hand on the pulse of Hollywood. I'm expected to know all the hot new and old writers and directors, actors, new financiers, etc. I've also just recently set up my first project at Warner Bros. Hopefully, I'll be producing that quite soon and starting to look for projects of my own to produce.

Continued

Andy Horwitz—cont'd

I've also recently, with the help of [my colleagues] over here at Atlas, started an independent film division of Atlas to expand our horizons, called Atlas Independent.

This book is about the soft skills a person has to have to survive in the industry—people skills, political skills. Can you think of any dos and don'ts for someone just starting out? Can you think of any examples?

I've seen people be amazingly successful off people skills alone. I've also seen amazingly smart people that know a ton about the movie biz fail horribly because of their lack of people skills. Hollywood is 75 percent relationships and 25 percent skills, intelligence, and business practices combined.

Also, your reputation is everything! People in Hollywood don't forget, and they LOVE to gossip. It's a small town, and everyone knows everyone. Hollywood is just like a big version of High School with all the drama.

What are the mistakes that you've seen people make? Any consequences?

REPLY ALL. I can't tell you how many times that button has fucked people out of relationships and jobs around town. Lots of times people love to make snarky comments about the stupidity of others as written in an email, or their lack of grammar or creative skills. Instead of hitting FWD to send it to a colleague for the sole purpose of talking shit, you hit REPLY ALL instead and let everyone on the email see your shit talking. It's never good when that happens. LOOK AT WHO YOU'RE SENDING YOUR EMAILS TO, PEOPLE! *BEFORE* YOU HIT SEND. I also can't tell you how many times I've seen extremely important and sensitive emails go out with the wrong people on them. When you try to put Andy Horwitz on an email about deal points for a project or story ideas for a very confidential project and you accidently put Andy blahblah on it, you've fucked yourself. Even if you call that person and kindly ask him to delete it, he never does without telling one or two people what he read. PAY ATTENTION TO DETAIL. One email that goes out to the wrong person or unintended recipient could have million-dollar consequences in this business.

Allison Ewart

Allison Ewart is Manager of Physical Production at Alcon Entertainment, producers of *The Blind Side, The Book of Eli,* and *Dolphin's Tale.*

Three months before graduating college I landed a job as a PA on infomercials and would make the three-and-a-half-hour round-trip commute to Orange County to work on set, on the weekends, or days I didn't have class. The second job I had was as an assistant to a talent manager. I finally landed the job I wanted as the Executive Assistant to the VP of Physical Production at Alcon Entertainment. I became assistant in a department I was passionate about, and that [passion] showed. Nine months after being hired I was promoted to Staff Production Coordinator, and two years after that I was promoted to Manager of Physical Production.

It's truly massive [how much there is to learn]. Each film has a team, creative and production. And those teams are made up of mini departments, and each

Allison Ewart—cont'd

department has people in different positions that all do different jobs. Then you have the insurance, guilds, travel, agents and managers, postproduction, delivery, etc., etc., etc.... The list goes on and on. And this changes on every film. You have films with VFX, children, animals, musicals, pre-records, post-apocalyptic, true story, etc. etc. etc. The opportunities to learn are truly endless, because no matter what you do each film is different and presents different circumstances, allowing the opportunity to build your knowledge database.

As someone who is now in the position to hire interns and/or assistants, what do you look for?

In physical production you are looking for an extremely detailed person and one who is not afraid to ask questions. I don't expect interns or assistants to know everything—or really anything—so there's no need to put a false wall up pretending that they do know. I'd rather be asked the questions and teach someone so that they grow, and while they grow I benefit from the quality of work.

What makes a good assistant?

A good assistant is someone who is detailed, timely, a multitasker, has excellent speaking skills, is good at time-management and on top of things (schedule, phone sheet, lunches, etc.). Someone who keeps a detailed "to do" list and can remind you about deadlines, urgent emails that may not be marked urgent, etc.

What makes a promotable assistant?

A promotable assistant is one who constantly asks questions in order to learn. An assistant who says, "What can I do to help you? What can I take off your hands?" That shows your boss that you have a desire to do more and a will to learn. And then following through when you do get the chance to do more than your assistant duties require. Again, don't be afraid to ask questions. Now with some bosses this may not work well, but you have to feel them out. No matter what, it's always better to ask rather than do something wrong. And you should never make the same mistake twice. The mistake is there to learn from, not to dwell upon or forget and make again. Another thing is knowing when you can find the answer yourself. As an employer, there is nothing more annoying than when you get asked a question that is right in front of the person's eyes. We have a saying in our department that is directed to those outside our department, which is RTFW—"Read the F***ing work papers!"

Every person is replaceable in the job world. You can never feel like you are entitled, because when you do people sense that. Attitude is everything; if you aren't enjoying your work, it shows. Finger pointing and pushing blame or just ignoring a problem is the absolute worst thing to do.

What advice would you give someone just starting out in the Industry who wants to be a director, a producer, someone working in a creative or development position at a production company or a studio?

If you want to be a director, I would recommend that you get a job assisting a director. That may be difficult to get right off the bat, so you might have to start out as a PA on-set and get some face time with the director. Once some time passes in the production, you can start expressing to people (director, producers, etc.) what

Continued

Allison Ewart—cont'd

you want to do. When you work with a team for three-plus months, everyone gets friendly. So it's great to speak up and not be too timid. You have to grab your opportunities when you have them. If you are the PA in the background just doing your job you will remain in that position. But if you are doing your job while networking, you have a better shot of getting hired again and in the position you want. In your off time I would suggest working on your own low-budget projects as well.

If you want to be a producer you really need to learn it all. Development, physical production, post, etc. I think working as an assistant to producers is a great way to start, because you can develop a close relationship with them, which will allow you to ask questions and let them know your goals. The people in the higher positions all started somewhere. That's what students and those starting out need to remember. When an intern wants to ask me questions or is looking for a job, I always keep them in mind because I remember being in that place. You HAVE to speak up for yourself and show how motivated and passionate you are about what you want to do. If you want to be a producer, I also think a creative/development assistant is a good place to start, because if you get promoted to development executive, you then get an opportunity to learn the production side if a project you bring in gets a green light. It's all about taking as much advantage of your starting out position as possible, going to drinks with other assistants, reading scripts day and night, and just consuming yourself in what you want to do. That passion will show to the right people.

If you want to work in creative or development, then you should definitely start out as an assistant in this department. An extremely outgoing, expressive, opinionated personality is needed here. It's an opportunity to use all the resources at hand. Read all the scripts, try writing coverage, and ask your boss to read it. Show them how badly you want it. If they want to outsource work to an intern to write coverage on a script, ask to do it and say you will do it on the weekend. This job is a lot of mingling and lunches and networking.

What would you have liked someone to have told you, any lessons that you've learned that you could have learned an easier way?

I guess the hardest lessons learned are the ones where you could have prevented them had you been a little more detailed and thorough. The lessons where you know that you didn't give it your all and you beat yourself up about them. It's never a great feeling to have those "Duh!" moments. Where you're just hitting your head wondering how you missed something.

Priscilla Elliott

Priscilla Elliott is a freelance Art Director. Some of her credits include the films *In Time, The Back-Up Plan,* and *The Invention of Lying.*

I started out interning for a development company and reading scripts. I became a director of development for a small production company, and I published two books. Then I went to film school for screenwriting. I designed a bunch of shorts

Priscilla Elliott—cont'd

at school when we were short-handed. Upon graduating, I PA'd for a designer I admired and became his researcher on a bunch of projects. I learned the ropes. I started art directing on a small movie, which got me into the union.

I like making movies. My dream from when I was a kid was to make movies. So I found a place within the organization where I can do that. I like problem-solving on a large scale. I like complex puzzles and challenges. I like the unknown, exploring, researching. I like collaborating with other people. I like paint and images and illusions. I like beautiful things and dreams and making things. I like storytelling. I like explosions and car chases. I like travel. Chaos. Being able to contribute creatively. It's incredible. What's not to like?

What is your advice for people trying to break into the business?

Getting along, and at the same time speaking your mind constructively, is the core of this business. Be on the ball without steamrolling others.

Get good at interviewing, and expressing yourself directly and clearly. Be honest about your strengths and weaknesses. I think it would be better not to get a job for being honest about something you don't know, than getting the job by covering that up and then making a mistake, which everyone in the industry will hear about, anyway.

Do learn the hierarchy of a set. Go through the proper channels. Try to appreciate what other people do, and understand where their focus and problems lie. Delivering information and communicating is a huge priority. Make sure everyone who needs the information gets it as soon as possible. But don't just throw the information out there. Give the right people the right information they need.

Chapter 5

Internship and Entry-Level Do's and Don'ts

1. Have a resume that is professional and appropriate to the industry.
The examples of resumes in most books are great for corporate, sales, or more general businesses, but don't use those as samples for your film internship or job. You must create a film resume. (For examples, see Appendix: "Your Resume.")

2. Don't send out hundreds of generic resumes.
Have a template resume that you constantly adjust and tweak so that it's applicable to each potential position.

3. Do your research.
If a person is looking for an assistant or an intern, get on imdb.com. Google them. Ask anyone you know in the business if they know anything about them. Understand their place in the business. If it's a company, know what they do—is it management, production, distribution, or a combination of all of them? If the company has released movies, know the titles.

4. Although you may really want to direct, produce, or be a screenwriter eventually, the reason you want to intern at or work for a company should be because you think you can learn a lot.
"I need to pay the rent," while an honest answer, is not the correct answer when asked why you're interested in a position. They know you need money. They want to hear that you are intelligent and can handle stress, that you're a hard worker and a team player, that you're responsible and reliable. If they ask what your long-term goals are, tell them, but be aware that by asking that question they are trying to get to know you and to judge whether you will be a good fit for them.

5. Don't have a juvenile, party-type message on your voice mail recording.
If someone calls you in for an interview and has to leave a message, you don't want to set yourself up as unprofessional even before they meet you. Don't have a long musical interval either. When someone calls you

for a job, they don't want to have to wade through 60 seconds of pop hits just to leave a message. People are in a hurry. They don't know you. They might hang up and go on to the next resume on their list.

6. If you get an interview, dress in a professional manner.
For guys, this means clean, nice jeans or slacks, a nice shirt (no T-shirts), and a sports jacket. You should not wear a suit unless it's a position at an agency, or in the business or legal affairs department of a studio. No tennis shoes, no flip-flops. If the interview is for some kind of on-set position such as a P.A. or an assistant in the Art department, you can be more casual, but jeans, a shirt, and shoes is a good start until you see what everyone else is wearing.

For women, slacks, a skirt, nice jeans, a blouse or sweater, and it is always good to finish your outfit off with a blazer or some other type of jacket. You don't have to look androgynous, but you shouldn't wear anything that calls attention to your body—no tube tops, no extreme minis. The idea is to project confidence, and competence.

Whether male or female, look around to see what everyone else at the company is wearing. Check out the clothing of the person who interviews you. That may be a clue as to what is considered appropriate dress at that particular office.

7. If you're called in to meet, get to the building early but don't appear for the interview more than 15 minutes early, and DON'T under any circumstances be even a second late.

If you are asked to wait, no matter how long, don't keep checking your watch, and don't start making calls on your cell. When you finally get in the door, if the person interviewing you says something about keeping you waiting, smile and say, "no problem." If they don't say anything, don't you say anything either.

8. Listen to what the person interviewing you tells you about the job and don't interrupt.
Don't overtly sell yourself. Don't tell them what an asset you'll be. When it's time to speak, speak to what they've told you rather than going into some pre-rehearsed speech about what you can do. If they're looking for someone who is good on the phone and you have experience handling multiple calls, tell them a little about it. If they want someone who is calm under pressure, you can give them a brief re-cap of something you've done that demonstrates that you have that ability. It doesn't have to be in an office situation. Maybe you've been on a sports team and you've been in tense extra-inning situations.

9. When you talk about yourself, be confident but not aggressively so.
It should never seem as if you're jaded, or that you'll be tiresome to have around. Be enthusiastic. Use the interviewer's questions as an opportunity

to show a little bit about the kind of person you are, but above all be calm. Don't have a big cup of coffee or a soda before you interview. You'll be speedy and won't even know that you're striking the interviewer as a bit over the top.

10. If you're at an interview for a paying job and not an internship, don't ask about money during the first interview.
If you're called to come in for a second interview, it will come up. If you're offered the job, it will come up. It's an entry-level position. Go in knowing that you're not going to earn a lot. The average starting pay for an assistant in the industry is around $500 per week. If it's a small company it might be $400. If it's a studio or more corporate type of position, it might be $600. An assistant to a major producer or director on a bigger budget film might be paid $600 to $800, but the job is only meant to last through production or postproduction and there are no benefits. On a low-budget indie, the same job will pay $400 or $500 and still no benefits. Some of these positions will pay overtime. Many of them won't. You have to grin and bear it when you're starting out. If it's any comfort to you, be assured that there are Harvard MBAs, Rhodes Scholars, and children of prominent folks in the business, all starting out, and most are making the same sad salary.

11. Try to learn something about the business at every interview.
Whether by following up on something you overhear in the waiting room, or by researching something the interviewer says, you will get better at these meetings. Knowledge and practice is what will help you to feel more at ease.

12. Know what your favorite movies are and try to remember the most recent film you've seen.
This may sound like an odd bit of advice, but it's a common interview question, an ice-breaker, and you'd be amazed at the number of interviewees who are so nervous and unprepared for the question that they blank out.

13. Try to get a sense of what department or position you're applying for—that may be more important than the company itself.
If you want to be an editor, you'll meet more relevant people working at a post or trailer house than you will in the development department of a studio or at the most high-powered agency. Go for the job, not for the company name. Once you've got one internship or entry-level job under your belt, you can use the fact that you have experience and rave references to move up to doing something you really like.

14. If you're interviewing for either an internship or a job at a production company or studio, realize it is customary for interns and assistants to be required to read a lot of scripts and to evaluate them.

If you don't like reading or are an unusually slow reader, avoid applying for anything in either the development or production departments. Go for an area where you'll shine.

15. Don't suck up to your boss, but if you know there's something he or she is interested in and you see something about it, cut it out and bring it in. It may or may not be appreciated but it will be noted that you're listening.

16. Don't ever ask when you can go home.
Don't make plans on work nights if you won't be able to cancel them. Don't ignore your phone when it rings and it is someone at work calling you on the weekends. Check your voice mail often. Don't be MIA. If you don't pick up the call to answer the question, someone else will become your boss's go-to person. Your days will start early and run late. Depending on the job and the temperament of the person you're working for, you may be expected to respond to calls at night and on the weekends. This is very rare and not appropriate for an internship but is often the case with jobs that are entry-level and higher. And if you're working on a movie rather than at an office job, it's virtually a certainty that as an assistant, you're more or less on call for the duration of the production. Put up with it. It's part of the deal.

17. Don't drink at professional functions.
OK, if you're of legal age, you can have a small one. But that's it. Whatever your personal recreational use of substances, forget about it if you're around anyone in the industry, no matter what they may be doing. Don't view business-related parties or drinks after work as anything but work. Don't lose control. Be careful about what you say, of the jokes you make. Never be in photographs or take photographs that show anyone in a "party" mode. It may sound ridiculously old-fashioned, but it's far better to live up to something than to try to live it down.

18. Don't do anything that violates your personal morals or ethics.
You can always find another job, but you're stuck with yourself forever.

Chapter 6

This Is a Great Idea, But Is It a Movie?

THE STORY IS EVERYTHING

If you are planning to make films, whether as a creator or as someone who is on the support side—development, production, marketing, or distribution—you must understand story. Without story you have no script, and without a good script you have no movie worth making.

What is a great story? It may be a matter of opinion, but it's safe to say that when we're looking at stories intended to become movies, there are some common elements. In general, a good story involves a journey, a mission of some kind. The journey can be emotional, mental, or a true physical journey, but there must be change—either a real or metaphorical—in getting from one place or mental or emotional state to another.

Whose Story Is It?

Often this is not as obvious as you think. If we think again about the journey, the simplest way to know whose story it is might be to decide whose mission we are on. Is it your main character? What if your idea is some kind of memoir— is a friend remembering an episode in the main character's life? Is the story seen through an observer's recall? If that's the case, whose story is it? Through whose point of view are we watching the action unfold? Is the subject of the story the observer or the character who is observed? What if it's an ensemble piece with a lot of characters, a group of friends at a high school or summer camp reunion? However many main characters are part of your idea or scenario, you must choose one as the primary character we follow. That character should be active, rather than passive. By that I mean, he or she should act, not simply react. We must want to join this person on the trip, not wait with this person while things happen to him or her.

What Do Your Characters Want?

Your lead character should have a goal, something he or she or it must accomplish. Whether the goal is to solve a personal problem, win the big game, fall in love, or save the world, there must be a mission. When you are looking at an

Make Your Movie: What You Need to Know About the Business and Politics of Filmmaking.

idea or story, it should be clear in each scene what the character wants. Usually, the more *conflict* there is between what the main character wants and what everyone else wants, the more interesting the story. What the characters want is the driving force that pulls them through the plot, from beginning to end. Examine your idea. Does the hero or heroine face obstacles? What is standing in the way of the goal? If there is nothing standing in the way there is no story. Someone wants something, they get it, the end.

Sometimes as the story progresses, the obstacles become increasingly difficult and threatening. This way the drama builds. Or the hero faces more or different risks. The peril can be physical, psychological, or emotional—it can be the threat of humiliation. But it must feel dangerous in some way, and it must be imminent. There must be urgency. Urgency is the motor that pushes the story. If the only danger is something that may happen in the distant future, the motor will slow and you will lose your audience. Sometimes overcoming one obstacle may be easy, but another momentous obstacle lurks right behind it. This can result in a pattern of relief, then surprise, then heightened tension. And there must be problems. An obstacle is overcome but the consequences are bad, or there is no way for the hero to overcome the obstacles and still achieve what he wants, or the hero gets what he wants but loses something equally or more important along the way. The obstacles can change. The hero thinks the problem is one thing or one person and it turns out that it's another. As one obstacle is encountered and dealt with another must arise. The obstacles should become more complex and interesting and possibly dangerous, *raising the stakes*. Along the way, we encounter other characters, side plots, and surprises until the story has run it's course and our hero either learns something or accomplishes the mission and emerges wiser, happier, or less happy, but transformed if only in a minor way, by the experience.

Three-Act Structure

In feature films, the story, the journey, is broken into a *three-act structure*. The first act of a screenplay introduces the *set-up*, the opening scenario. In the first act we usually meet our hero and additional important characters, and we get a sense of the *world* of the story (fantasy, futuristic, contemporary reality) The *rules of the world* are introduced. We see the way the Hobbits in the shire live in *Lord of The Rings*. It's not the way the family in *Juno* lives or the way King George VI lives in *The King's Speech*, and it's not the way any of us live now. But in order for the screenplay to draw us in, we must gain an understanding of the environment of the story so that we can actually understand the motivation of the characters, the obstacles, the conflicts, and what is at stake. There is an *inciting incident*. This is the turn of the key that starts the motor. The set-up usually presents us with the mission—the goal.

Act two is where the fun begins, as the hero is beset with complications. Danger looms. The hero progresses. Act two is usually where the most dramatic opportunities present themselves, because the story is developing while the hero is moving ahead. There is the possibility of layers of plot, of motivation, and of behavior. There may be misleading information. Added plot points. Like may progress to love or at least flirtation to consummated sex. A friend may be revealed as an enemy. In the best cases, the second act ends with exhilaration and anticipation. How will this all be resolved?

The third act is the resolution. There are usually one or more *climaxes*, high points that occur after elevated tension. Then, the tension seems to fade only to rise again. Finally, we are at the final climax, the roller coaster ride is over, and there is the end. Depending upon the story, an epilogue can tie up any messy unanswered questions; it can be the punctuation, or the final punch line. Sometimes it can be there solely to avoid an abrupt ending.

There are several great books on screenwriting. These books go into all the elements of film story and character in much more detail, and every person who writes has a different way of looking at the structure of a film. But for our purposes, let's accept that the three-act structure has been the industry standard for decades. As we look at the most common reasons an idea or screenplay is turned down, it will become clear that many of those reasons come back to poor structure. We're reviewing the basic components of an effective screenplay here not because you're going to run off and write a formulaic script but because you must competently speak the language. There are variations. Sometimes a film moves a bit off this path. But you must accept the fact that this structure serves as the underlying blueprint for most successful screenplays for a few reasons:

We—audiences, executives, all of us—are comfortable with this rhythm of storytelling, whether we're hearing it, reading it, or seeing it projected or on our TV or computer screens. We have learned to be drawn to this structure.

In order to think of something, write something, find something that is new enough and different enough to grab the attention of someone who might help you get your movie made, you have to understand the game. Your strategy is to either embrace this structure but find a way to be original and surprising within it's boundaries, or to know it so thoroughly that you can play with it and come up with something that feels fresh but that is not so radical that it will turn off the people who are looking for material. A new story told an old way (*Fight Club*), an old story told a new way (*500 Days of Summer*, *Black Swan*, *Inception*)—that's what can help get you in the door.

THE WIND UP AND THE PITCH

A pitch is a sales tool.

A pitch is a performance.

When you bring your idea to someone who might help you get your project made, you must be able to present your idea quickly, succinctly. You must be prepared with an extremely brief summary of your idea, an *elevator pitch*. Imagine you're in an elevator with someone who may or may not be interested in hearing what you have to say. You have only the time between when the door shuts to when the elevator reaches the lobby to sell yourself and your idea. The elevator pitch is a quick hit of what your story is and how well you can tell it. Think of a pitch as the verbal 30-second trailer of a film, told in present tense to an audience of executives who have already spent hours that day listening to dozens of pitches, and you'll understand why it's important to be warm, self-assured but not cocky, have energy that is appealing (be *good in a room*) and to acquire the ability to seduce. Seduce? Yes. Someone has to *want* to hear your idea. They must want to accompany you on the trip.

The reasons for the extreme brevity of the pitch are:

These people have no time. Their job is to sift through literally hundreds of ideas, treatments, screenplays, books, and magazine articles to find the one story that might be worth pursuing. If you can't knock the ball out of the park in 30 seconds, why would anyone assume that you can do it in twenty minutes?

The executive hearing your pitch may know something you don't. For instance, the company already has a circus movie in the works. They don't need another one. Or the executive has been charged with finding a project for a specific actor or actress and your project is not it. Or the idea just doesn't have any appeal for the person listening. Don't take it to heart and don't argue about it. Not everybody likes everything.

Ideas are cheap. Investing in an idea is not. If you can't tell your story effectively, why would they think you could write or find someone else to write it effectively?

A quick pitch should communicate the feel of the world of the idea. Your audience should know immediately whose story it is and what the main character wants, the set-up and the obstacles. The highlights. The pitch should be compelling, funny if it's a comedy, intriguing if it's a mystery. All this in no more than 30 seconds. Then you can use about 3 minutes to fill in the holes. Longer is not better. Longer feels like you don't know what you're doing. If you are interrupted by a ringing phone, an assistant knocking on the door, anything, mid-pitch, it's unsettling, but you have to live with it. You must recover quickly and regain your ground. If the person listening to you interrupts you to ask a question, that's good news. If the person cuts you off, don't fight it. Realize that this time, it's not happening for you. Say thank you and move on. The person listening may like you but not your idea. You might ask if there's time for you to pitch a second idea, or he or she may ask *you* if you have anything else. This is a good reason to have several ideas rather than only one prepared—in case your pitched is shut down but you're asked, "What else you got?"

You've probably seen films about the movie business where someone describes an idea using an elevator pitch. The 30-second pitch is a teaser, a shortcut. *27 Dresses* meets *The Hangover*. *Lord of the Rings* meets *300*. *The Parent Trap* meets *Spy Kids*. Some industry veterans have their pitches down to five words. Years ago, producer Alexandra Rose sold her Academy Award nominated project, *Norma Rae* as "A female version of *Rocky*." *Rocky* was a huge box office success at the time. She could count on the fact that everyone in the room had seen it and was salivating at the thought of another film that championed the "little guy," who this time happened to be a woman.

The people who constantly hear pitches want you to cut to the chase. They want to hear about things first in a matter of seconds (the elevator pitch), then if they're interested, in a matter of minutes (the full pitch), then if you're lucky, in a more detailed way (a written treatment.) If anyone's attention wanders while you are making your pitch, you're going to have a major struggle getting it back, so before you meet anyone to talk about yourself or your idea, you're going to rehearse. Like an actor. You're going to have your elevator pitch down pat, so that when you're told Go you will hook them right away. You're going to watch the reaction of the person you're speaking to so that you can *tailor* the slant of your pitch. If your story is critiqued, you're going to appreciate the comments and advice. (If you receive the same critique from several different sources, it's time to start listening very closely.) In short, you're going to be prepared and have something relevant to say or say nothing at all.

DO YOU OWN IT?

If you have an original idea, you might think you own it. After all, it was the product of your imagination. Say you're sitting in your room the day after graduation. You're feeling wistful, and you're remembering some wonderful time from your childhood. You think, "Boy, things were simpler when I was a kid . . . If I had only known then what I know now . . . ," and you get your idea.

You Can't Own an Idea . . .

What if there's a guy who somehow switches bodies with a little kid or a teenager. And there's a kid who can't wait to grow up. The kid is switched, and he's now in the body of the guy. The guy goes back to school, the kid goes to the office, and there's potential for humor and sweetness. Or maybe somehow he's actually himself, but himself as a kid, reliving his life. Eventually he learns that you can't change destiny (or that maybe you can), and he appreciates what he had then and comes to appreciate what he has as an adult. He has to find a way back. That's a movie.

Good idea. But what if I don't know you, and I'm thinking about my nephew. A cute kid, wise beyond his years, often described as an old soul. I'm thinking, it's funny how some kids are so grown up and some adults act just like little kids. What if there's a kid who somehow switches bodies with an adult, and vice versa. After comedic encounters and maybe a poignant romance, the boy/adult and the adult/boy realize that there's no place like home, and the rest of the film is about how they get back to where and who they are.

We've come up with similar concepts and we both own our ideas. Other people have had and will have similar ideas to ours. We all own our ideas, and none of us can protect them. You can't copyright an idea. If you could, the movies

Big, *Freaky Friday* (the original and the remake), *Vice Versa*, *Eighteen Again*, and *Like Father, Like Son*, would not have been made. They would have been mired in lawsuits, and production would never have begun. In fact, a couple of those titles were adapted from novels, and those authors didn't sue each other either.

You can own (and copyright) the execution of the idea. That is, how the story is told.

The characters—who they are, what they think, how they react—is part of the execution of the idea. Specific incidents, lines of dialogue, and individual story turns are all part of the execution of your idea.

Think about it. Almost every romantic comedy originates from the same seed of an idea. Two characters meet or hear about each other. They don't like each other. They become friends, but it's platonic. Or they don't become friends, they really dislike each other. We get to know these people, and at some point it becomes obvious that they belong together. The rest of the story is the "how." How they interact, how they irritate each other more and more, and eventually how they irritate each other less, then fall in love. The successful execution of a romantic comedy depends upon an original approach to a familiar formula—clever twists, snappy dialogue, some "oh no!" moments, and very likeable characters. The audience must find the characters appealing and be able to identify with them, because in the case of romantic comedies, the audience has to really want these people to get together. You could easily reel off the names of ten romantic comedies that share the formula. Some you liked, some you didn't. Why? The execution of the idea.

How Do You Protect Your Idea?

The first thing is to get it down on paper. On paper, the approach begins to become more specific, and it becomes clear what your individual execution or take on the idea will be.

The traditional steps towards an idea becoming a script are:

The *outline:* a short plot summary (one or two pages), written in prose form. An outline is a description of the story, written in the present tense. No dialogue, camera direction, etc. The outline starts at the beginning and brings the reader through the three acts of the film to the conclusion, with only as much detail as is necessary for the reader to understand what happens, how it happens, who it's happening to, and how it's resolved. It's a shorthand description of the character's journey and the *arc* (build, shape, and resolution) of the story. The outline is a blueprint that can be referred to as a guide when a more detailed *treatment* or *first draft screenplay* is written.

Step Two is the *treatment*. The treatment is the entire story in detail, in prose not screenplay format, in the present tense, and usually each paragraph describes the pivotal scenes. The treatment should delineate the spine of the plot and the feel of the characters. The treatment can be short (five pages) or very long (30 pages), and it is intended to serve as a step-by-step guide for the first draft of the screenplay.

You can find samples of outlines and treatments and pitches online and in books on screenwriting. The reason I bring up these steps is because when we're talking about the ownership of ideas, it is important to know that there are several phases of development before an idea becomes a screenplay. At each stage, the idea may change, and the ownership of the idea or treatment or screenplay may change with it.

Why Ownership Is Important

An idea is a tiny spark. A beginning. You may have a character or a situation in mind. "What if . . ." You may have an entire scenario, from beginning to end. Perhaps your idea is based on something you read or heard, or on something that happened to someone you know. The first question anyone in the industry is going to ask is, "Do you own it?" If it's an original idea, it makes everything easier. If it is not an original idea, and you don't own the *underlying material*—the book, the magazine article, the game, the stage play, the song—you have nothing. There is no reason for anyone to deal with you because you bring nothing to the game. Your most important job is to come up with and/or own a great story. If your idea is based on something real or on someone other than you, you must acquire the rights before you even begin to discuss it.

How do you acquire the rights, and what type of rights do you need? That depends on where the idea comes. In the case of written material, whether a book, a screenplay, or an article, you are dealing with *intellectual property*. The material you are going after belongs to someone else, and just like a more tangible form of property—a house, a car—you can't just go ahead and use it. You have to obtain permission, and usually that permission will cost at least a little bit of money. As a script progresses towards production, the production company will want to be sure that there is a clear *chain of title*. This is the documentation of the path and transfer of rights and ownership of the idea: of the book or article if the script is an adaptation, and of the script, including all related contracts, agreements, options, etc. No company wants to make a film that is going to be stuck in neutral as the owners or originators fight it out in the courts.

I Just Read Something Great . . .

You read a book or a script and think it would make an outstanding film.

For a book, look at the inside of the first page of the book to find out who the publisher is. Call the publisher and ask for the *subsidiary rights* department. The subsidiary rights department of a publishing company deals with additional uses for the material—movies, plays, TV shows—anything beyond the book itself. Someone in the subsidiary rights department will give you the name of the author's agent or attorney, or tell you that the rights have already been optioned or sold to a film production company and are not available. Sometimes the publishing company holds the rights, sometimes the author. If the author is dead, sometimes the author's heirs or estate holds the rights.

For a script, where did you get it? Whether through a friend, a relative, an agent, or a manager doesn't matter. You must know who actually owns the work, because you want either to option or purchase the material from the owner.

An *option* is a contractual agreement between the owner of the rights and a producer or production company. The person who is doing the optioning has the right to hold material (the book or the script) for a specific period of time, presumably to see if he or she can drum up interest (cast, money) in the project. You can think of an option as a lease. When you option a piece of material, you don't own it, but if you can do something with it in a specific amount of time, you will move on towards the next step of the contract, which would be ownership. This is called *exercising the option*. While you have the option as long as it's *exclusive*—and it should be, otherwise why have a contract?–no one else can do anything with it. The cost of an option can run anywhere from a small fortune for a bestseller to $1.00 if you're a good talker and there has been no other interest. An option runs for a specific period of time, usually a year or 18 months. When you option material everything that can or will happen with that material should be contractually spelled out ahead of time, usually as part of a *step deal*. A step deal is a set of progressive financial commitments. For example, a script purchase agreement with a writer might have the following steps: $X amount upon the completion of a first draft, $X amount upon financing, $X amount when the project is *green-lit* (given a "go" and funded). If the project stops at any point along the way, there is no financial commitment beyond the steps that have already been reached.

If nothing has happened with the project and the option period runs out, depending upon the way the contract is written the person optioning the material might be able to *renew the option* (usually for additional money) for a set period of time. The owner of the material (again, depending upon how the contract is written) can say yes to the renewal or can take the project elsewhere.

When you purchase a script or a book, you can either own the right to make a movie from the material or you can negotiate a purchase agreement to own all rights to the material. All rights might include novelization of a script, the right to make a stage play or create a television show using the underlying material, toys based on the characters, etc. Of course, this should be your preference. If you hold all rights you truly control the material. This kind of overall purchase is not always possible, but it's the best way to go. This way nothing happens to it without you being included in the deal.

When you think about optioning a book that has already been published, don't forget that there are people whose entire job it is to scout books before they even come out in order to snap up the rights in case there might be a movie there. If you're thinking about a bestseller at this point in your career, put it out of your head. On the other hand, if you went to a yard sale and found an out-of-print book by someone no one has ever heard, or you found a short story by an unknown writer that is part of an obscure collection, it could be that it's a hidden gem that was overlooked. Starting with a book that has already seen success in the marketplace probably isn't for you at this time—not until you've established yourself or actually have a source of funding beyond your own savings.

In addition to a true option, there is a trend towards an arrangement called a *shopping agreement*. A shopping agreement allows you to obtain the right to shop the script around for financing or investors without an option. There should be an agreement in place (written by an attorney) in case financing is found. A well written agreement will protect the person shopping the script from being cut out if a deal is made, and will also protect the screenwriter's interest by getting the script to potential investors, as most screenwriters don't have access to sources of financing.

You read an article in a magazine and think that it could serve as the basis for a terrific screenplay. This is more complicated, but the action you take is the same. You call the publisher of the magazine, and they will give you information. Sometimes the magazine owns the work of the writer, and sometimes the writer owns his or her own work. Your job is to track down the true owner of the material and check on the status of the material in terms of availability.

Depending upon the nature of the article, you will likely want to option it so that you can use it in part as the basis for your screenplay. The writer has done the research and you want the writer's collaboration. Be aware that because you have the journalist's blessing doesn't mean you have the blessing of the people mentioned in the article. Which brings us to another kind of rights.

Based on a true story. Something happened to someone, or you are interested in making a narrative theatrical (non-documentary) film about a real person or real events, or the material you found is based upon real people or events.

This is much more complicated. You must find the real people involved, decide whose story you want to tell, decide who else's stories you will need in order to tell your story effectively, and then approach all of these people for their *life rights*. These are the "based on a true story" rights. Life rights give you the right to use something that truly belongs to someone else—their personal story. In this case you are dealing with *privacy rights*. Unless they are public figures, people "own" their own lives, and they are entitled to privacy. You obtain someone's life rights because you would like cooperation. You can invent characters, but if they are recognizable to the person whose story you're telling, you can bet that your project will be held up with legal proceedings. Even if you win, the cost of it all can break you.

All three of these situations require the hiring of an experienced entertainment lawyer. You'll have to pay somebody, then take your chances that your investment will be recouped when you interest a financial backer. Even if you are able to persuade someone to give you rights for free, these are complex agreements that must be negotiated. You need an attorney who is schooled in the entertainment industry, not a lawyer uncle or cousin or family friend who is happy to help. Entertainment law and intellectual property are specializations. You want someone who can outthink and outmaneuver the other guy—that's how you will be protected.

Can you and should you write it yourself?

Can you write? It is surprising how many people believe that they are writers because they have read a lot of scripts, received As in English, and can use Final Draft or who want to produce or direct and think that writing a script is the easiest or least expensive first step.

You're a storyteller, and you may have a sense of how to make a story work, but that's a long way from being able to write a good script. In fact, writing a good script is a lot more difficult than finding a good script, and you will be more objective when talking about, critiquing, pitching, and negotiating a project that you did not write. Other people will be more straightforward with their critiques and notes if they are delivering the news to a third party. Being creative doesn't mean you have to be creative in every area. As a producer, your biggest asset might be your ability to spot promising raw material, to work with the writer to massage it until it's the best it can possibly be, then to use your personal passion and skills to get the script seen and made. If you're a director, and you have the acuity to spot material that is special, the best road to take may be to find a script and bring your personal vision and sensitivity to the telling of story.

On the other hand, if you have always written, whether you're a journalist, have been published, have studied screenwriting and not only received good feedback (not the same as a good grade) and have had your work read by someone actually working in a creative capacity in the industry and have been consistently urged to show them more—then you may want to think about writing your own script.

Be prepared for heartache. You will have to toughen up. It hurts deeply to labor for months on a personal drama only to be told, "This is a great idea, but can you change the lead from a 20-year-old woman to a 40-year-old man, and can you make it much funnier?" Particularly if the story is personal and autobiographical.

Finding a terrific script means you have taste; optioning or attaching yourself to a terrific script means you understand the way the business works. Even when the script you've brought to someone is not a home run, if it's an interesting project, you've paved the way to meet them again with something else. If you've written a script and they don't want it, the door may not open next time around. Owning a great script is often the only currency that will get a newcomer a seat at the table, so whether you write it or find it and option it, it can't just be good. It has to be brilliant, engaging, great, or you're wasting your chance.

WRITING WITH A PARTNER

Maybe you want to work with a partner. Screenwriting partnerships are common. The collaborations all work differently. One partner may be more disciplined, and because of that he or she pushes the other to be more productive. Sometimes one half of the team will write a part and then send it to the other to rewrite or continue. One may be more of an idea person, and the other is the one who does more of the actual writing of the scene. One is better at plot, another at dialogue. One is better at pitching and meetings, the other doesn't want to leave his room. However the partnerships work, the team has come to the conclusion that two heads are more effective than one. Writing can be isolating. Writing with a partner can help relieve that "sitting and staring at the blank page" syndrome.

Writing partners don't even have to be friends. In fact, sometimes the team spends little non-work time together. Writing with a partner is most successful when the partners have complementary skills and share sensibilities as to what is good and what should end up in the rubbish. A partnership won't work if you are a "my way is better, I'm always right" kind of person. It's OK to have that unwavering, singular faith in your brilliance. In order to survive sometimes you must have that. But a partnership is like any relationship—there has to be synergy, a benefit gained from the pairing, and a willingness to view a project as *ours* rather than *mine*. If that's not you, it's better to write alone.

If you are going to write with a partner, you should be sure that your business arrangement is on paper. No verbal agreements. No so-called understandings. You must, must have something in writing that details the structure of the partnership. There is a saying that "good fences make good neighbors." Well, good contracts make good partnerships and can help prevent a relationship from going down the tubes when there is interest in a script the two of you have written. People interested in your work may find it profitable to try a "divide and conquer" strategy, and in the thrill of the moment one of you may be tempted. Think of your written agreement as the contract that keeps you both honest.

How to Find a Writer

What if you know you're not a writer but you have an extraordinary idea, or you've optioned a book or an article? How do you find someone to write it?

It's easy to find people who call themselves screenwriters, but it's not easy to find people who are talented and pleasant to work with. Return to those friends and contacts you've been accumulating. Ask around. Look at graduate screenwriting programs at the top film schools. Read samples. Ask anyone you meet who works as an assistant to a literary agent or manager or who reads *spec scripts* (scripts that are not commissioned or contracted by a production company in advance of the writing) and writes coverage as part of their job. Contact past winners of screenwriting awards. If you're hoping for a career as a producer, director, or any kind of executive, you should make it your goal to meet as many writers as possible, to read as many scripts as you can find, and to learn to weigh the merits of the writing even if you don't care for the actual story.

This is one of the reasons why early on, finding an internship where you read scripts and have the opportunity to read coverage written by others is paramount. The ability to read a script and analyze the basic premise, the way the story unfolds, and the talent of the writer is of supreme importance. Whatever you do in film, you have to be able to understand what is worthwhile and what is junk, what is well-written but not a great premise, and what isn't working in it's present form but is twenty drafts away from outstanding. You will develop the ability to separate the story from the writing. Sometimes a script will be a genre piece or will deal with an issue that is not your cup of tea, but something keeps you from putting it down. That's the skill of the writer. The more scripts you read, the more people you ask, the more it will become evident that there are many terrific undiscovered writers out there, but you have to dig through a pile of scripts to find them.

How to Persuade the Writer to Work with You

Since you have no money, how can you find someone to write for free, or for very little money? You're going to have to make a deal. You cannot expect anyone to work with you day after day without a contract. This means you must negotiate a fair "if this happens, you'll get this" contract. Your agreement should be in steps: "If A happens, you'll get B": "If the project moves on to the next step, you'll receive C." Any agreement you create must address ownership and must be specific. Although it may be your idea, when someone else writes it they can rightfully claim ownership of the script. If a screenwriter is contracted to write a script based on someone else's idea, an important part of the agreement between the writer and the person paying is who owns the project and how much of an interest in the project each person controls. This must be committed to paper before anything happens with the script or you can lose ownership of the project. Remember that ideas are cheap and plentiful—it's the execution of the ideas that count.

When you write up your agreement be certain that you are not making promises you can't keep. For example, if the writer does drafts 1 through 5 then decides he or she is sick of it or has to make some money and you're left with finding another writer, what kind of interest in the script does the original writer hold? What if draft 5 is the basis for a new (9th) draft that another writer does? What does writer number 2 receive if the project is *set up* (funded) by a production company? Do not guarantee that any of your writers will be kept on the project once a deal is made with a production company, or that the original screenwriters will receive a specific credit on the finished film. At this stage of your career you will have no control over who receives what credit, especially if the production company is signatory to the Writers Guild of America (WGA), and it is even more likely that whoever is funding the project will want a more established and better known writer to do a rewrite. The only thing you can guarantee is money, and the appropriate amount of money can be determined by consulting an experienced entertainment attorney. Since your reputation is important, you will want to come up with a realistic but fair amount. You don't want to begin your career by being the producer or director who screwed over the people who helped you get something going.

Chapter 7

The Politics of Development

DEVELOPMENT HELL

There are several stages to making a movie, and each can be brief or take years. There is the crafting or finding of the idea, then the writing of one or many drafts, or the optioning of the material that is the basis for that writing. These are the first stages of *development*. When a project is in development, it means that the idea/novel/article/script draft is being transformed from whatever it was when you started to a ready-to-shoot project. Development usually includes *attaching creative elements*. An attachment is an agreement that links a director and/or cast member (the elements) to the project in order to enhance its value and hasten the decision that it will be worth the money to move ahead.

If the project is funded by a major production company or studio (which means there is a *development deal*) months and even years can pass between the point where the company decides that the project is one that they want to be involved with to the point of production and a firm \ go.\ In the past, some writers were able to live quite well on development money. These days more than ever, there is very little money paid out for development. Producers want more and more work done on the script for less and less money, because they themselves are not seeing a payday until something is close to a green light. If the project is an independent, you can usually count on a very long search for money somewhere just after the development stage. For independent films, it is often the case that the script is where it should be, but it's a matter of finding someone to pay to make that script.

Many more scripts are optioned, purchased, and even slated for development than ever get made. "Development Hell" is how industry people describe it when the project is in limbo, awaiting a better draft, a rewrite of the draft, a name whose involvement can take it from a yellow light to a green one. The project is sitting, waiting for something that may never happen. If you are the force behind the project (producer, writer-director, executive), it is your responsibility to create and maintain momentum. You must push or pull the project from each stage to the next. The project may falter or stall at any point, and you must bounce back quickly from each rejection or problem and get on to the next step. Without an enormous amount of personal enthusiasm behind it, a project can easily get lost as energy flags and obstacles slow things down. You must stay on top of what is happening by touching base with your contact on a regular basis so that your project is not consigned to the bottom of the pile due to lack of heat. Is there something relevant to your project that's just happened in the news? Bring it up. Is there an audience trend or a break out picture that might help you or your project with a little reflected glory? Maybe someone involved with your team just got one of their other projects accepted into Sundance...make everyone involved with your project aware of it.

WORKING WITH YOUR WRITER

Working with a writer will call upon every ounce of tact and people skills you possess.

You must think of the work as a team effort but always acknowledge that without the writer there is no movie. A writer tries to create something special—not just words on a page, not just a blueprint for a movie, but a living, breathing, original work that will jump off the page and into the psyche of the reader. Some writers blitz through an entire draft of a screenplay in a few weeks just to get it on paper then spend the next several months changing, editing, tweaking. The finished product might end up nothing like that first draft. Some writers obsess over every word. They are ritualistic in their fussing and shredding of pages until they feel settled into the work at hand. Your job is to learn how your writer does his or her best work and to create a safe environment so he or she can focus and can give birth to something special and unique.

What is a safe environment? It means that you are there when your writer wants to talk but you're not hanging over her shoulder while she writes. You allow her to explore new ideas that might not exactly be what you'd thought of but that might work—sometimes even better than the original plan. You don't call every day demanding to know what she has accomplished, but you touch base so she knows she hasn't been forgotten. Your job is to keep your writer on track—unless the tangent is an improvement. You discuss everything calmly and supportively, and when you disagree, you must find a way to express precisely what doesn't work, not just, "I don't like the second act." You may think this is purely common sense, but screenwriters get emotionally and intellectually beat up all the time. The last thing you want is for your writer to feel victimized or bullied. That can result in all kinds of passive-aggressive retaliation ("I just don't feel like working"; "Sure, whatever. I don't care.") and ultimately it will be the end of the relationship.

How can you be precise? First, read every word and think before reacting. Second, pinpoint exactly what is lacking. "I don't think the mother would react like that, and everything hangs on the boy's response to the mom." You're constructive. You discuss the problem, but you don't tell a writer what you would write to "fix" the problem. If you could do it, you'd be writing! Your comments are called *notes,* and they should be brief and specific, not rambling and general.

No one enjoys hearing his or her work being criticized, but a screenwriter has to get used to it. If your writer can't take criticism at all, you're going to have to decide whether the relationship is working for both of you or if it should be dissolved. Before you take that step, though, remember that there is a reason you wanted this person involved—talent. You should be prepared to put up with a lot of hand-holding and tears if the pages you're reading have promise.

I'LL GET BACK TO YOU (GETTING THE SCRIPT READ)

Unfortunately, it is not enough to be in possession of a great script. It's one of those if a tree falls in the forest and nobody hears it things. For a script to make it anywhere close to production, it must be read by someone who has the clout to do something with it if they like it. Studios and production companies are constantly looking for the next hot property. Producers and directors have multiple staff people who read and read, hoping to find that golden script. You just have to find a way to place your great script into their hands and hope that it strikes them as a potential winner.

The catch is that most studios and production companies will not accept the submission of a script from someone who doesn't have representation (an agent, an attorney, a manager). There are several reasons for this. One is that if someone is represented by someone they know or know of, it can be assumed that at the very least it will not be a complete waste of time and effort to have the script read. Another is that in this litigious society, everyone is always claiming credit and suing for a piece of the pie. Win or lose, lawsuits are costly and suck up a lot of personnel. Even when a script is properly represented, there is the danger that someone who pitched Fox his story about a driven tap dancer will decide that the script for *Black Swan* was stolen from him. The preliminary filter of a known representative helps to fend off a few of the frivolous or misguided lawsuits that might be brought by Bob in Ohio (because he mailed his script to the studio Production department) or Jill (because she went to a party in L.A. and told someone who worked at Disney that she'd read a really good book, then heard that the book had been optioned by the company.) It's cleaner, easier, and less legally precarious to have a flat policy of "no unsolicited screenplays will be accepted." In fact, the rule in many industry mailrooms is not even to open up the binder, but just stick the script into a larger envelope with a form letter describing the policy and return it to the sender.

Then how do people without representation get in the door to pitch or get a screenplay read? Once again, it's about those people you've been meeting. If you know an assistant, he may be willing to read a script. That's a personal exchange. If the assistant likes it, he can bring it to the boss. Someone might know someone who knows someone at a company and is willing to vouch for you if she likes the script and knows that you're not a stalker in the making. Individual producers and directors accept unsolicited screenplays all the time. The writer might have to sign a release but can rest assured that no one is trying to steal an idea. Ohio Bob's script, on the other hand, was never read. It was tossed in the trash because it came through the mail with no release form and no attached representation. The book that Jill was so excited about? That one was optioned in *galleys* (unbound manuscript form) by the literary agent who scouts books for Disney. By the time Jill read the book, the deal had long since been negotiated, consummated, and a screenwriter already hired for the adaptation.

If you are interning at a company, ask if you can get a script read before you finish your internship. If you are taking a course with someone in the industry, ask for advice on how you can get something read. Go to seminars. Meet people. As long as you're affable and pleasant, if you have a good script, people will help you. One caveat to all this is to be careful to whom you give your idea and your script. There are many ways you can be scammed in the industry. There are a few legitimate pitching events—the better film schools hold them, but they are not open to the general public, and *Fade In* magazine holds an event a couple times of year—but there are several that are not legitimate. These events charge the participants a great deal of money, and the pitch recipients tend not to hold the type of positions that can do any good, so you'll want to check them out thoroughly before you decide to invest. Your reason for attending one of these pitch events is to make contacts who will be willing to give you their card and will accept a script from you. This will not happen unless you ace your pitch—so again, practice.

BEFORE YOU SEND OUT THE SCRIPT

Before you give written material to anyone in the business, you must be sure that you are legally *attached*. This means that you are the official source of the material, whether or not you wrote it. You hold the option or you have purchased it outright. You have a written agreement, drafted by an entertainment attorney, giving you (a) the exclusive right to "shop" the project from company to company, and (b) the right to continue on with the project if it is set up—meaning that someone wants to finance the project.

When a script is set up at a major company often the first thing the major players will want to do is purchase the script from the attached rights holder, replace the writer with someone with more experience, and thus relieve themselves of any obligation to involve the person who brought the script to the party. You may choose to "take the money and run"—that is, have your lawyer negotiate a credit of some kind for you, then leave. If you really want to be in the business, though, you will want to hang on and have your lawyer negotiate an active position for you on the film. You will have no power, but just by being around you'll learn enough so that you can take the reins on the next one.

Do not accept a verbal agreement of your involvement. Even if the initial intention is an honest one, you will soon find that a person without an official job to do on a film is considered an encumbrance, is not taken seriously, and is soon left out of meetings and phone calls simply because there is no real reason to include them. You must start to define your contribution and amass some power. The industry is full of people who received some kind of producer credit on a single film, but because all they did was bring a project to someone else, they are back at first base, unable to get meetings or to make anything happen. People in the industry always know who really is involved and who is just hanging out. Don't willingly allow yourself to be cut out of the mix, but be realistic. No studio or major production company is going to give you control over your baby. There is just too much money and too much risk involved.

The money for bringing in a project comes in the form of yet another step deal. There is some money up front; some money when a final draft is approved by the financial entity; some money upon production green light; some when talent (cast, director) is attached; some the first day of production; some upon delivery of the finished film. By spreading the money out this way, the financial entity is again avoiding possible losses. At any point, the project can stop its forward progress. When that happens, the payment obligations come to an end.

When a script is submitted to a company or to an individual, the first thing that will happen is that someone will be assigned to read it and write coverage. As mentioned previously, coverage is often written by an intern or an assistant. Ever write a book report in elementary or middle school? Coverage is like a book report. The format varies slightly from place to place but basically follows this outline:

The title of the script (or if it's a book, the title of the book)
The screenwriter
The format (screenplay, book, magazine article)
The number of pages
The genre (thriller, suspense, teen comedy, family drama)
A log line (not unlike a pitch, a log line is a one-sentence summary of the material)
A synopsis (a page or two written in present tense describing the plot)
A comments section (Usually a few paragraphs of critique, both general and specific points about whether the script works, doesn't work, has appeal—if so why, if not why not.)
A final choice: Recommend or Pass.

A script should never be handed to anyone at a studio or production company or to a source of funding until it is the best draft the writer can achieve, because a script doesn't usually get a second reading at the same company. There are too many scripts pouring in. When a script comes in to an executive, an agent or manager, a producer, a director, anyone with any sort of elevated position in the industry, it is covered. The decision-makers at a company rarely read a piece of material without having first read that coverage.

Anything that will shrink the immense load of reading material down to a manageable level for an executive or a producer is a huge help. The assistants and interns are not only trained to read, but their taste and take on a screenplay matters because it is often indicative of whether the material will ultimately succeed with the target audience. If they really love a script, chances are that it will be passed up the food chain, intern to a first assistant, assistant to a development executive, development executive to his or her boss.

Every Friday, everyone takes home a pile of scripts. Each week a meeting is held, and all participants are expected to report as to the merits or lack of merit they found in their weekend *reads*. Sometimes there is a vested interest in the meeting. An agent is looking for a project for a certain client, or someone has heard about a new project needing a rewrite and a list of potential writers is being compiled. More often than not, the screenplays are all found wanting. These readers are looking for the proverbial needle in the haystack, the unexpected jewel that will make the reading process worthwhile.

To put it in some kind of context, know that most of these scripts come in with references. These are not blind, unsolicited submissions. These are sent by agents, managers, people with experience, or people who are attached to the Industry in some way. During the heyday of the Seventies and Eighties, there were hundreds of projects in active development, with producers and writers receiving substantial monies in order to work on getting a script from idea to production, but that landscape is now completely different. Due to the current economic climate and all the unknowns in terms of where the industry is heading, of the several thousand screenplays read at any given company every year, possibly fifty will ultimately be involved in some kind of financed development deal, and possibly ten will actually become movies. Most movies that are made now come from scripts that are packaged and nearly ready to shoot.

The cost of developing, casting, prepping, producing, finishing, and most of all marketing a film is so high that everyone has got to be enthusiastically on board. There are lots of reasons why a project dies. The production company is not only looking for a great story, but for a great story that will interest the level of cast that will bring in financing or make financing worthwhile. Is it a project fraught with complicated production issues so that it can be made only for a very high budget? Do the marketing and distribution people feel that this is something an audience wants to see? Is there a reason right out of the starting gate (the script stage) that passing on the project is the smarter way to go? Remember that it's easier to say no.

WHAT HAPPENS DURING DEVELOPMENT

If a script is in development it usually means that someone has put up some money to option or purchase the script, that it is being written and notes on ways to improve it are being communicated, and that it is then being rewritten. Over and over again. The structure of a development deal is usually (a) an option agreement is signed, and (b) the script is critiqued and extensive notes are given either by a company development or creative executive, or by a producer or director. This depends upon who has done the optioning. The intention of a notes session is to help the script morph from a really good piece of written material to an outstanding, visual film with impact and commercial appeal.

The job of the note giver is a strange one, because although the person giving script notes has read many very good and many more truly awful scripts, he or she is not a writer. This person probably has a knack for negotiating, for dealing with writers, producers, and directors, as well as a wonderful sense of story, structure, and character, and hopefully good taste and great communication skills. The belief is that this person has the experience and ability to guide a project from idea to screen. That's why many producers are former creative executives. There is a natural tension between a development person and a writer, and it is often a volatile relationship. If a producer or director has brought the project to the company and is attached to the project, the notes will be channeled through that person, which makes the relationship a little easier.

Sometimes this process works, but sometimes the specialness of the story is diluted once all the changes are incorporated into the script, and the story that was once deemed great enough to start the process in the first place, seems to get weaker over time. *CEs* (Creative Executives) and investors can run out of steam on a project. If you brought the script in, it is your duty to champion that script and keep it alive through all the comments and drafts. If the notes make sense, it is the obligation of the writer and/or producer of the project to give them a try. If they don't make sense, the producer must smooth the way, maintaining the integrity of the project without causing the CE a loss of enthusiasm or respect. Even once a script is in active development, it can at some point be left foundering, never to become a movie.

It is not enough for a script to be really good. *The Black List* is an annual list of great unproduced scripts. The scripts on the list have been nominated by key creative executives, and the list represents their favorites. These screenplays have made the rounds, received outstandingly positive coverage, been passed up the food chain from reader to development exec to production exec, but for one reason or another still have not been made. Often inclusion on the Black List spurs a script into production but sometimes the screenplays just sits there, praised, respected, but not made.

If all this comes as a shock and seems too depressing, you can take heart in the fact that this process is a learning experience for everyone when they are starting out. Most experienced, successful writers tell me that their best shield is humor. They try not to take it too seriously, because it may be art, but it is after all, a job. The trick is to find a producer, director, or development person who first and foremost understands and admires your work, and who is able to remain supportive while edging the material bit by bit towards the finish line.

THE TOP TEN REASONS SCRIPTS ARE REJECTED

Assuming that so many screenwriters are literate and talented, it may be surprising that even highly experienced successful writers often can't sell their scripts. Consider this: Many readers, development people, and producers read five to ten scripts per week. Multiply that by 50-odd weeks. (They do occasionally take vacations.) That's a lot of reading. Taking an informal poll among my friends, former students, and colleagues, here are some of the many reasons a script will end up on a shelf in a storage room:

1. Took too long to get going
2. Didn't care about the characters
3. Writer didn't know the world
4. The tangents or subplots were more interesting than the main action
5. Nothing new, seen it before
6. Writer didn't know what the script was really about
7. Loss of energy in the second act
8. The Stakes are not high enough
9. Didn't know how to end it
10. Why would anyone want to see this movie?

Let's take these one by one.

Took Too Long to Get Going

Although the ideal is for each reader to complete the full script, the common wisdom is that if the script has not piqued a reader's interest by the first thirty pages (the first act), it's not going to get better, and chances are that script will land on the finish-when-I-have-the-time pile—and the reader will never make the time.

A script should start strong. Sometimes you may feel that in order for us to understand a character or an event we have to get his or her entire history, when in reality part of a writer's job is to find a way of letting us get to know a character without giving us the whole birth/marriage/death cycle. This must be done through revealing action and dialogue, not *on the nose* (obvious) speeches. Think of the opening scene as the first possibility to intrigue the reader. It had better move us quickly into the set-up and the world of the story. Don't creep up on the story. If it takes too long for us to get into it, the fight has been thrown before it has begun.

Starting strong doesn't mean there has to be a gunshot or a suicide. It means that right from the first scene, we want to hop on board and take the trip. Who are these people? What is the situation? We have short attention spans. Movies must compete with TV, gaming, and the internet. Readers and executives know this all too well. It doesn't matter if it's a drama, fantasy, romantic comedy, or a suspense thriller, the story must hook us right away or we get distracted and find other things to do.

Didn't Care About the Characters

We must be able to relate to your characters, especially your leads. We don't have to like them, but we do have to be able to identify with them, to see traces of someone we might recognize. If we don't have a sense of what a character wants or what a character feels, then whatever that character does seems random and without meaning. Why would we care about what happens to her? Again, it's about getting us to want to go along with the character for the ride.

People are multidimensional. As lovable as some people are, they have their faults. As boorish or despicable as some are, there is something or somebody they care about. They are motivated by love, hatred, greed, sex—all the stuff of real life. The characters must be motivated, and we must know what drives them. A character can't do something just to support a plot point. If a character must do something senseless just to help get them from here to there, then there is more work to be done on the screenplay. Even if the character is insane, there must be a sense of the parameters of his insanity. When the actions of a character feel inauthentic, we immediately become bored because there is nothing to grab on to. When that happens a reader is just looking at words on a page, not seeing the action unfold before them. If a reader is bored with the character, he or she is bored with the story, and that's when it's time to pick up the next script in the pile.

The screenwriter must be able to find the humanity in the world of the characters. We don't have to admire criminals in order for a crime story to work, but if none of the criminal characters have a bit of humanity to them, what are we watching? A standard good guy/bad guy film is far less unique than a not-so-good hero and a not-so-bad villain. When we know why a character feels and does things, then we care about what happens to the character. If we don't, and the character does something only because she is good or bad, we don't care. It's not interesting. If we don't care, we'll stop reading if it's a script or stop watching if it's a film. When a reader is covering a screenplay, if there is a point where that reader feels that the story has gone from interesting to ordinary or by the numbers, then the comment on that script is going to be Pass.

Writer Didn't Know the World

You don't have to be a gang member to write about gang life, but you must have an understanding of anger and of brutality. However the writer gets the information—maybe through research, maybe through truly experiencing whatever the subject or situation—doesn't matter.

We must believe that the storyteller comprehends the environment, the mood, and the events of his story. We must believe that the storyteller knows what he is talking about. When we find a script gripping, it's because the writer has created a world that feels truthful, whether the script is an urban thriller, a high school comedy, a fantasy, or a western. Without this element of truthfulness, a script feels clumsy and unconvincing.

The Tangents or Subplots Were More Interesting Than the Main Action

A good story is like a train ride. The storyteller must keep the audience on the track from the minute the train leaves the station to the very end of the line.

There can be all kinds of twists and turns to the story—characters and situations the audience might want to get off the train to explore. But they must not be permitted to get off that train. A script may introduce subplots or characters that seem to be from out of left field. These plots and characters must enhance the main action in some way. The second the audience wants to spend more time off the train than on, you lose them. Ever feel as if halfway through a movie, the feel and tone of the story shifts and it's as if you're watching a different movie? That's often because the story took a turn, threw you off the track, and now you're trying to figure out what or who the story really is. The weight and originality of the turns must energize the audience's ride, not derail it.

Nothing New, Seen It Before

If people are going to take a chance on you, a newcomer, they are going to do it because you have something they want—an original idea or script or concept.

The genre—drama, comedy, thriller, horror—is irrelevant. If your project is like a hundred other projects, why will anyone want to give you a shot? They can find more reliable veterans to make and remake the same old thing. They're listening to or meeting or reading a newcomer like you for one reason only: You may have something new.

Writer Didn't Know What the Script Was Really About

How is that possible? Perhaps the writer thinks the big story is the murder while the reader thinks the story is the mother-son relationship. Of course the story involves both, but a choice has to be made. What moves the story forward? What is the point? Is it that someone has been killed, or is it that the mother thinks the son did it? In a drama (think for instance of *The Fighter*) where is the emotional weight? Is it the relationship between the brothers, or does the victory or loss of the final boxing match carry the most weight? If the most compelling path offered is not the path the writer chooses to follow, the reader will not be satisfied and will pass on the script.

Loss of Energy in the Second Act

Great start, but then it fizzles. We have a situation, we have characters, but whatever made the beginning work so well isn't sustained. The reader loses interest. Because the beginning is strong, the reader is anticipating good material. The script has a cool set-up, but the writer has not figured out where to go from there. Maybe she has written herself into a corner because she didn't go into enough detail with her outline and treatment. Possibly the story got lost somewhere (see reasons number 4 and 6). In the second act, we need more conflict, more barriers, and maybe there aren't any.

You must keep the reader laughing, squirming, alert. If there is any excuse at all, the reader will pass. The writer must raise the stakes. This leads us to reason number 8.

The Stakes Are Not High Enough

Simply put, there is not enough jeopardy. There is not enough conflict. There is no building tension. It's not enough that a criminal wants to go straight and his buddies want him to continue with his life of violence. That can make for a powerful conflict, but a single conflict won't carry the film. There has to be an emotional conflict. The guy owes his buddies. That pushes the stakes higher. Then there is a romantic or family relationship. The main character can't maintain one relationship without betraying the other. Higher stakes.

Whether the threat is the loss of trust or love, the physical risk of imprisonment or death, the threat must be ever-present, looming in the background but often subtly brought to the foreground. Stakes push the action. Raised stakes keep the reader turning the page to see what happens—and helps get a meeting for the writer, producer, or director who found the story.

Didn't Know How to End It

The final scenes of a film are decisive. The third act of a screenplay should feel inevitable but not predictable. Even an intimate family drama should end in a way that feels organic, natural. No sudden unrelated revelations that make your audience feel they've been conned. Revelations belong in the first and second act where they set the story in motion, not as explanations for a plot that would not otherwise make sense. The days of a film ending with a psychiatrist explaining that Norman Bates killed people because he had a domineering mother are over. We don't want after-the-fact explanations. We want to understand events as they happen.

Tying up loose ends must be done with a light hand. In a romantic comedy, you know the characters are going to get together (it's inevitable), but the way the various obstacles are resolved must be inventive. In a thriller, if everything points to a certain culprit and in the end he did indeed "do it," then the turn must be how he is trapped. If there's a surprise at the end, the audience must think, "Of course! How could I have not seen that coming?" not "What??"

If everything just rolls on as expected or as we've seen in dozens of other films, why is anyone going to want to invest time or money in your film? If an audience is let down by the ending of a film, they feel tricked and leave feeling angry. An audience should feel as if they've just had an amazing dinner—sorry that it's over, but full and satisfied. If the film is intended to be disturbing or thought-provoking, that's fine. We're not talking happy endings here. We're talking about a sense of completion, rather than just the end.

Why Would Anyone Want to See This Movie?

This is about marketing. It is possible for a screenplay to be well-written, with great roles and the requisite structure, and still be a hard sell. Remember that *selling* is what this is about. Distribution and butts in the seats. There are certain films that a reader or development executive or a marketing executive just can't imagine attracting an audience. It's all well and good to think, "If we make it and it's good it will sell," but that's just not true these days. Sometimes it's the genre, sometimes the subject matter. If no one can figure out how to sell your Victorian-era brother-sister feud, they're not going to help you make it. If a screenplay is a sci-fi western and one came out last year and bombed, it may not matter that this is the better version. They aren't going to go that way again anytime soon. If it's G-rated family fare but then the kid dies, an executive or investor is going to ask, will anyone want to see this? If you're dealing with a difficult subject you must at least be sure that the film will not be too expensive to make and that there are some fantastic roles in there so that you can attract known name talent, or your project will almost certainly not get made.

Finally, sometimes a screenplay is good—just not good enough. Or the company already owns something like it. Or they're just not sure of it. All you can do as someone starting out is take a good hard look at your material and see how it stacks up against other work out there. There can also be reasons that actually don't have much to do with the script itself—a screenplay is developed, but then there's a change of management at the company. The new head of production wants to start with a clean slate and dumps many of the projects that were on track just . . . because. Or it has become known that there's another project out there that is similar to yours and it's further along. It's rare for an audience to want two films, one after another, that are so close in type—unless the first one is a big hit for another company, in which case you might find your project resurrected.

What happens when a script is sold, developed, but then for some reason the right cast says no, the director loses interest, it's too expensive, another film with the same concept is released and does poorly, and the film is not made? Sometimes it just dies. And sometimes the script goes into *turnaround*, meaning that it is available for someone new to buy it. Turnaround costs can vary from a percentage of the original purchase price to much, much more. Depending on how far along the project was when it was pulled, in addition to the original price of the script, the costs of development are added in because the original owners want their losses recouped. This means that any money paid to additional writers for new drafts, any money spent on getting a tentative budget made, any location scouting (if the project got that far along), all these expenditures are added on to the original price. And if a company does want to purchase it with all these additional costs attached, there may be additional issues to be negotiated between the new buyer and the old owner, such as credits, or possible profit participation. It can become quite complicated. In rare cases, a studio may have purchased a script with the intention of shelving it because it was too close to something they already owned, or it's a novelty film that they want to pull off the market. Can you, as a writer do anything about that? Will you be in control of your script? Once you sell it, it's no longer your script. That's why you need that razor sharp lawyer—so you'll understand all the possibilities and consequences of what you sign in advance.

Cornelius Uliano and Bryan Schulz

Starting as a Screenwriter—Talent and Luck

Cornelius "Neil" Uliano and Bryan Schulz are a successful young screenwriting team. Neil Uliano, 26, graduated from the film school at the Brooks Institute of Photography in 2006. Bryan Schulz, 30, is the grandson of the *Peanuts* creator, Charles M. Schulz, and lives in Northern California. He graduated from the film school at the Brooks Institute of Photography in 2005. I asked them to tell me about their first steps into the industry.

Neil begins: When I first started working in the industry I realized a lot of people were frustrated that they were stuck doing a job they didn't want to do. They were no longer following their dreams. They had become comfortable. A lot of negativity comes from that. I wanted to make sure that did not happen to me. I made a promise to myself that I would not stay at a job for any longer than six months. This plan made my parents very happy. (That was sarcasm for anyone that missed it.) By doing this, it always kept me on my toes. It made me always hungry to succeed.

My first job was working at a reality TV company. I was assigned to be a director's assistant for a documentary they were shooting on the Griffith Observatory. I loved the job and I loved everyone that I worked for. It was an amazing opportunity, and it allowed me to hire a lot of my friends who were looking for work at the time. The company offered me a more long-term position at the end of the shoot. It was so tempting to take it, but I knew if I did, I would be there for a very long time. I had to decline.

I was desperately trying to find work. I decided to call the head of the scoring stage at Paramount Pictures. My composer and I scored all of the music on that stage for my thesis films in college, and we established a connection with the staff. The scoring stage has since been destroyed. I asked if there were any openings on the lot. I said I would do anything. Mop the floors. Cook the food (I didn't know to cook). Anything. She got back to me and said they were looking to hire someone for the mailroom. I thought, how cliché. I applied that very day. I got the job.

Working at Paramount was one of the most amazing times in my life. I was so excited to have the job. I don't think my parents knew what to think when I called them all excited about how I was hired to deliver mail. For me, it was the best job I could have. I got my own Paramount mail shirt, a golf cart, health insurance, any Paramount DVD I wanted was only 5 bucks, and it was only a six-month commitment job.

I would wake up at 5:00 am, get in at 6:00 and deliver the trades [*The Hollywood Reporter* and *Daily Variety*]. We would get the mail in at 11:00 am, sort it, and filter out any crazy letters from teenage girls or inmates at the nearby correctional facility trying to have a romance with Tom Cruise. We would do an afternoon

Continued

Cornelius Uliano and Bryan Schulz—cont'd

run and get to go home by 3:00 pm. This was a perfect job for an aspiring writer/-director. I was able to get home and work on my script before going to bed and repeat the same thing the next day.

The most valuable part about the job were the days I would stay late on the lot. The only thing that made us stick out as mailroom folk were our shirts. Our ID badges, however, were the same as everyone else on the lot. So, I would bring a change of clothes and keep my badge on. I was able to go anywhere at anytime without question. I would sneak onto sets and watch them shoot, trying to learn as much as I could. The most memorable experience was walking into the soundstage while they were shooting *Charlie Wilson's War*. Watching Mike Nichols shoot a scene with Tom Hanks was truly an awe-inspiring event. It did not last long, though, as I was caught and removed shortly thereafter.

At the end of the six months, it was time to move on. I did not have another job lined up. I did not have any connections to other work. And because I was working in the mailroom for so little money, I had nothing saved up to hold me over. I just took a leap of faith and left. I look back at this as one of the stupidest things I have ever done. I had nothing. I could not find work. And it got a little ugly.

After being rejected by everyone I was desperate for anything. I applied to a job at Fox to be an executive assistant. It said you needed five years of experience. I sent them my resume and I was called in for an interview. I'm pretty sure somebody made a mistake. They asked me three questions when I arrived. (1) Have I ever been an assistant before? I answered No. (2) Do you know how to roll calls? At this time, I did not even know what that meant. I answered No. (3) Are you sure you're interested in this position? I had to lie on this one. I said, "Of Course." I was not hired.

It was one of the lowest points in my life. I had nothing. No money. No job. I felt really discouraged. I thought I had made a big mistake. But then I got a phone call. A dear friend of mine from film school was working as an assistant to a very high-profile producer in Hollywood. He was meeting a lot of new people, especially agents. He called me one day and asked if my writing partner and I were interested in meeting an assistant/up-and-coming agent at CAA [Creative Artists Agency]. When I heard CAA my eyes opened wide. I had researched them when I was little, trying to find out who repped all my favorite filmmakers growing up. I didn't care who he was at the agency. I agreed to meet him. My friend told me that before he set up the meeting he would have to give him a script of ours, and asked if we had anything. As it turned out, we had just finished a script we were excited about.

I was very cautious going into the meeting. I had heard a lot about agents, and most of what I heard was not very good. Meeting a potential agent is a lot like a blind date. You don't start off talking about your script or the business. You talk about yourselves. You get to know each other. You have to have that connection. On my end, I wanted to make sure I trusted and respected the person who would be representing us and speaking on our behalf. I wanted to make sure we were going to hand our baby (script) off to someone who would treat it with the utmost respect. Who really believed in it. Who believed in us. On his end, he wanted to make sure we were serious. He wanted to make sure we had the passion for the job. That

Cornelius Uliano and Bryan Schulz—cont'd

we would keep working hard. That we would keep creating. He wanted to make sure we had good character. When you talk somebody up on the phone, trying to sell them, you better make damn well be sure when they get into that room for a meeting they live up to the hype.

We hit it off right away. I loved his story, how he came into the business. It showed he had a lot of heart and character. He had experience. He was somebody I could be friends with, not just a business associate. I trusted him from the start. He was only an assistant at the time but I knew he was going to be a great agent one day. There was only one thing wrong with him; he was a Yankees fan. But, I let that go. He told me he had read our script, and it was something he thought he could sell. I kept my cool, but on the inside I was dancing with joy. He was going to give it to an actual agent at CAA, and they would get back to us. We signed a release and let our baby out into the world.

A few days later I was at Paramount. I still had no job. I would go there and hang out with my friends who worked on a television show that shot on the lot. I got a call from an agent at CAA. She talked to me on the phone for about an hour. She told me she loved the script and asked who I saw directing the movie. I said Robert Zemeckis. Her immediate response was that she had a meeting with him the following Tuesday and would pitch him the story to see if he would be interested in reading it. Things were getting more exciting by the day.

Tuesday came along, and by the end of the day we got a phone call telling us that Robert Zemeckis had taken our script home to read for the week. It was exciting news. That week came and went. And so did another. We were getting worried. Finally, we got a phone call. We were told that Robert Zemeckis had passed on the script. It was heartbreaking news, but we were happy he even read it. They continued to tell us that they decided to pitch the story on the phone to Steven and see if he'd be interested. I was like, "Steven who?" They said, "Steven Spielberg." My heart froze. They said he heard the pitch on the phone and liked it and wanted the script sent to his plane so he could read it on his flight. By the time he landed, he wanted to buy it. At this point in the conversation I was having a mild heart attack. It was the most exciting news I had ever received. The only problem was this was the day the writers strike started and no projects could be sold.

For the next four months we had to wait for the writers strike to end. We could not work. I still could not find a job. The only thing that got me through was hoping that after all the madness was over, Steven Spielberg would not have forgotten about us. Three days after the strike ended, DreamWorks acquired our script, *Imaginary Friends*. It was one of the best feelings in the world. We were signed by CAA. The assistant who brought us in was promoted to agent and continues to represent us today. A lot of doors started opening for us.

This book is about the soft skills a person has to have to survive in the Industry—people skills, political skills . . . can you think of any dos and don'ts for someone just starting out? Can you think of any examples?

Bryan: The most important thing is to always stay open and positive, whether it is about the people you're meeting with or notes on your project, there will always

Continued

Cornelius Uliano and Bryan Schulz—cont'd

be things you won't agree with. The most important factor in your ability to keep getting work is how you handle these situations. Always be open in receiving new ideas, and never just dismiss anything there on the spot. On the flip side, do not be afraid to share your concerns or talk out other possible fixes in the room. As long as it stays open and positive.

There is nothing to prepare you for the highs and lows of this business. You get news someone loves your script, it's an amazing feeling! Then you learn there is another project out there that's just a bit similar, thus no studio will make your movie, and it's over and there's nothing you can do about it. That has happened to Neil and me more than once.

Here is another example. You fight for a writing assignment at a big studio. You win the job, spend a year or more developing the movie, and finally write the script. You get feedback that things are looking good and this movie might go into production soon. Then, totally out of the blue, you get a call saying the head of the studio has left, and now the incoming person wants to look at everything in development before moving forward. So, what the first person liked and what this new person likes might be totally different, as was the case for our project. In a matter of a few days we went from thinking we had a movie about to go into production, to learning it was going back in development with a new vision for it and a new writing team assigned.

Neil: When we sold our first script we had to join the WGA. The WGA has a meeting for newcomers hosted by a panel of working writers. I remember in this meeting that many of the writers were talking about how they don't start writing a single word until their commencement check comes in. They did nothing for free. The meeting was fantastic, but this one comment stuck with me mainly because I didn't believe in that. And as a newcomer in the writing world, I think it's smart to write a little bit for free.

Whether you are a new writer or a veteran writer I think it's important to show people that you are hungry and passionate for a project. When we go up for a job we always work with the producers and try to understand what it is they are looking for. We will then write out a beat sheet or an outline or a character analysis for what our vision of the film is. The producers will come back with notes, and we continue to work with them to perfect it so everyone is happy. As soon as we are on the same page as the producers, that's when we take it before the studio and try to sell it. This worked out for us specifically on two projects, one for Warner Bros. and another for Sony Animation.

There will be times where you do a lot of work on a project with a producer and it ends up falling through. Even though nothing happens with it, the producers always remember the effort and time you put into the project for free. They remember your passion. One of the most important things to have in this business is a good reputation. Writing for free in order to get a gig goes a long way.

What would you have liked someone to have told you, any lessons that you've learned that you could have learned an easier way?

Bryan: Our job in this industry is way more than just the words on the page. Work on your public speaking skills. I cannot tell you enough how key a skill it

Cornelius Uliano and Bryan Schulz—cont'd

is to have. Whether in general meetings or studio pitches, having those skills will make you that much stronger of a writer, and with all the fierce competition out there vying for jobs, it could mean the difference from getting it or losing it.

How do you work as part of a writing team? What is the process?

Neil: It's always funny to hear how other writing teams work. Everyone has a different process. It's also the most commonly asked question to Bryan and me in a general meeting. We live seven hours away from one another, so we never write in the same room, and I think that's a good thing. We would NEVER get ANYTHING done. We like to be alone and in our own element when we write. We have our own schedules, and we have our own times that we like to work.

The first part of the process is talking out the story and the plot and creating a beat sheet. This involves hours and hours of discussions via phone, email, iChat, Skype, and video conferencing. As soon as we have an outline that we're both happy with, we begin converting it to pages. Typically, I will write ACT I and ACT III while Bryan writes ACT II. As soon as we are done we switch and edit each other's work. Once we're done with the editing process, we put it all together and read it as a whole.

After reading the script as a whole we get a good idea of what is working and what isn't, and we begin another discussion on how we want to make changes. We'll also discuss the edits that were made to our sections of the script. We have heard stories of many writings teams and how they fight and argue all the time. Fortunately, Bryan and I have never reached that stage. We certainly have lengthy discussions on how a scene should play out or how a certain line of dialogue should be written, but we've never broken each other's bones or hearts.

I think it's fantastic to work as a team. Writing is a lonely job. It's good to have someone to spitball ideas with. It's good to have someone to call when you're stuck on a scene. Most importantly, it's good to have someone to tell you the truth, that what you've just written is a pile of garbage. A writer's best therapy is to talk about his story to anyone who will listen.

How do you feel about getting notes? What are useful notes and what are not?

Bryan: All notes are useful, period. I've never had a problem with receiving notes as long as they are constructive in some way. Some writers are too emotionally attached to their work and take each note as a personal attack on their being. This will prove exhausting and ultimately lead to a short and painful career, I imagine.

The best notes for me are the ones that make me see the material I've been working on for months, or even years, in a whole new way. It's very easy to get so ingrained in the material and how that world is constructed that it takes an outsider to pull you out and help show you it from a whole new perspective. This is also why I like taking some time after I get notes to sit with them for a while before jumping right back in. It allows me to come back to the material fresh, with new eyes, and ideas.

We all know getting notes you agree with are the easy ones. The ones you don't agree with are trickier, but there is a reason the note was brought up. It's up to the writer to see behind the note and fix the real issue. It's not always the exact thing the note addressed that's the problem.

Continued

Cornelius Uliano and Bryan Schulz—cont'd

How do you like to work with a producer (or a director)? What is most constructive, and what doesn't work for you?

Bryan: My favorite producers to work with are the ones that really understand the project and connect to it as I do as the writer. I know this sounds simple, but it's not always the case. I love the ones that can jump right in with you and spitball new ideas about the plot, or the characters, or what have you. The most important aspect about any new project Neil and I begin is the heart of the story. We have to be emotionally invested in this thing. If the producers are able to invest emotionally with us, it shows they are seeing the movie as we do. This is key in building the foundation of the movie right from inception and will prove invaluable as you move through the process from idea to a finished script.

What should writers know and understand about the pitching process?

Neil: The most important thing writers should know about the pitching process is that THEY are the pitching process. THEY are the ones in charge of selling the film. When you go into the studio to pitch, the producers accompany you but all eyes are on the writer. As writers, we have to take the executives through the story in an exciting and timely manner. We have to make sure they understand what the movie is about.

Typically, we work with the producers on developing the story and formulating an outline. Once we are all on the same page, we turn that outline into a pitch document. A pitch document is essentially exactly what we are going to say in the room to the executives. You want to try and write it out so it is as conversational as possible. It gives you something to resort to in case you need it, but you never want to have to look at it when you are actually in the room.

From a personal standpoint, pitching is one of the most nerve-racking things I have ever done. There is a lot of responsibility involved in it. A lot of things run through your mind when you are pitching. Primarily, you are always wondering if the executives are enjoying it. It's hard to read people sometimes. Also, there is the fear that you will forget what you are talking about or stumble on the story. The best thing a writer can do is know your story. If you know the story, no matter what happens, you will be able to pick up where you fumbled and make it through.

Another reason you should know the story is because executives will ask a lot of questions. Sometimes they will ask you as you're pitching, but for the most part, after the pitch, there is a session where the studio executives will ask all the questions they may have. It's important that you're able to answer all their questions. It could be a matter of selling your movie or not. If they feel you don't know the story or have unanswered questions, it puts doubts in their minds. Not being able to answer a question about your story could cost you a job.

A lot of people ask us how we pitch as a writing team. The first movie we ever pitched for was with Warner Bros. At first, we broke the story up into many sections between the two of us. I would say this part to this part, and then Bryan would come in after I said this particular word and then I would come in after he said this

Cornelius Uliano and Bryan Schulz—cont'd

particular sentence. It was kind of insane. Back and forth and back and forth. When we did a practice pitch with the producers it looked like they were watching a tennis match. So we scrapped that and decided to divide it into bigger sections so it wasn't so back and forth. We got the gig but wanted to try a different approach on our next pitch.

The second pitch we did was for Sony Animation. For this one, I was going to pitch the entire thing, and Bryan was going to work the slideshow presentation we created. Because it was an animated film, we wanted to have visuals to showcase the tone of the movie and what the characters were going to look like. This process worked out very well. I was able to take them through the story and Bryan would change slides as I reached a particular part of the pitch.

What can you tell us about generals (getting-to-know-you meetings)?

Neil: It's important for a writer to take as many general meetings as possible. It's a great way to get your name out there and establish relationships. It's also a great way to find out what kinds of projects people are looking for. We always make it a point to ask what the company is looking for first. It gives us a sense of what projects of ours to mention and what to keep to ourselves.

I remember one time we took a general at Sony Animation. We had a great meeting and exchanged a lot of ideas. There wasn't anything we initially connected on, but we established a great relationship. Six or seven months later we got a call from our agent mentioning a project they were looking for writers for and remembered us. We ended up pitching for it and got the job. Generals are great meetings to take because you never know what will come out of them. You just have to make sure you be yourself, tell your story, and get to know one another on a personal level.

Chapter 8

Agents and Managers—What's the Difference?

DO YOU NEED AN AGENT?

At the Oscars, everybody thanks their agent. When you put together a film for financing, often you will be asked if your project is being represented by an agent. Even production designers and cinematographers have agents. Everybody seems to have an agent—but what does an agent do?

You have probably heard of the big four agencies: CAA (Creative Artists Agency), ICM (International Creative Management), WME (William Morris Endeavor), and UTA (United Talent Agency). The client list of each of these companies is a who's who of the media world. Each department of the big agencies concentrates on specific areas. There is Talent (actors), Literary (directors, writers), TV-Literary (same, but specifically for television), Music (musicians, composers), Below-the-Line, Sports (athletes, coaches), and Branding (the representation and promotion of the images and activities of major companies). Big agencies do it all. There are also boutique agencies that are equally established but more specialized in size and client range. And there are lots of even smaller agencies and one-person offices that have been around for decades.

It is difficult to ascertain the legitimacy of an agency unless you speak with reputable people in the business. If you're thinking of aligning yourself or your project with an agent for any reason, you should take a look at his or her client list to see whether the people on it are working members of the film and television community. You can also check them out with a reputable entertainment business attorney.

The primary responsibility of an agent is to get work and to negotiate the best possible deal for his client.

In order to do this an agent must be the ultimate insider. He must not only have an ear to the ground about what is happening in the business as soon as it happens, to enable him to pitch the client the second an opportunity arises, but before it happens, so that he is on the fast track and can somehow implant the idea of meeting and hiring the client into the consciousness of whoever might be hiring in the future.

A great agent is a consummate salesperson who can make you think that his client is the perfect fit for the project and how incredibly brilliant you are to have thought of him! Then the agent will try to negotiate the highest rate of pay for the client, thus establishing a specific standard rate (*quote*) for him. An agent will try to raise a client's quote with each new project. Let's say Jeff is an unknown actor. He is cast as the "buddy," the second lead in a tiny independent film. His fee for the entire four-week shoot is $5000. Then let's say that this film is accepted as an official selection of the Sundance Film Festival. Most everybody who is anybody in the U.S. film industry attends Sundance. Jeff is suddenly on the radar. If the film does well at Sundance, he will be on the receiving end of a lot of attention. He's not the leading man, but now people in the business know who he is. When a casting director suggests, "How about this Jeff guy for the best friend?" and calls Jeff's agent, Jeff's agent will be ready with a higher quote because this is her chance to strike while Jeff is hot. She knows that within the next couple of months, after the film is accepted to Sundance but before there are possibly insignificant or even weak reviews or word of mouth, there is a window of time where she can push Jeff out from the ranks of the often-unemployed to the level of the cool new talent on the block. Assuming that Jeff is a fine actor with some kind of charisma going for him, a good agent will go into overdrive to get Jeff signed to a film that will move him up to the next level of work, recognition, and money. A really good agent will be able to get Jeff into meetings with people who weeks before would never in a million years have even thought about seeing him. A great agent will get Jeff seen, will persevere, and seal the deal, allowing Jeff to leap frog over other equally talented, charismatic actors. This great agent is able to use her expertise to position Jeff in the minds of casting directors, producers, and directors. This agent is shrewd, has a wide net of contacts, and understands when to nudge, when to urge, when to lay back, and when to give the final push and close the negotiation. For all this work, the agent (or the agency where the agent works) receives a commission (10%) of the client's paycheck for each project. This commission acts as an incentive for the agent to negotiate for highest paycheck possible for the client (as 10% of $500,000 is more than, say, 10% of $150,000.) Most agents have several clients. The good news is, they want to see them all work as much as possible. Their livelihood depends upon the livelihood of their clients.

The bad news is, because the agent has several clients who presumably would be capable of getting the same job on a film, how does an actor or a writer or a director know that her agent is truly going to bat for her, getting her seen for the best jobs, pushing her unique ability or look as opposed to going for the easy deal with one of the other possibly more visible clients? More possible bad news: the biggest paycheck may or may not be the best overall career choice for the client.

For instance, Beth wants to show the world that she can carry a prominent dramatic role even if it's in an ultra-low-budget indie and she'll earn a much smaller paycheck than she usually does. She has told her talent agent what she wants, and the agent has been supportive. An agent wants a happy client, and the agent believes in Beth's ability and sees her potential. The agent thinks that Beth could someday become a major serious, actress. Beth has just been offered that perfect indie film. Two months work, March and April, and not the lead but a substantial role. The problem is, Beth has also been offered the "girlfriend" role in a big-budget action-thriller where she'll be on the screen a lot but get only a few lines of dialogue. She'll earn fairly big dollars as the girlfriend, but she's been the girlfriend or the beauty in peril in two other films. She's thirty and getting on as far as the babe factor is concerned. She knows the starlet roles can't go on forever. She doesn't want them to—she wants to act, not pose. The girlfriend role will tie her up for the months of March and April. Should Beth grab the money? It's a good offer in a movie that will have high visibility. She'll be seen by a broad audience, which may or may not lead to the meatier role that she's looking for. And even though the indie seems to be fully financed, with indies you never know. The money could fall through midway through production, something much more unusual on a studio film. And there's the money: $175,000 rather than $8000. With the $175,000 in the bank, Beth can comfortably bide her time and wait for another low-budget indie if that's what she wants to do. From many agents' points of view, there would be no contest. It would be seen as a win, win. And this is what Beth's agent advises. If Beth takes the girlfriend role, she gets the money and buys herself some time and financial security. But from Beth's point of view, the answer isn't so clear. She's been through this before, and one of the indies she turned down went the festival route, made a splash, and the woman who ultimately was cast seems now to have embarked on the type of career that Beth wants.

The agent is doing a good job, because the agent's job is to procure work for the client and to negotiate the deal. If the indie does fall through, or if it doesn't turn out to be a festival darling, Beth is no further ahead and she could be $175,000 behind. Beth trusts her agent, and in this case, there is no reason she shouldn't. She's concerned that if she opts out of this girlfriend role, her agent will hesitate before putting her up for the next one. She's also aware that her face is beginning to become known in part because of the girlfriend roles she's played in the past. Will she lose momentum? Should she take the risk? In the long run, is doing what the agent advises the best choice for Beth?

Then there is Andrew who has been laboring over a script since he graduated from film school. A friend of his cousin knew an assistant at a studio, who read the script and passed it on to her boss, a major producer. The producer has optioned Andrew's script. Andrew is ecstatic. He knows that this is the chance of a lifetime. His former professor, an established screenwriter, has helped Andrew by introducing him to his own agent, who in turn has introduced Andrew to an up-and-coming agent at the company. Now Andrew, a first-time screenwriter, has a solid agent at a big agency. Andrew meets with his agent and tells him that eventually what he wants to do is direct. He understands that his first shot as director won't be on this particular project as it's ambitious and expensive, but he just wants the agent to be aware.

The agent understands but says, "Let's take care of you as a writer first. Then when you have a couple of script sales under your belt, you'll write something small and we'll start on the directing thing." Makes sense to Andrew.

The script is sought after by a well-known producer/director team. While the option and sales negotiations are in progress, the agent explains to Andrew that he will try to get him top dollar at every step of the deal so that when they bring in another writer, Andrew will still do well financially. Andrew is aghast. Why would they bring in another writer? They like what he's written so far or they wouldn't be buying his work. His agent explains that the reality of the business is that almost always another writer is brought in to do at least one draft, maybe more. "They often feel that the original writer goes stale and has taken the project as far as it can go."

But Andrew will get money and his first big credit—that's something that the agent can control. The agent promises Andrew that now that he's part of the team, he will be sent out to lots of meetings to pitch his ideas for future screenplays and to listen to production companies, executives, and producers pitch *him* what they have to see if any of those projects strike a chord. He also tells Andrew that he'll be going to *generals* so that everyone will be aware of him and keep him and his work in mind if the appropriate idea or project comes up. Andrew is rather shy. One of the reasons he likes being a writer is that he can hide away in his apartment and not force himself to be social. Now he is hearing that a major part of his career will be spent meeting with strangers and impressing them so that he'll get work. The agent tells him not to worry. He'll work with him, rehearse his pitches, even rehearse meetings with him. The agent says that because Andrew has a nice way about him, he'll do well in meetings. Andrew doesn't understand why his personality is important. "It's not as if they won't know what they're getting. If they've read my work, they'll know exactly what they're getting—so why does liking me matter?" The agent explains that when Andrew sells another script or is hired for a writing assignment, he'll be working with the executives and/or the producers. There will be notes. More meetings. More drafts. "You have to present yourself well. They have to believe that you can handle it, that you won't freak out, won't argue over every comma. They have to want to be in those meetings with you. You have to be able to play well with the other kids."

This is not what Andrew had in mind, but he appreciates his agent's insight. The agent tells Andrew that he will need a good lawyer right away but not to worry. The agency will recommend several with terrific relationships with the agency. He'll set up some appointments, and Andrew can figure out who he likes the best. Andrew is grateful. The only lawyer he knows is his cousin who works with insurance companies.

Is Andrew's agent watching out for Andrew's interests? He is explaining the realities of the business while reassuring Andrew that he will be there for him, coaching him, easing him into the routines of a Hollywood screenwriter. He's being honest with him, and he's trying to get him the best deal that he can.

Where's the concern? Think about it. Andrew needs an experienced entertainment attorney. He needs someone who is completely on his side. If an agency recommends an attorney, where does the loyalty of the attorney lie? With a client who is just starting his career, or with the agency whose client roster produces millions of dollars? So Andrew would be better off asking his former professor for the name of an attorney who is not affiliated with the agency and doesn't owe the agency for the recommendation. It's a small industry, and no doubt the paths of the lawyer and agent have crossed, but hopefully the relationship is not so tight that there is the temptation for any kind of conflict of interest in looking out for Andrew.

Does any of this make Andrew's agent a bad agent? No. He's doing everything he can to expedite Andrew's first step into the big leagues. But in the film business, you can never completely abdicate responsibility to your advisors or representatives, no matter how veteran they are. As much as you, as a creative person, might want to, you should never put your business life entirely into the hands of another person. You must pay attention and understand the implications of your decisions. It's not that everyone is out to cheat you. It's that everyone acts in their self-interest and you must act in yours.

DO YOU WANT TO BE AN AGENT?

Where do agents come from? There are a few paths to becoming an agent. Many of the agents at the big agencies begin in the mailroom. Why? Why do hundreds of college grads, MBAs, and even attorneys decide that it is worth their while to spend a year or so sorting mail, delivering scripts, and generally doing something that seems far below the appropriate level of their education and training, with no guarantee of promotion? It's definitely not the money. Mailroom employees (and even agents' assistants) earn a paycheck that is not much better than minimum wage.

Agents often begin in the mailroom because there is the belief that the only way someone can understand the agency business is from the ground up. Working in the mailroom you hear things, read things, meet people, start to sort out how the business works, and you learn the etiquette of dealing with clients. The idea is that after you're in the mailroom you have a feel for the industry in general and the agency in particular. Once you've been in the mailroom for a while (several months, a year), you may be promoted to a desk. This means that you'll be working as an assistant to an agent in a specific area—Talent, Literary, etc. Working a desk means that you will be privy to all kinds of financial information, the inside scoop on the clients your agent currently services, and the people your agent hopes to sign in the future. You will see and hear everything.

An assistant position at an agency is a coveted steppingstone, and many assistants go on to work at studios, major production companies, or become producers. Since much of the business activity of a film is filtered through one or several agencies, you are in a position to observe the evolution of a project from script to casting to financing to production.

Working at an agency puts you at the nerve center of the business. An agent's assistant gets to know the people who make the deals and the people for whom the deals are made.

Part of an assistant's job at an agency is to listen in on their boss's phone calls. This is not a secret, everyone knows that it's happening—that's part of the training. The assistant takes notes. An agent is on the phone for hours each day, finding out what is going on around town, who is up for what job or role or writing assignment, what project is being boosted or dropped. An assistant listening in learns how to structure a deal, how to reassure a client, when to be gentle, and when to go for the jugular. It's a grueling job, the hours are very long, the pay is low, and the expectation is that you will always be alert, good-natured, and grateful for the experience. Although it is a stereotype, there is some truth to the reputation agents have of being volatile. The pressure is always on. If the clients aren't working, the company is not earning. An agent is a salesperson first, and salespeople are aggressive and competitive.

MANAGERS

A manager does much of what an agent does, but with a long view.

A manager does not necessarily come up through the ranks the way an agent does. A manager should first and foremost be a trusted advisor. Unlike an agent, who might have a list of 20 clients who do what you do, a manager will usually have just a few. An agent wants to get you a job now. A manager wants you to work but will probably be more careful about exactly what projects you do, considering if the project is part of your greater career plan. In the example of Beth, a manager would not only serve as a sounding board for Beth's concerns, but would act as the middleman with her agent, conveying her feelings about the pros and cons of the indie versus the girlfriend roles. Presumably, the manager would be more inclined to spend the time helping Beth assess her situation. In the case of Andrew, a manager might have been the one to find Andrew his own attorney, rather than encourage him to sign up with a firm the agency suggested as his agent did.

A manager deals with the client on more of a day-to-day basis. If you're on top, an agent might call you every day, but if you're not, you won't hear from your agent constantly. He or she is busy with the clients who are making a lot of money for the agency. It's not personal, but there is only so much time in the day, and an agent is not going to call to say hello. A manager will call often, to see how you're doing on that script, how you felt you did at that meeting, did you hit it off with that director. Like an agent, managers are paid a percentage of your earnings, but the idea is that they are there for the long haul. That's why many managers are their clients' family members or friends before they are managers. Their job is to take care of their clients, rather than just find them work.

An agent's 10 percent commission is regulated by law. There are no laws regulating a manager's fee. Agents don't usually receive credits on their clients' films. On occasion, managers receive some kind of producer credit. Managers tend to be active in the development of their clients' scripts and in the production of their projects. Agents are not; that's not their job.

Some people have an agent, a manager, and a lawyer. Some operate best with an agent and a lawyer, or a manager and a lawyer. If you are out there working all the time (and you probably aren't, or you wouldn't be reading this), you can probably afford to carry an entire team of representatives. Starting out, you don't need that.

PACKAGING

One more thing you should know about agents and agencies. You need to understand the concept of *packaging*. Packaging has been important in the world of financing and production for studio films for a long time, but in the last several years it has come to play an increasingly key role in the world of low-budget independents. If an agency represents Actor A, it is in the interest of that agency to be sure that A works. If an agency also represents Director B, who has a script that is a good fit for A, wouldn't it be extra profitable for the agency to team A and B and to find Co-Star C and to represent this package to studios and financiers? In a packaging situation, the agency has done part of the producer's job. The agency has helped to gather the key creative elements. And even if much of the talent is not an agency client, if the agency packages the film, that contribution qualifies them for a major fee.

In a packaging situation, the agency becomes, in a sense, a de facto producer and has a much stronger financial interest in the profits. Rather than wait for someone to call about hiring one of the agency's clients, by packaging, they take a more active role in the filmmaking process. The agency benefits, and because the agency is behind the project, the project has more star power and more industry power, and thus has a better chance of being well-financed and well-distributed.

On occasion an agency that would not ordinarily sign on many of the creative elements involved in a small film will put considerable push behind a project because it might be a vehicle for someone on their client list—such as Beth from our earlier example. Although the powers that be at the agency may not want to sign each screenwriter or director, it may still be in the interest of the agency to load up the package with some additional talent on the agency's list to help get the project made.

WHO DO YOU NEED ON YOUR TEAM?

Often newcomers to the industry are so thrilled that someone has agreed to represent them that they really don't examine who the potential agent is, what they really do, and who else they represent. If you're a beginning screenwriter or director, and you don't have a connection that can get you in front of an experienced, established agent, you're going to have to do some thinking. You have to examine the motives of this person who wants to represent you. How did you find him, or how did he find you?

An established agent will usually take on a new screenwriter or director if and only if there is already a deal pending. That means that you'll have somehow found your first job on your own. Sometimes an agent will take on a new screenwriter because someone has gotten a script to the agent and the agent thinks there's promise there, or she will sign a new director because she's seen a festival film the director has made or because prizes have been awarded, or (very rarely, but I've heard of it happening once) because there was an extraordinary pitch at a reputable pitching event. But usually the agent wants to be reasonably sure that her clients will work often and soon. That's how agents make money. An agent makes money only if you make money. You would never pay an agent anything but a commission on money you're earning. There are no fees, no retainers, no expenses.

Trying to find an agent can be wearisome. You're looking for someone to help you find work, and they're interested only if you've already got work. Of course you're thinking, "If I'm already in the midst of selling a script or getting money to direct a film, why do I need an agent at all?" Although you have a point, you will still need someone to negotiate your deal for you and to help you get the next deal and move up. If an agent at an established agency wants to sign you, you should sign. By having an agent you will have access, and that access will lead to future work. If an agent at a less-known agency (not one of the major or well-known boutique agencies) offers to sign you, check them out thoroughly before you move ahead. Signing with an agent who doesn't have access or contacts will tie you up and could in fact hurt you in the future.

The same theory holds true for managers. Where did you find them? What have they done for other writers or directors? Who else do they represent and why? Does the manager represent his own successful, well-known brother? That's great—he's a trusted family member. How will that work for you? You're not a relative. Will this manager invest himself in your career in the same way he would for a cousin? Is the manager part of a management group who all have tentacles out into the Hollywood community? That's as good as if the manager is an agent. Is she just starting out? You're just starting out too. Do you want your manager to be learning along with you, or do you want your manager to be a veteran of the industry to help you survive the journey?

If you're an aspiring producer or executive you will not need or want an agent or a manager, but you will want to get to know all of them. Strong relationships with agencies and management companies can put you first in line to see the fabulous new screenplay that's come down the pike. If you have a list of agents and managers who know and respect you, you'll know the latest on who and what are the next big things, and information is power.

Harry Ufland

As an agent, Harry Ufland represented a veritable who's who of superstars, including Martin Scorsese and Robert De Niro. As Producer and Executive Producer, he has been involved with the production of several major feature films, including *One True Thing, Crazy/Beautiful, Snow Falling on Cedars, Not Without My Daughter, Last Temptation of Christ,* and *Night in the City*. His next project, *Big Wedding,* starring Robert DeNiro, Diane Keaton, Susan Sarandon, Robin Williams, Amanda Seyfried, and Katherine Heigl, will be released in early 2012.

What is a good agent?

A good agent is somebody who is going to be honest, who is not going to be afraid of telling you the truth. They don't tell you that you are great, that something is great if it is not great. I never lost clients, because they knew I was telling the truth. Your first obligation is to the client. Keep your feet on the ground about what it is you are doing. If you believe in something—first of all, please have something that you believe in, and don't give up because some people tell you to forget about it. If you believe in it, and you feel it, then you stick with it.

While you were at William Morris, did you ever have a client about whom other agents would say, "I don't know why you are even representing this person"?

Almost every one of my clients. When I found Scorsese, I thought, this is amazing. I said the same thing with De Niro. To me, a bell goes off and you feel it in the pit of your stomach and you know this is sensational... Then you realize that not everybody agrees and not everybody sees what you see. But you stick to it. I had all my associates at William Morris ask me, why are you wasting your time ...

When someone decides to take someone on as a client, what is the next step?

You bring them in, and you would like to get help because it is a big business. You cannot cover it all yourself, but be prepared if they're not going to give you the help, you need to do it yourself. There wasn't anybody I wouldn't call. There are ways to do that. You don't have to be a pain in the ass, but you can call and say I really believe in this person. I show them the work, show them the film ... if there is a script, show them the script ...

If you believe, you can't let anybody say no and stop you. You've got to keep coming, which is what I did with clients, with Bobby De Niro, Martin Scorsese, Jodie Foster, any of them ... They certainly would have emerged without me, but it would have taken longer.

As a producer who has found, acquired, and developed lots of material, what do you think defines a good story?

It is like something hanging on the wall on the museum. You know. I tend to go for true stories and character. If I see something that is a familiar concept, some action picture, not to put them down, I think there is a great place for them, but it doesn't excite me. What excites me is getting into real-life characters. That also makes my career and my life harder, but they are the most rewarding things to do.

Continued

Harry Ufland—cont'd

I love books. But you've got to be careful with books, because books and movies are two entirely different mediums. In a book, you have hundreds of pages to show what a wonderful writer you are. Movies are visual, and the writer has to tell you a story visually. Because it's a bestseller doesn't mean it would make a great movie. Usually, they don't. Usually, it's books that people have passed over [that make good films]. There is no rule. There is no right or wrong way of doing this. If there were, everybody would have success all the time, and God knows none of us do. We all need different stuff to get up in the morning, and for me, it is character and truth and reality, honesty.

How do you see that the business has changed? We know about the economy and that kind of change, which has affected things, but in general, how has business changed?

The business has changed in a couple of ways. . . . Just as an example, [studio X] has four non-sequel, non-comic book slots. They've got a lot of producers [on the lot] getting a lot of money. They are paying a lot of money, both for overhead and upkeep of that situation [the producers and their staff]. This studio is going to be very reluctant to take on a project from me because I don't have a deal with them.

So if you're going to come in to this, then you better not ever give up just because studios don't want to do something. The other way a movie will get made is you go to HBO, cable operations, AMC. You put it all together yourself. You've got to hire a sales agent who is going to sell the foreign rights. You get equity investors. You get banks. You advance, and then the money you thought was there isn't there. I did a movie a long time ago with [a studio]. They said, we want you to use this private money, and there was no private money. They never did the research on them! When you go into putting a movie together with rights and foreign rights and equity, it is very difficult, because you think you have the funding, but you don't. Monday is good, Tuesday is bad . . . it is a very difficult way to do it.

Now, you're teaching film students. What advice do you give them?

This is a 24/7 business. If you are not prepared for that, don't get in the business. This business is loaded with daily, hourly rejection. Don't think it's personal, it is not. When I was young, I had to get over that, because it drove me crazy.

Also, I've had students who don't understand the need to see classic movies. One of them said to me, how is a classic movie going to help me get a job? I said, when you are going to a job interview and somebody references a movie that you haven't seen, do you think you're going to get that job? See all the great movies. Go director by director. It is so easy now with Netflix and streaming. We cannot, as educators, coddle these kids [film students], because this business does not coddle. I don't want to hear they can't do something because they have a thesis. Screw that. There are no excuses. If they were working for me and they came in and said something like that, I'd fire them. Find a way to do it. Just do what you are supposed to do. There is fierce competition out there. If you don't, believe me, somebody else will.

Brent Lilley

Brent Lilley worked in independent finance and packaging for Paradigm before leaving to take a more hands-on and creative approach as a manager at Foursight Entertainment. He currently works for Mosaic, where he manages publishers and talent for both film and television. Mosaic is a management/production company with a TV deal at HBO and a film deal at Sony.

Describe your career/employment path from the time you started in the business until now. What if anything has changed?

I would argue the path hasn't changed, but the market has. It's simple—make them money, become a valued member of the culture, or be of added value in some way that makes them realize it's in their best interest to promote you . . . and you are in. But what does "in" mean, and how have slashed budgets and reduced overall deals affected the path of employment, is a much larger topic. A promotion used to mean off a desk, [an] office, assistant, expense account—the company essentially accepted you were a loss leader for two years, an investment that needed time and support to grow. More and more in this climate a promotion simply means the dreaded "slashy" title of assistant/story editor. You are at that point expected to act like an exec till you produce results like an exec. Nature of the biz and a shrinking marketplace.

What do you do, and how did you get your first few opportunities? Why do you enjoy what you're doing?

The job, in its purest form, is—I find scripts/movies/shorts/books I love and get feverishly excited about . . . and then get to tell all my friends. It's a basic brand build—I take all the execs I have met and find effective and then make my friends your friends. All the while keeping your career and business constantly pushing forward. The first few opportunities were earned through stupidity and tenacity. It starts with Robert Luna, who ran the mailroom at Paradigm when I was applying for a job. Luna was a true old-school, one of a kind. He believed in building people and taking chances. [He] was not happy with the easy hires, he built it like a superhero team . . . finding people that didn't really make sense on paper, but had "something" intangible that he thought he could invest in. It created in turn employees that were fiercely loyal to the company—and more importantly him—for the opportunity. Which in turn just made us work that much harder. And of course, every once in a while there would be the complete oddball that backfired. Thankfully, I was the former, not the latter.

The first desk I was ever on, I should not have gotten. I was simply undertrained and by no means qualified. It was a dual desk [two agents sharing an assistant due to space issues] to two mid-level lit [literary] agents with rather large [client] lists. It was a slaughterhouse. It was the wood chipper. It was a desk whose volume would chew up and spit out most kids. At the time, I had a sum total of three working days as a floater on a desk. I barely knew how to answer the phones. But I also knew there was a logjam of trainees in MP lit [the motion picture literary department], so desks didn't come up often, and when they did, they were hard to jockey for position. The assistant before me was let go, and the desk became available. They

Continued

Brent Lilley—cont'd

put the floater on it who was quite simply the best employee/assistant they had, Jen. But the secret being, Jen hated MP lit and liked me.

So I aggressively (she might say annoyingly) hounded her for information—Who were they going to replace her with? Who were the clients she dealt with? What were the agents like? When were they hiring a permanent assistant? On and on for days, maybe even weeks. But while I had done the proper political push—talking to the agents about being their assistant, talking to Luna in the mailroom, talking to HR [Human Resources] . . . the company line was simply "you don't have the experience, you aren't ready." Later I would learn there was a political struggle: they were two agents on the rise, making too much money to be sharing an assistant, and neither would commit to a new shared assistant as a sort of protest till they would hire each of them their own.

So the coup comes when the owner of the agency's assistant is also "transitioned" (euphemism for fired), and he calls in his favorite floater, Jen. The agents are miffed, but there's nothing to do. Jen tells Luna, "You know Brent knows the list, he seems to want it." Luna tells me, "It's just till they get a new assistant, so don't get comfortable, you can't have the desk." And I tell all of them "it's mine." Because here is the secret to this town—if you want it bad enough, you will make it happen. The assistant gig is essentially a monkey job, anyone with common sense can learn the entire soup to nuts of assistant-ing in a matter of weeks. So I committed to proving everyone wrong. Got in when the doors opened at 7:30. Left after the last submission was sent at 9:00. I simply willed it into reality. It was the desk in the department I wanted, and I just squatted on it—nailing down the job so hard, there was no leverage or way to complain about me.

After weeks of the standoff between the department head and the agents to get their individual assistants, I was there by default. And the desk was mine. If you want it bad enough, just take it and do the work. Regardless of outcome, at the end of the day, they will respect the work.

What should job and/or internship hunters know before they walk in the door for an interview? As someone who is now in the position to hire interns and/or assistants, what do you look for when you interview them?

Always, always, always say you want to be the job you are interviewing for. It doesn't matter if you want to produce and you are interviewing at an agency. Everyone in this town has an ego. We ALL either are mentors or perceive ourselves to be mentors—regardless of the reality. People will invest in you in a different way when they perceive they are investing in the future of their business/company. The second you consciously or subconsciously tell them you are a short-timer and not a lifer at that company, they will distance themselves from your learning curve. If only because they take one eye off you and put their busy thoughts back to their business at hand. So tell them you want to be in their seat one day, and they will impart a different sort of learning and teaching to you. And then, years later when you decide to leave, put as little lead time into that as possible—don't tease a departure or say you are waffling about your future. Just commit and do it. They will respect you and help you more for the clear vision you present.

Brent Lilley—cont'd

Can you think of any do's and don'ts for someone just starting out?

It's a digital age. Clear up your online profile. Just do the deed. Google yourself and see what comes up. It's literally the first thing people will do when you are a serious contender. And be aware of that digital thumbprint. There's a story of a girl that called in sick while her boss was in the midst of crunch time/production, bailed on work at 9:00 in the morning. Then [she] posted her status update in Facebook from the beach in Mexico. But [she] seemed to either not care or not know that she was friends with the head of her HR department on Facebook. She was "transitioned."

Don't be a bully. We are all aware of the monsters. We all talk about them. It's practically a hobby in this town. And you will be allowed to treat subordinates and others with disrespect and defiance . . . in so much as you are producing and earning. But one hiccup in that momentum or revenue, and the chickens will come home to roost. Karma's tough in this town. Clients and projects will come and go, but the relationships are what can carry you through the tough times and maximize your potential in times of growth.

What have you learned about the film industry that you did not/could not have learned at school?

How little is has to do with "the best" script or book or idea. If you have the BEST script in town and have zero ability to communicate your vision or passion for the material, or more importantly why/how someone will make their money back when they give it too you, you don't have a script, you have 90 pages of scrap paper.

What surprised you about the industry?

That projects and ideas really can appear at the same time and have ZERO nefarious theft behind them. I had never heard of the term *Cryptozooligist* before. But I did have a client developing a script—only to be scooped just days before we took it out by a second (then third) Crypto script . . . as well as a month later, a TV show. Sometimes ideas just bubble to the surface at the same time and enter the marketplace at the same time. There's surprisingly very little idea theft. On the outside looking in we would hear all these stories of shady producers and agents twirling their moustaches, chomping at the bit to try and steal your IP [intellectual property]. Oddly I've never witnessed it. And can't remember the last time I heard a story of it.

What are the mistakes that you've seen people make? Any consequences?

See the Facebook story above.

The market's shrinking. Don't be in too big a rush. It used to take three years to get promoted—now it's not uncommon to hear five or six. Subjugate the ego. That isn't to say, don't have opinions—because you should ALWAYS have ideas and thoughts and learn the politics of when/where to voice them . . . but it's a buyer's market—more kids want in than jobs are available. Which means you will have to pay your dues.

What advice would you give someone just starting out in the industry who wanted to direct, produce, or someone with an independent project looking for funding?

Continued

Brent Lilley—cont'd

There is no other way to become a director than to just direct. Be the guy/girl that has a camera in your hand every weekend just experimenting and trying to grow. Weird thing they don't tell you, 90 percent of the work you do in your career will be for free or because of a relationship. So don't ever expect to get paid for it, and figure out how you can be the best and most cohesive storyteller in a room. Do the work.

For a producer—find the 800-pound gorilla. You can either take the ten years to put together your small indie film that will see a festival circuit and maybe break even. To then repeat. Or you can find a Scott Rudin that will (if you play the game right) get it done in four [years] and build a bigger, larger, better quality of network for you. Don't be afraid of the 800-pound gorilla. They can teach you a lot of things and make you better at your job. If you want to learn to play tennis or chess, you always have to play up. If you only play people at or below your level, you will never get better.

What would you have liked someone to have told you, any lessons that you've learned that you could have learned an easier way?

Raise your hand.

You'd be amazed, shocked even, if you realized how much you could get done by just asking. Like I said, we all have an ego in this town—we all want to help if we can, we are all looking to have favors out there, ready for the day they can be cashed. But you have to be unafraid to raise your hand and ask. Ask for help, ask for advice, ask for a favor. But most people won't ever get over the fear of asking. Took me years to realize that's what the bosses/mentors are there for. They WANT to invest in your career if they are good people.

What predictions do you have about the way the business will change due to the advances in digital technology, reproduction, and distribution?

I just spent $23 (me plus a date) for a $10 million, dark political thriller. If I'd waited three months I could have gotten it on VOD. A month after that I could have PURCHASED the film for $14.99. We have priced ourselves out of the market. Kids see less and less films and have more and more options. Audiences will get older and older. The film experience is changing. And the migration of filmmakers to TV has only elevated TV to a place where it looks and feels like film. But it's free and there are ten times the amount of hours of your favorite story. Consider this—anyone under the age of ten will spend more money incrementally, $0.99 cents, $1.99 at a time, off their iPad/Tablet/iPod/handheld whatever in their lifetime . . . than they will EVER SPEND in a movie theatre. Don't be a filmmaker—be a storyteller, and tell the best stories you can, regardless of how they are delivered to the viewer.

Chapter 9

The Money, Part 1

WHERE DOES THE MONEY COME FROM?

You have a script, a director, and a producer, or you have a script and you are the director or producer. Where will the money come from to make your movie?

Let's look at a simplified description of how the big boys do it. Studios and major production companies are publicly held corporations. They sell stock, they have shareholders, they have operating funds, and they often have *revolving lines of credit* from investment banks. These are loans that can be repaid continually, then reborrowed. They produce and distribute *slates* of several films per year. The idea of producing a slate of films rather than just one or two is that the odds are with them. If one film sinks, another may soar. The president of production is the person making the final decision as to the slate, and he or she seeks to balance each risk with a sure thing. This year, a slate might include the big-budget sequel of a megahit, a family-friendly adaptation of a bestselling children's novel, an edgy military thriller with a star in the lead, a teenage comedy of questionable taste, and a quirky drama. The drama and thriller would represent the risks. The theory is that if one of them does exceptionally well and two of them do fairly well, the profits will cover the losses. If they all flop there will be a new president of production.

There are international investment banks and funds that specialize in making business loans to major companies. Until fairly recently, several of these banks were involved in financing films. With the onset of the current economic downturn, many of these banks have decided to focus on businesses where the outcome is a more predictable than the film industry. Still, studios have preexisting long-term relationships with banks and can access hundreds of millions of dollars. Studios not only distribute their own productions, they distribute films they do not produce. Because the studios have a vast international distribution network, independent films seek distribution deals with these studios and the studios earn a fee. These days, it's fairly safe to say that one of the main reasons studios produce films at all is for the revenue they earn through distribution. Studios can raise funds by the pre-selling of their films to foreign territories. They can also finance a film in part through *negative pick-up* deals—arrangements where they contract in advance to pay to pick up a film for distribution once it's been finished.

You, on the other hand, don't have most of these options. You have only a few choices:

Approach the big agencies about helping you package your film. If a major agency is interested in your project and takes it on, you will have access to cast, funding, and distribution situations that you would not have otherwise. You'll be a little film getting big film treatment.

Find a distributor who is willing to make a deal with you. The way this could happen for a first-time filmmaker is if there is an important element—almost always a cast member—attached. The distributor assumes that one way or another the film will make some money back. It's unusual to get that money up front, but a guaranteed distribution deal would help you to secure a loan. But without some type of distribution in place, it is unlikely that a first-time filmmaker will be able to convince a bank that his or her project is a solid business investment.

Pre-sell foreign territories. Again, it's unusual for an independent film to be able to do this before the film is actually made for the obvious reason that no one knows how the film will turn out or *if* it will.

Find private investors. This is the option that is most realistic for any film with a budget of a few million dollars or less.

FINDING ANGELS

If you're making a small independent film ($1–5 million), unless you're already aligned with a major production or distribution company and unless you have some heavyweight star-power attached to your movie, you're going to have to go out to the general public for help in raising funds for your movie.

It's often said that everybody has two businesses—their own business, and show business. That's because everyone sees movies, watches television, and has an opinion about the quality and type of material they see. The general public doesn't recognize the names of the vice president of a company that manufactures sporting goods, but they recognize the names of directors and even minor actors in New York and Los Angeles. People read and hear about the goings-on of the industry, and they find it fascinating. Many, many businesspeople go to the movies and think, "I can do better." Sometimes they are people who want to participate in what they think is a glamorous and possibly profitable investment.

And there are also online fundraising possibilities—crowd-sourcing sites where you can pitch your project to the public. Don't count on raising a huge amount from these sites, though. A micro-budget project with a great website might do fairly well, but the most I've heard of people raising is $20,000, and that was huge.

Finally, there are people who know you, who may support you in what you're trying to do, and they or someone else they know might have money. Depending on the size of your budget, you may want to raise money through a combination of family and friends and friends of family and friends. Often people will make introductions to other, possibly interested investors. Some people want to invest in films because they think it's exciting to help young creative people, and some want to do it because they love movies and have the wherewithal to be a part-time producer. They have other businesses but they like the idea of being involved. The bottom line, though, is that none of these people except maybe your family, are doing this completely out of the goodness of their hearts. They all want the movie to succeed financially.

So you want investors. Your next step? Setting up an LLC (Limited Liability Company.) Why not just set up a company called "Tim's Film Company"? A couple of reasons why you should not do this:

1. **The money you raise will be taxed as private income.** This means that if the budget for your film is $1 million and you raise $1 million for "Tim's Film Company," the IRS will look at the money raised as if you just struck it rich and you will be taxed appropriately—which will leave you owing more money than you've ever earned. If you set up an LLC, the earnings of the LLC will be taxed on its earnings but not on the money raised.
2. **You will be personally liable for the company's debts.** You will not be if you are one of the owners of an LLC.
3. **You will be personally liable for any legal issues and lawsuits brought against "Tim's Film Company."** Maybe you own a condo or a house. If "Tim's Film Company" isn't set up as "Tim's Film Company, LLC," your assets will be vulnerable.
4. **If you are going to seek investors, they will want to have some profit participation in the company. The company will own the final product—the film.** That participation can be more easily set up without your losing control of your film if you create an LLC.

The chief reason not to set up an LLC is that it's expensive, but the pros completely outweigh the cons.

To simplify a fairly complex business structure, an LLC allows for the raising of funds for an *entity* (the production or production company) rather than for a specific person (Tim). When you've created an entity, none of the participants are expected to pay personal income taxes on the money that is raised for the company, because the money is not income. It's investment money that belongs to the LLC. Setting up this kind of company will somewhat protect the personal assets of Tim and his investors in case of any sort of lawsuit. The assets of the LLC are the funds raised for the movie.

Understanding the legal and tax obligations and restrictions of an LLC and dealing with investors requires the services of both an attorney and an accountant. This is not something you should handle on your own. If you are forming an LLC to raise funds for your film, you are restricted in terms of who you can approach, how you can approach them, and what you can promise. You must know from the beginning how expenditures, debts, and assets must be accounted for, and how profits will be determined and distributed. You need professionals to counsel you every step of the way. You must be aware that once you begin raising funds for your film, you assume a load of legal and financial responsibility. An unintentional misstep can cause a chain-reaction of long-term legal and financial grief.

Once the LLC is set up and you want to raise money for your movie, you will create a *Business Plan*. Your business plan will include an overview of the LLC, a description of the film, and a summary of the fundraising plan. It will address where the money is coming from, and if the production will be taking advantage of any *Production Incentives, Rebates,* or *Tax Credits*. It will specify the management team, the production team, and the cast, if there is anyone attached. It will describe the marketing and distribution plan, and what you are actually looking for in terms of investment. If the film makes money, what will the *return on investment* be? How will the moment when (and if) the film goes into profit be determined? How will the true amount of profit be determined? You will include information on any deals you've already made, and of any backend deals you intend to make (a percentage of the profits for the star, for example.) You will have charts that reference other films that are the same type and scale of the film that you want to make. These charts are called *comparables*. The charts will list the budgets of those films and their earnings, not only at the box office but from ancillary markets—DVD sales and rentals, TV and cable sales, etc. You will use the financial histories of these films to create *projections* (predictions) of the potential earning capability of your film. These projections are often referred to as *the waterfall*, because the charts you will make to represent a financial picture of the *revenue stream* of a film from start to finish start with a gush (feature film distribution) and end with a trickle (online profits).

Caution! A business plan is a legal financial document. You should not be writing your own business plan. Even if you have been trained, you should have your attorney review it. There are several possible ways for an attorney to go when setting up an LLC. The management of the LLC must be clearly delineated. There are variations in the ways the LLC can operate. You are a filmmaker, not a lawyer. Bite the bullet and hire an attorney who is experienced in setting up this kind of production structure for individual films. Spending the money now can protect you from much more expensive mistakes later.

HOW TO ASK FOR MONEY

When you approach someone to invest in your film, you are really asking them to invest in you. Of course they should feel great about the project, and they will note that you somehow persuaded a known actor to play your lead, but ultimately it's about whether they are convinced that you are the one to successfully shepherd this project and whether or not they feel that they want to gamble on you. You must present a left brain, professional, businesslike plan to potential investors while maintaining your right brain passion for filmmaking in general and your project in particular. Try not to get too bogged down in the fact that you're pleading for money. If a potential investor hears your energy flag, he is going to start to worry that you'll fizzle out before you've even begun. Would you invest in that person? You must demonstrate confidence without arrogance, you must be able to speak to people with respect but not as if you are begging. No one who is looking to make a profit on this kind of venture is going to invest in someone who is weak.

You must let your investors know up front (both verbally and as part of your business plan) that there are inherent risks in the film business and that there is absolutely no guarantee that they will even make their money back. Then show them your plan for turning those odds in your favor—your cast, your budget, any kind of potential interest you've received from distributors you've contacted. Show them a detailed budget, not just a final number, and be capable and prepared to discuss it. If they ask how much you need, tell them a little more than you expect that you might get from them. You might be surprised, and if they come down closer to what you anticipated, they'll feel that they didn't give away the store and you'll still be where you expected to be. If they want to think about it, leave them the business plan and also the phone numbers of anyone in an established business or creative position who is willing to vouch for you. Follow up a week later. If they can't invest, ask if they are willing to help you find people who can. For years, groups of doctors and dentists have been investing in small films. Who do you or your family or friends know who knows the kind of people who love movies and can afford to take a chance on something new? When you're dealing with low-budget films, often you will find one investor who might bring in other, small investors, or you'll have lots of minor investors and then perhaps because you seem closer to the finish line, you'll relax and along will come a major investor to complete the funds.

Fundraising for a film project is arduous and can be disheartening, especially in our current economic climate, but first-time filmmakers do it every day. The upside is that your budget is not very large—the downside is that you are most likely to work as hard to find that million dollars as you would to find twenty million.

A few pieces of advice:

You don't have the money until the check is deposited and cashed.

Promises are cheap. Intentions may be good, but the money isn't there until it's really there. I can't tell you how many people I've met who swear they are just "fifty thousand away" from making their film, and they've been that same $50,000 away for five years.

Don't be profligate with credits.

If someone gives you a really big chunk of money, then go ahead and give them some kind of executive producer credit. But be certain that it's worth it, because you can't give that credit away very many times without diluting its attraction. You may, for instance, want to give the credit to that well-known actor who might be willing to be in the film because he likes the script, likes the role, and is interested in getting his feet wet as a producer. You may want to give the credit to a big money investor. At a certain point, no one will be interested if they are part of a list.

Don't state a specific date for the commencement of shooting your film.

Give an approximate date. That way if you still don't have the money and have to push the date back, it doesn't look as if you don't know what you're doing, or as if you were just saying what you thought people wanted to hear.

Don't make the mistake of talking only about money to your investors.

Money is one of the reasons they're helping, but there are more secure ways for rich people to turn a profit. Talk about the movie. Talk about your cast. Help them envision the film. Give them a good time. Your potential investors could easily take the ten or twenty thousand dollars they are giving you and spend it on an amazing vacation in China. You must make this an investment experience that's fun and worth it for them in other ways. Every year, thousands and thousands of businessmen and businesswomen travel to Las Vegas and other gaming meccas and routinely drop thousands of dollars at the tables. Do they all think they're going to come away winners? Maybe a little part of them does, but most of them are fairly realistic. They hold out hope, but many of them do it for the thrill of a possibility of beating the odds. It's your job to make anyone who is involved in your project feel that thrill. I had a friend who was constantly in contact with his investors, making them feel as if they were part of the project. When the film was done, the investors flew in from out of town and attended a gala screening and party he organized at a theatre at one of the major studios. He invited potential distributors, press, anyone he knew in the business, and of course the cast and crew who had worked for next to no money. It was a mob of excited, happy people, and everyone had a unique, wonderful time. Did the investors make a lot of money? Not a lot, but no one left angry that they hadn't struck gold.

PRODUCT PLACEMENT MONEY

Your lead actor wears a T-shirt with a company slogan on it throughout your entire film. He wears a ball cap with a team logo and watches pro football nonstop. Your beautiful lead actress loves her sports car and drinks only a special brand of beer. You say to yourself, these logos, these brand names, they reveal something about these characters, and they are on screen for several scenes. Your actors are appealing, and although not big stars, they are recognizable faces. Can you get money for your movie through the advertising these companies, teams, manufacturers, and brands will get?

It depends. If you have distribution in place and name actors wearing the clothing, smoking the cigarettes, drinking the soda, etc., and the characters are behaving in a way that is consistent with the aims of the product brand (doing something that positively mates the product with the brand's desired demographic), you may be able to negotiate a little money. That money would arrive when the final version of the film is released if the product is still prominent in the movie. How prominent? Depends upon what your producer negotiated. More commonly you don't ever receive cash, but during production you might be given samples of the clothing, the beer, and soda for your wrap party, or if you're lucky, a few days loan of a picture car for the lead character to be filmed driving, which will save you the cost of a vehicle rental. These donations can help offset production costs, but it's not cash.

The big product placement deals are made for big films. Companies want to be sure that there will be major returns if they are tying up advertising and promotional dollars in a film, and product placement is an iffy business at best. There is so much lag time between the investment and the release of the movie, and there is no way to predict how the movie will turn out. The contracts for cash product placement deals almost always specify amount of time on screen, whether a label must be clearly visible, and what happens to the product. Does the lead actress have to mention the brand name? Most filmmakers don't like that. They don't want their films to feel like commercials. It's a battle for the companies, and even when the dust settles it's never a sure thing that the product will make the final cut. The companies don't have control, and why spend money on something you don't control? All these factors make a big investment of upfront money in exchange for product placement a less than desirable option, even for studio pictures with assured distribution.

When does product placement work best? When the demographic for the audience of the film is obvious and closely matches up with the market for the product, and the star has a fan base that also matches the demographic. Then you might have the basis for a strong argument for product placement fees. Additionally, if the movie is the right one—a kid-friendly, family film for instance—the marketing and promotional opportunities expand to merchandising involving toys, games, clothing, product tie-ins with a burger chain, etc.

Intellectual Property—Again

By the way, that T-shirt your hero is wearing? The one with the company slogan? You will probably not only *not* receive payment in exchange for the nod, you will have to get permission to use the slogan at all. That slogan is intellectual property, and that company owns it and may not want you to use it, so get a signed agreement before you start filming. The team logo and the games on TV? You will have to obtain permission from the team or from the sport association that governs the team, and you will have to obtain an agreement and purchase the footage of the games. It's usually a per-minute cost, and it's not cheap. You may have thought you were doing these entities a favor, but they collect a lot of money for the privilege of using their logo, colors, and design, and they are VERY litigious.

COMPLETION BONDS

A *completion bond* is a type of insurance. Let's take a hypothetical scenario: You have raised the money for an independent film, and you've got a great script and maybe one "name" cast member. You're ready to go. You want to get a distribution deal in place, possibly bring in some money in advance from pre-sales. Or, you are going after some big money investors. They're intrigued, and you've got them on the line for several thousand or even $100,000 dollars.

The first thing either the investors or the distributor will want to know is how they can be sure that in the end, there will be a movie? In other words, why would anyone financially back a film, loan you money, or advance money towards production on the basis of being able to sell the film and make money later, if they aren't sure that you will finish the film?

Independent films run out of money all the time due to inexperience, mismanagement, and too much optimism. Things sometimes fall through and the production can't recover. If you're an investor hoping for a return, a sales agent who has pre-sold the film to foreign distributors, or a distributor who has advanced money to the project counting on a profit, what do you do when in the end, there's nothing there? You can't finish the film on your own. That's not what you do. You're stuck. That's where a *Completion Guarantor* comes in.

For a percentage of the budget—somewhere around 3 percent but it varies—a Guarantor will insure that the film is completed. A bond does not insure that the film is good, or even that it is sellable. It just insures that in the end, the elements necessary to release a film will be there. Those elements are a completed film with all the necessary delivery requirements. These requirements vary according to where the film will be delivered and on what format it will be exhibited, but usually include the master; the separate components of the audio mix (with tracks separated in a specific way, so that there can be a dubbed track for foreign sales); all contracts and agreements including clearance paperwork; a complete cast and crew list; publicity stills; a music cue sheet and all music license agreements; backgrounds (for subtitles); and everything must match the technical specifications of your agreement. For foreign television, each country has different delivery specifications, and if you have multiple foreign sales, you'll have to find a way to reconcile the different requirements.

Because a bond agreement is for the benefit of a bank, distributors, and investors, it specifies two things:

1) If for some reason the project runs out of money, the bond company will take over and either finance the completion of the film or repay the investors
2) If the bond representative thinks things are getting out of control and the production is running into trouble, the bond company can take over the production of the film and make whatever changes they consider necessary in order to get the film finished and sellable, including replacing the director. "Running into trouble" is defined as not sticking to the approved shooting schedule and/or budget.

A bond is also viewed as a sort of seal of approval. It means that the very knowledgeable production accountants, production managers, and line producers working for the bond company have scrutinized your plan, your financing, and your track record and have found it solid enough to be sure that your project won't go too far astray. Again, it doesn't say anything about the artistic or creative quality of the film, just that there will be a film.

If a bank is involved in the financing of your film, they don't care about the movie. All they care about is that a movie is delivered so that you can repay your loan and the interest on that loan. So they require you to get a completion guarantor.

What do bond companies look at? They check out the people involved in the project. Does anyone have experience? If you're a first-time director, they may require that you hire an experienced First AD who they approve. If it's a first-time producer, they'll want an experienced accountant and line producer. They will look at the DP and the Production Designer. Why will they care if the AD is your cousin or the Production Designer is your boyfriend? Because these positions and the management of these departments are crucial to whether or not the film stays on schedule. An AD creates the schedule and his or her job is to stick to it. A slow Cinematographer can cause hours of delay and those hours can cripple a shooting schedule. A Production Designer who is an amazing talent but can't stick to a budget can cause terrible cost overruns, and the overages will have to come from some other department, which will in turn cause other, serious problems.

A bond company examines the script, the schedule, the budget, any contracts, insurance policies, and agreements that have already been negotiated, and they decide whether or not the project is bondable. Once they agree to bond a project, a contract is signed. If they have to shut the film down or take it over, they stand to lose a great deal of money. If everything runs smoothly, you'll rarely see them.

The important thing to realize about the bond company is, they don't want to take over your movie. They aren't a studio or a production company. They would much rather sit back, earn their fee, and not have to do a thing. As long as you cooperate with them, are open and straightforward in your dealings, and are prompt with both good and bad news, they can be extremely helpful to first-time filmmakers. Bond company representatives often have decades of practical experience doing what you're doing for the first time. They may have all sorts of suggestions, contacts, and resources that they are willing to make available to you. Listen to them, be forthcoming with the information they require, and try to see them as allies.

Caution! Often inexperienced filmmakers decide that the bond representative is the enemy and act accordingly. They hide information, they give the rep the cold shoulder when he or she comes to a meeting or comes to set. It's as if it's high school and the bond representative is the outsider. They try to convince everyone else to behave the same way. This is absurd. The rep doesn't want you to fail. If you fail, the bond company loses money. As mentioned above, the bond representative probably has lots more experience than you do and could actually help solve problems. There are very few bond companies. Everyone knows everyone else. If you get a reputation for being disorganized and uncooperative, and don't stick to the budget and schedule, the other bond companies will know about it within a matter of weeks and you will find, as a director I know did, that you are not bondable, meaning that no company will insure a film if you are directing. This is a tough restriction, and it will greatly hamper you in terms of financing and distribution.

FINDING MONEY AND WORKING WITH AN ATTORNEY—WHO CAN YOU TRUST?

At several points in this book, I advise you to consult a lawyer. Not just any lawyer. An attorney who is experienced in the film industry. How do you know if an attorney is good? Get referrals from people in the business. Do as much research as you possibly can. An experienced entertainment attorney will cost several hundred dollars an hour. Some attorneys will work with filmmakers to help them create a business plan (more about that later), put together financing, find distribution, etc. They will charge a retainer (a sort of down payment), and ultimately, if the money for the budget is raised, a percentage of the project budget. This type of attorney is often the best way to go for a first-timer. They know the lay of the land and they will work to protect you and to help you act strategically.

Robert Kaplan

Robert Kaplan has been an entertainment lawyer for over 40 years, starting with the preeminent firm of Kaplan, Livingston, Goodwin, Berkowitz & Selvin. He has represented producers, production companies, directors, writers, music groups, agencies, financiers, and Internet startups. He's been Production Counsel on over 20 independent films and was a Business Affairs Executive at Warner Bros. His current practice is focused primarily on independent production and financing. He has produced or executive produced films and has several films currently in development.

Why should a filmmaker form an LLC or a corporation?

Let's start with this—the insurance company won't give you insurance unless you form one of those companies. The completion guarantor, the distributor, even the actors' agents and the director's agents, everybody involved is going to want to know, "Who's the production company, and who am I making a deal with?" It's nothing to lose sleep over. There are two questions. One is when do you form it [the LLC], when do you spend the money? If you want to option a script in your personal name, that's fine, because the only person that you really have any obligation to at that point is the writer. If you have a free option [no money changes

Robert Kaplan—cont'd

hands, or just a dollar seals the deal], or you pay him $500 or $1000 for an option, and you paid it and now you have a year[to get the script set up], you don't really have to worry about any other liabilities.

But when you start to hire somebody to do a budget, or when you start to make a deal with a director, or when you start to go out to investors and it looks like this thing is turning into a real business, that's when you really have to sit down and look at spending the money to form the LLC or the corporation.

For people who have to find private investors and who are not at all knowledgeable or experienced with this, what do you suggest as a strategy?

There are several different ways to go about it. The question is, how do you get to the people? How do you put the deal together? How do you structure the deal to make it even minimally attractive to people?

Let's say you have a $2 million movie and you have no distribution. With a $2 million movie, maybe you can get a couple of actors with names. Let's say you don't have them. You have a list. There are two major roles, and you have a list of five or ten actors who could be in the roles whose names mean something and who would maybe be attractive to distributors or foreign films companies.

One question is whether or not you are prepared to go to the investor and say, we want you to invest the money in the movie, and we want to make the movie before we go to distributors. [For] most people who make a $500,000 or a $1 million movie, there's no choice. You're not going to get a distribution deal before you make the movie. When you start to get to the $2 million area, you actually have a choice. One big mistake that most young producers make is they think that it's better to get the money and make the movie before making the distribution deal. Most people think that they're going to make a great movie and that the movie is going to be more valuable after it is finished. "We can make a better deal when the movie is done than we can right now." I am totally, utterly against that... What's the most ideal state of a movie? It's the screenplay before it's shot, because you can say, "Look at this great script. We're going to have these great vistas, and there are going to be great actors." It's 100 percent of the movie's potential.

But movies, particularly low-budget movies, are nothing but a series of compromises. The question becomes how much of the 100 percent can you hang on to before the movie is over. You're lucky if you can hang on to 80 or 85 percent. And what about movies where you don't have a lot of money to play with, and you have a tight schedule, and people are not getting along, and... you're making more compromises. For people to say that they think the movie is going to be better when it's done—"We'll make the distribution deal later"—it's crazy. I always say to people, here's the order: Get the money [first]. Get the money subject to distribution, meaning the investors don't have to put the money up unless you bring them a distribution deal. Maybe a sales deal for just the foreign [sales] is enough, but [bringing them] somebody in the distribution world who is saying, "I'm in" tends to give investors comfort—that there are professional people, not you the producer but a professional person out there who is vouching for the movie. Even if it's a

Continued

Robert Kaplan—cont'd

foreign sales agent who's only taking foreign, and even if the foreign sales agent isn't guaranteeing any minimum amount of sales or pre-sales, just [the fact that] a foreign sales agent has agreed to handle the movie is going to give an investor more comfort.

My ideal scenario is to get the investors to say yes based on bringing in the distribution deal. If you don't bring in a distribution deal, the investors don't have to invest. But that's not always possible. There are a lot of movies where you're just not going to get a distribution deal in advance.

The second thing that I would do is make sure that you're going to shoot the movie in a state or in a country where there is a tax rebate plan. Most of them [rebate plans] are in the area of 20 to 25 percent of qualified expenses, which usually turns out to be somewhere in the area of 15 to 20 percent of the total budget. What you should do is try to maximize that. When you read the script and you're determining whether to commit to a movie or not—this is a strategic matter—you can't just read the script and say I love it. You've got to look at how well the financing is going to go, what kind of budget [it is], are the actors going to appeal, are the foreign sales agents going to be interested, can it be a movie where you can get pre-sales, can you shoot it in a territory or in a state that's going to give you the maximum rebate for the budget.

Let's say you have a $2 million movie, and you figure that you're going to shoot it all in Louisiana or Michigan or New Mexico or Georgia. You can figure that you're going to get the crew and you're going to get pretty much everything locally so that you can maximize the tax rebate. That ends up being 20 percent of the budget. The way you talk to the investors is that you say you're putting up $2 million but 20 percent of that is collateralized. The tax rebate is actually stronger collateral than the pre-sale. It's payable within six months after the movie is done, and it's payable regardless of what happens to distribution. That's money you get back from the state of Georgia, so that's solid money. So right away, the pitch to the distributor is you're investing 100 percent of the cost to the movie, but you're really only risking 80 percent of your investment, because we've already covered 20 percent without even thinking about distribution. Then if you have the foreign sales agent or maybe a domestic deal, you can even pre-sell digital rights.... Between the tax deal and maybe a distribution deal and maybe some name actors, those are three major things you can do to put a positive gloss on the movie.

In addition, you'd better make sure that it's a movie that's got foreign potential, since that's two-thirds of the world's revenue for movies now. If you have a domestic-only film [dialogue-driven comedies, domestic dramas, coming of age movies], it's hard to be able to do projections that show an investor that they're going to make money.

Let's say you've got the right genre. You've got a cast member who's not a household word, they may not drive box office, but someone will know who they are. You've done that. You've set up your LLC, and now you want investors. What do you do?

Robert Kaplan—cont'd

If you are a producer, and you have no background in this area, and you yourself don't know any rich people to tap into, you're really a blank slate. If you know one rich person and you can go to [him or her] and say, put up 20 percent of the budget of the movie, instead of 100 percent, that's a really smart thing to do... How do you get people to do this? You get your lead person. You don't have to get one person to put up all the money. You don't even have to get one person to put up half the money. One person to put up 20 percent of the money is enough to start building on.

If you really have nobody that you can turn to... what I would recommend is that you go find somebody who does have sophistication on the business side. You will need somebody in your group who, if you have meetings with investors, whether it's an investor who potentially can put up the whole budget or whether it's somebody who's just going to put up a little part of it, you generally are going to need somebody in the room who can talk business.

Whether you bring them in as a partner [or] as an executive producer, there are people in Hollywood who do this for a living. There are definitely a bunch of lawyers who are able to do that. They [these lawyers generally] don't work for producers because it's much more lucrative to represent actors and writers and directors. If I [as a lawyer] represent only actors and I get a 5 percent fee from all of those actors, I don't really have to work for those actors unless they get a job offer. And maybe some of the job offers fall through and the deals don't close but enough of those job offers will go through where my 5 percent will be something, and frankly, I don't have to do a lot of work for it.

If I'm representing a producer, on the other hand, in order for me to get to my payday, I have to do an agreement to acquire the rights, I have to do an agreement with a director, I have to help write a business plan or put the thing together for the money. I may have to do a whole bunch of deals before the movie goes and before the producer gets paid and before... therefore I can get paid. So there are a lot of lawyers that don't really like to represent producers, or if they do represent producers, they say, I can't really do that on a spec basis. They say, I'll represent you, but if I'm going to be the lawyer putting everything together on this movie, a typical fee for a lawyer to do that is about 1 percent to 1½ percent of the budget of a movie. If somebody comes to me and says I've got a $2 million movie, we're looking at a $20,000 or $25,000 fee. That's really the minimum, because even [on] a $1 million movie, my work as a lawyer is going to be the same.

A lot of lawyers say, I'm not going to get that [much money] on this $2 million movie. I'll charge you $25,000. But the producer doesn't have that $25,000 right now, or maybe a minimal amount, and most lawyers would say, my work as a lawyer is all before the movie starts. You've got to get the financing, you've got to get the director, you got to get the script, you've got to get the actors, everything has to be done before you start shooting. My work is very front-loaded. The lawyer has to come in very early on, and there's a real grinding kind of a conflict there, because the young producer doesn't have any money, and he needs a lawyer to put all this together.

Continued

Robert Kaplan—cont'd

What most lawyers do is they'll say, I'm not going to charge you my full rate upfront, because the movie may never go and it's just unfair. What I do need is a retainer. Let's say on a movie where the attorney's fee would be $25,000, give me $2,500 or $5,000 and I'll do all that early work, and if the movie collapses, I'm not going to get the full value of what I did, but at least I'll have that retainer. And that will be our compromise deal in case it doesn't go forward.

If you're a producer who has no experience raising money and you want to go find that other person to bring in, maybe you have a lawyer and the lawyer says, "I'm doing the legal work, but I can't help you raise money. I'm not a producer, and I'm not a financier. I don't know money people." Then the producer goes to somebody who is connected to money people, and there is probably going to be a similar issue with that person. That person might say, "I'll do it on a total contingent basis." It's like a finder's fee—"I'll take from my fee 5 percent of the money raised." Something along those lines—2½ to 5 percent would be the range of finder's fees. (I don't like the idea of the 5 percent, because that's money not going on the screen. I would rather make a deal with the finder that says 2½ or 3 percent plus a couple of points of the profits on the back end in case the movie is successful, rather than paying the finder 5 percent upfront.)

When you're talking to somebody like that, here are the strategic issues: on one extreme, there is "Let's go to one person who puts up the whole $2 million." On the other extreme, there's no one person who's going to give $2 million or even $1 million or even $500,000, so what about a situation where you say, "We're going to go out and find a group of people, and if each person puts up $50,000, that would be 40 people. Or if each person is going to put up $25,000, you would need 80 people."

Then you have a situation where you can look at fewer numbers of investors putting up more money each, or a larger number of investors putting up less money each. The advantage with the latter category is that if either the producer or the guy who the producers brought in to raise the money says, "Let's go to a number of smaller people because there are more people that we can hit up," it's not as much of a problem, you know, "We can open it up to people who are not billionaires or hundred millionaires. We can open it up to the doctors and the dentists." Then you're not limited to Beverly Hills anymore.

But [there is] an SEC, a Securities and Exchange regulatory issue. Back in the Depression of the 1930s, there were people out there saying, "I've got this great gold mine in Nevada, and I want you to buy my stock in my gold mine company." But it was a sham, it was BS. A lot of widows in New York or Boston [bought] stock and then found out that they had been ripped off. So the Securities and Exchange Commission was formed, and they set rules about what you can and cannot do when you're selling stock. And the basic thing is the following: If you're selling a profit interest in a movie, it's a sale of a security, which means it's a stock. If you're selling a security, you're under the rules of the SEC, and what the SEC is saying is that if you're going to go out and raise money from a bunch of different people, you're going to tell them, "Here's the deal. You put up this much money and this is what you'll get for it."

Robert Kaplan—cont'd

There's no negotiation in the deal. That's the deal, because you're giving the same deal to everybody. If you're doing that, then you'll have to follow the rules of the SEC, and you have to give the investor a complete disclosure of what the deal is, what's the movie, what's the budget, we don't have distribution, we don't have this, we don't have that. You have to disclose everything good and bad about the movie.

On the other hand, if you go to one person and say to one person, "Will you put up $2 million," or even two people to say, "Would you put up $1 million each," in that situation, you're going to end up negotiating a deal. Let's say that a producer comes to me and says, "I've got this film, and I know a couple of rich people, but what I don't know is how to close the deal. What do I offer them? What do they get back?" And if there's one guy putting up a million and another guy putting up another million, you could do two different negotiations. One guy might get his money back first, the other guy might have a bigger share of the profits. One guy might be active in the production and get a producer credit, the other guy might not. You can negotiate those deals.

The problem is that if you say instead of two people for $1 million each, let's go to 10 people for $200,000 each, or let's go to 50 people for $40,000 each. The greater the number of people you go to, the more you can't negotiate the deal. How can you go to 10 people for $200,000 each and say, I'll have 10 negotiations? The only way I can do this is by telling you all that you're all going to get the same deal and there's going to be no favoritism. And the minute you do that... now you're under the SEC. You don't have to file anything, but you have to move ahead according to the rules of the SEC. You have to write up a business plan, a written plan that discloses the dangers, all the risks.

So it's easier if you know people. Would I want one person to put up all the money? If one person puts up all the money, that person tends to have a real proprietary interest, and all of a sudden, you could have an investor who really doesn't know about the movie business, or they want to be on the set, or they want their girlfriend to star in the movie. The ideal scenario would probably be to have two people each putting up half, so that no one person can rule the roost.

Up to about three or four investors, you can do individual negotiations. The SEC rule is that as long as you can have individual negotiations, you don't have to follow those disclosure obligations. Why? Because the minute a person has the ability to negotiate a deal, then the SEC looks at them as they're big enough and smart enough to take care of themselves. If you can negotiate a deal, you're a big boy.

Now, you've got your money guy, you brought in that executive producer, and he says, "I don't really know any really rich people, but I know a lot of different people in Orange County, and I know investment bankers and... all these money managers. I think that the way to do this is that you don't want to go out and sell units that are really expensive, because I don't know how many people are going to go for it. I think that if we sold $50,000 units or $25,000 units, there [will probably be] a lot of takers." This is a big philosophical decision that has to be made. If a unit is $25,000, you have to sell to 80 people. The rule used to be that you have to go

Continued

Robert Kaplan—cont'd

visit somewhere between 5 and 10 people in order to get one to go. So that would mean, if you need 80 people, you'd have to go visit 800 people. That's hard to do. Even if you had a couple of people that said "I'll take a big chunk" and you reduce that 80 down to 50 or 60, it's still a lot of people. And it's a dog and pony show, you've got to have a million and one meetings... That's the hardest way to raise money. It becomes a full-time job.

We were talking about the attorney for independent filmmakers as a strategist, and I wanted you to walk me through this scenario: Someone is an independent filmmaker, they made their film, they've gotten into a festival—let's say, they've gotten into Sundance or not even Sundance. They want to get distribution, and they don't know anything about distribution deals. They don't know anything about the things that can really screw them over. How you would counsel them in what you would do, and how you would work with them?

I would put film attorneys into two categories. There are guys or women, too, who are lawyers. They're comfortable negotiating deals, drafting agreements, and being lawyers and don't necessarily want to be much beyond that. Then, there are entertainment lawyers who go beyond that, and you can look at them as strategists, you can look at them even as agents. There are a lot of entertainment lawyers to whom a client will say, "Can you get this script of mine to this agent or this actor or director?" Entertainment lawyers are performing that kind of agent function all the time. But it depends on the personality of the lawyer and whether they want to get into that kind of area of business.

You may get involved in packaging the project or—

Yes. Or instead of writing scripts on spec, "Let's see if we can get you a commissioned job at the studio." If it's a director who's got his own project that he wants to get made, then it's almost like representing him to a producer. Let's say that we've got a fairly young director, a guy who's maybe made a movie or two that he's written and now wants to direct his own favorite project. It's a $5 million movie. The lawyer as well as the agent might want to get involved in helping him to get that. Maybe there's an actual producer attached, or maybe, on an interim basis, the director is actually his own producer until they get it to a producer. Maybe that's part of the strategy. Let's take it to these five producers who have deals somewhere, or have access to money, or who are good producers for you to be teamed up with.

There seems to be a lot of private money coming into the business now. We had 20 years of the foreign sales agent [plus] bank loan methodology of independent financing being the dominant way. What that led to was too many movies being made. Maybe more movies being made than should have been made, because most of them were not very good. What happened over a long period of time is that a lot of those movies didn't perform, and a lot of buyers around the world have gone out of business.

"Buyers," meaning distributors?

Studios have always financed movies. They financed movies in order to have them for their distribution channels. They'd rather not finance movies, but they have to finance them in order to have the movies. In the Seventies, somebody had the bright idea of saying, "We can use that same method but go to foreign

Robert Kaplan—cont'd

companies. [We can] get them to put up money against the distribution rights." The problem in the foreign market is that you have a distributor in Spain. You have a distributor in France, and a distributor in Japan, and all these countries around the world. So, in order to sell the movie to enough parties, in order to gather the financing together, you have to be able to have somebody who knows the distributors in all the foreign countries and could go make maybe five or six or seven or eight different deals, which would total the budget of the movie. And the distributors in those foreign countries are looked upon as the buyers of the film.

And the sales agents, the foreign distributors and sales agents, get what for their trouble?

They get a distribution fee—a type of a distribution fee, not the same distribution fee as at a studio. If you go to Warner Bros. and they finance the movie, they're basically going to charge a 30 percent distribution fee. That is actually higher in some areas and lower in other areas, but across the board, just assume for simplicity's sake about a 30 percent fee. The sales agents when they say, "I will take your movie and I will sell it to a bunch of distributors around the world," they generally charge a bit less than that. It's 15 to 25 percent.

They only get paid if they produce results?

Right.

Are they paid a certain something plus the percentage?

Recently, it's beginning to happen that foreign sales agents are now starting to ask for some advance against their fee. That's been a development only in the last few years. Generally speaking, with this "foreign sales" way of making movies, the sales agent fee or commission, like the studio distribution fee, is based on revenues. If there are no revenues, they don't get any money. If there are big revenues, they get big money. But it's a bit more complicated than going to Warner Bros. or Paramount and making one deal that covers the whole world. Let's say you have a $5 million movie. In order to get $5 million through this foreign sales methodology, you have several problems. One problem is that there is no one foreign territory that's big enough to get the whole $5 million. So, you have to sell Japan for $1 million, and then you sell Germany for $1 million, and you sell the UK for $1 million, whatever. Multiple deals have to be made in order to assemble enough money. But more than that, you now don't have the centralization of financing. You have these contracts with four or five or six buyers. If I'm the Japanese buyer I'm saying, "I'll put up my million dollars, but I'm only going to put up my million dollars when I know that everybody else is in." So, it creates much more complexity in terms of the management of the deal.

You go to a sales agent. The sales agent comes back and he says, "Good news. I have a $1 million dollar contract from Japan, five territories for $1 million dollars." Actually, you need six territories for $1 million dollars, because of what I'm about to tell you. So, you have these contracts. Now the question is, how do you turn the contracts into cash? If you make a deal with Warner Bros. to fully finance your movie, Warner Bros. is the only party you're dealing with. They have approval rights. They say, "We like this." The script is ready to go. The actors are ready

Continued

Robert Kaplan—cont'd

to go. And when the movie now has a green light, they start advancing money. They put money into the bank account, maybe—if you're the producer, you've got a cash flow schedule, so there's a drawdown schedule—but basically Warner Bros. starts advancing the money. When you have these multiple buyers, it becomes much more difficult. The way these deals have ended up working is the foreign sales agent says to the Japanese buyer, "Here's the deal. You give me a contract for $1 million dollars. You don't have to give me any money until I deliver the film to you. That way, you don't take any risk. I'm not asking you to put up any money when I'm not getting money from anybody else. You don't have to take any risk. I have to deliver the movie before you have to pay any money."

I'm oversimplifying things a little bit. There's usually a small down payment in order to secure the deal on both parties, but for simplicity's sake, let's say, the sales agent makes a deal with the Japanese buyer for a million dollars payable on delivery of the movie. The sales agent's job is to get five or six deals for that. He now has enough contracts, where… it adds up to the budget of the movie. Now the sales agent[has to] turn that into cash, because all these contracts are payable on delivery. He goes to the bank… and borrows money, because these contracts now have a defined amount of money payable on delivery of the movie. They can be viewed by a bank as collateral for a loan as opposed to going to a bank and saying, "I want to make this $5 million movie, can I give you the movie as collateral?" Because there are no guaranteed amounts, no bank will loan money on that basis, because they can't value the collateral. But a contract from a good buyer that says, "I'll pay you a million dollars on delivery of the movie," a bank can deal with that.

And just to clarify, the buyers we're talking about, say the Japanese buyers, would be a Japanese distribution company which has then got its own arrangements with exhibitors and all that. So it's basically a foreign sales agent to a foreign distributor—

And the reason the foreign sales agent only takes 15 or 20 or 25 percent is because the distributor that he's selling to, the buyer in Japan or the UK or Germany, is also a distributor. So, when they make their deal, between the two of them, it's going to be, "I'll put the movie in the theaters and I'll take a local distribution fee and pay you 70 percent or 80 percent." Then the sales agent gets that 80 percent and then he takes his 15 or 20 or 25 percent on that 80 percent. From the producers' point of view, you can say, it's kind of like a double fee… But the system works.

You were saying that you really don't want $5 million for a $5 million movie because you're going to have to pay interest to the bank. So you really want $5 million plus.

There are several hidden issues with using this foreign sales approach to financing that producers are not always aware of. I've seen producers make this mistake over and over again. They say, "I have a $5million budget, so what I have to do is go and get $5 million in presales." If they do that, they're not going to have enough money to make the movie, because the banks don't get profits. They get interest. If they're only going to [make the loan] for interest, they are going to want to make sure that they are in a risk-free situation. That's why they have to be able to

Robert Kaplan—cont'd

judge the collateral. They look very carefully at who the company is that's giving this presale contract. They want to make sure that company is going to be around six months or nine months or a year from now when the film is finally delivered. If the company is in a shaky state, the banks won't loan at all. In addition, the banks will calculate the amount of time they think the loan is going to be outstanding. They're going to calculate what they think the interest rate is. They're going to give themselves leeway, and they're going to figure out what their interest is, what their profit is, and they're going to build it into the deal, and it will become part of the loan. And they will actually take that money and put it into a segregated account when the loan closes and pay themselves the interest as they go. And they will pay themselves their own legal fees, their own commitment fees, and other fees that they charge. I'd say, on average, depending on the budget of the movie, if you were going to use this method and borrow 100 percent of the budget of the movie based on this method, then a bank loan alone, the cost of doing business at the bank, is probably going to be about 20 percent of the budget of the movie. So, you have to figure a $5 million movie is going to cost $6 million when you're done with the bank.

If you're a producer and you don't have private financing available, you may not have a choice. That was certainly the case for the last 20 years. That's why there were all kinds of producers with all kinds of projects, many of them not very good, and a lot of lousy movies were made. Distributors around the world... went out of business. In the last 18 months or two years, the thing that's new and different is that the supply has dwindled because the recession has shrunk the business. It's a very good correction in the Industry, because now we don't have a glut. Now demand may be greater than supply, and... when demand is greater than supply, prices go up. There are now buyers for the right project. It means that only movies with good elements are going to get made. If you're a producer with a good project, this is not a bad time to be getting into the business.

At the bank, they don't read scripts. They don't look at who the actors are, and they frankly do not care who the producer is. They really only care about one thing... and that is who's the sales agent, because they are going to be looking to the sales agent to make sure that the sales agent delivers the sales. If you're a producer and you start going around to sales agents, a very important thing to try to find out from a strategic point of view is, what banks does the sales agent have relationships with and is that sales agent in good standing. If the sales agent just got three movies in a row and they didn't sell anything, it isn't really very good. You have to look at your sales agent carefully. If the sales agent has a good relationship with the bank and can really get the bank to make the loan, then the sales agent's fee of 20, 25 percent is worth it, because you aren't going to get your movie made unless you have that sales agent.

There's more pressure on producers [now], even in the making of the deals with foreign sales agents. The demand being greater than supply, at the last market or two, the prices of presales were up. The last Sundance, I think, there were something like 32 movies that were actually sold at Sundance compared to the previous year, where maybe it was a handful. So, it's coming back. It's a good time for people to be entering this industry.

Michael Paradies Shoob

Michael Paradies Shoob is the writer-director of *Driven*, which premiered at the Toronto Film Festival, where *Screen International Magazine* called him "one of the new directors to watch in North America." He was also a director of *Bush's Brain*, the documentary about presidential advisor Karl Rove.

I was determined to try to make my first independent film as a director. So [my partner and I] took a script that we had rewritten back in Key West. We partnered with a friend who wanted to produce the film, and it appeared we had found the financing. We put together a terrific cast and crew (Dennis Hopper and Mary Elizabeth Mastrantonio were in the cast) and went to location with everybody and the financing fell through. Our first investor lost nearly a million dollars, and we had to give the script to him when the project went down. I came back to L.A. devastated. How do you recover from losing a $3 million film that falls apart on location? I was young. It took some time.

I took a job writing "behind the scenes" documentaries, primarily for movies produced by Cannon Pictures. I also was working as a researcher for an ABC miniseries. Again, lots of jobs and a pretty long period trying to pick up the pieces.

Eventually, I partnered with an older Emmy-winning writer and a financier from Australia, and we set up a company that financed the development of new screenplays we would write. We also began the arduous process of setting up a business plan, and we went out raising money for a film—which, through various twists and turns, became my first feature, *Driven*.

After that partner left the partnership, I decided that if I was basically going to "go this alone," I should have a project that was uniquely my own. So I wrote a completely new script based on my experience as a cab driver in L.A. The investors seemed not to mind the change in project.

During this time, I kept the investors' money in an escrow account drawing interest. [I] didn't touch the money. I also wrote a regular letter to the investors, telling them about how the project was going, apprising them of all major developments. I believe it's very important to keep your investors informed along the way. The process can take a long time, and it's important to show a responsibility to them and their investment. I also discovered that the regular correspondence not only kept them informed, but it served to bring us closer together. I think many of them began to root for us. They became part of the team. Our original selling idea was that this should be more than an investment, it should be, "win or lose," an interesting and memorable experience for the investor—which I think it was. I believe that can be a selling point for independent filmmakers.

In the end, we had raised about the half the money we needed, and the project was at a standstill. I didn't want to break escrow without an adequate budget. I had a lunch with a filmmaker friend who said to me, "Make it for what you've got. Give yourself a green light." Another director friend eyeballed the script and said, "I'm afraid you're going to need more money."

It turned out that they were both right. We decided to start the film, and we eventually needed more money, which we raised during production. So it wasn't unusual for me to work a 12-hour day directing on the set, and then get on the

Michael Paradies Shoob—cont'd

phone and try to raise money. My producer was working to raise additional money as well.

Since it was my first feature, I took probably more time in postproduction than I should have—but I was determined that the film should be the best it could possibly be when we went into the marketplace. I didn't want to cut any corners, but, in hindsight, I probably took too long. When we finished, the first question we faced was, Should we do a big screening and expose the film, or keep it under wraps until it played its first major festival? Since we finished really too late for Sundance, our goal was the Toronto Film Festival, which was six months away.

My producer became aware of a small screening event on a cruise ship. It was called the Floating Film Festival, but it was really a gathering of critics and festival programmers and film aficionados more than a "festival." We were introduced to Kathleen Carroll, the former film critic for the *New York Daily News.* Kathleen liked the film and wanted to take it to the festival (she and critic Roger Ebert and a few others took a few films of their choice as part of the "programming" of the festival). The whole thing was started by the founder of the Toronto Film Festival. So our idea was that the film could be exposed to some of the Toronto people and a few critics. The Toronto programmers who were there loved the film, and critic Ella Taylor wrote in the *Atlantic Monthly* that *Driven* was the "highlight of the festival."

To make critical marketing decisions during this period, Dan [Daniel Linck, the producer] and I would sometimes assemble our "kitchen cabinet," a group of our other producers and key "friends of the film." Now we were faced with a major decision—whether to have a big industry screening, which might create buzz for the film, or keep the film under wraps before it had major festival play. It was tricky—if we let the film out of the bag and word of mouth was poor, it could hurt us before Toronto. But, if it was good, it would be great for us. We were excited about the film, so we decided to have a big industry screening and see what would happen.

One new investor stepped up and offered to finance a screening and after party at the Paramount Theatre on the studio lot at Paramount Pictures. We printed a flock of invitations, and we must have sent them to everyone in Hollywood. Literally more than a thousand invitations went out the door. The theatre seated 600, and we were determined to fill it to capacity. We brought friends and some of our crew over to our offices and had mail stuffing parties. We left no stone unturned.

We invited our investors from around the country, and many of them flew in for the occasion. We rented a couple of limos for them (a relatively inexpensive gesture that went a long way). When the limos drove onto the Paramount Lot, one of the investors climbed out of the car and walked up to me with a starry-eyed look: "This is like the movies. . . " There was a beat, and she corrected herself: "This *is* the movies."

It turned out that we needed the second studio theatre as well. We had a thousand people filling the two theatres on the Paramount Lot. We treated this like a

Continued

Michael Paradies Shoob—cont'd

major industry screening with an RSVP line and a half dozen staff at the door signing people in. Some distribution people flew out from New York. Kathleen Carroll, who was becoming the "godmother" for our film, flew out to join us. All the cast members were there. We paid to have a huge reception in the lobby of the theatre which cost us plenty, but we were determined to pull out all the stops. It was a memorable evening. There were no immediate rewards or offers after the screening, but I do think we had created some significant buzz for the film around town.

After the screening, we set our sights on the Toronto Film Festival, and we began meeting with producers' representatives to see who could best help us get into the festival and get the movie sold. At the same time, we began interviewing publicity firms in L.A. and New York who specialized in festivals and independent film. The idea was to have a rep and a publicist in place as quickly as we could.

We finally chose a producer's rep, and he went to work trying to cement our participation at Toronto. Whatever people tell you about the importance of having a "producer's rep," I believe they are critical to the sale of independent films. Despite all of the preparation we had done—the interest we had gained at Toronto from the Floating Film Festival, the hard work building word of mouth for the screening at Paramount, and the support of critics like Kathleen—this rep made a huge difference.

In the end, despite being on a number of lists as one of the top ten films at Toronto (my memory is that there were more than 250 films at the festival) and being chosen by *Screen International Magazine* as one of the new directors to watch in North America, we were not able to sell the film at the festival. It was a terrible market for films at Toronto. Only one film sold that year. We followed up Toronto with the Hamptons, Slamdance, Taos, Palm Springs, and others. We received Honorable Mention at Slamdance. All of the festival play increased the visibility of the film, and it was great to meet new filmmakers and producers.

Eventually, my producer found a foreign sales agent who continues on the film to this day. We made a cable deal, and the film showed on the Sundance Channel and Showtime.

Sometimes the "best laid plans" don't yield financial success. But here's the silver lining: The film was a creative and critical success. There isn't a month that goes by when I don't hear some kind word about *Driven*. It's a film I'm very proud of to this day. It remains one of the great experiences of my life.

Section II

Production:

No Such Thing as a Free Lunch

Chapter 10

It's a Collaborative Medium—Exactly What Does That Mean?

It takes a village to make a movie. In addition to all the people who search out material or write the script, and all those who play a role in the decision of whether or not to finance a film, and those who represent the people involved in all of the above, there are the people who actually physically make the movie.

Because of the mesh of creative, technical, and financial elements involved, making a film has always been a collaborative process. Everyone has a job to do, and they must all work together whether they want to or not. This doesn't mean that everyone is equal. There is a definite hierarchy. At studios and in production offices there are the bosses and the boss's bosses, and even the assistants of the big bosses have more status than the assistants of the lesser ones. On the set there is a fairly rigid chain of command. There is even a specific protocol in the editing room—who sees the *cuts* (edited versions) of the film and when.

Most members of a film production crew are *freelance* employees, *independent contractors*. This means that they are self-employed, hired to work on a movie on a per-project basis. When their part of the work on the film is completed they are unemployed again until they are hired onto a different film. This means that almost everyone—including the producer, director, casting director, actors, and cinematographer—has a vested interest in someone saying Yes to a movie, rather than saying, "We'll think about it," or "It's not completely together yet, let's wait until it is." Until a movie gets a green light, no one is hired, therefore no one gets paid.

HOW STORIES CHANGE

It is often said that a film is written three times—once on paper (the screenplay development), once on set (production), and once in the editing room (postproduction.) A film can change radically as it moves from one stage to the next. The success of the finished project depends on the script, on the execution of the production, what worked during shooting and what didn't, on the performances of the cast, on the order and pacing of the way the film is assembled, on the music, even on the marketing and distribution plan. There are many stages to the process, and very few people are around for the entire process, so it is vitally important that everyone at each stage is making the same movie. Exactly what does that mean?

Let's say that Jessica has written a script, a courtroom drama. Everyone is excited about it. It is optioned by a producer, Taylor. Taylor loves the dialogue, the clever set-up, the plot twist ending. Taylor looks for financing. Taylor brings the script to his friend, a production company development executive. The exec respects Taylor's taste and ability to get things made and is a good buddy, so she bypasses the intern and assistant and reads the script herself.

She loves the script! She comes to the Monday morning meeting, where the creative and production executives discuss what they've read the weekend before. She says, "I read a great thriller." She describes the script. "Could be a terrific role for Jane," a star. "Let's send it over to Harry," Jane's agent. The marketing executives around the table agree that it could be a big picture for Jane, but will a female lead be able to *carry* (ensure an audience for) this kind of film? This will be an expensive project that cries out for "names" and Oscar-caliber performances. Is there a role for a major male lead also? Not really. There's a juicy secondary role, though. One of the marketing VPs at the table asks, "Is there any chance that the lead could be male and the secondary role could be Jane?" And that's the way a story about a corrupt female attorney having a crisis of conscience becomes a movie with a major male star and co-starring Jane. The assumption is, women will go to a courtroom picture with a male lead, but men won't be eager to see the same film with a female lead.

OR:

Let's say that Dustin's script is a comedy, witty and smart. Samantha, the producer, is thrilled about the interest she's gotten from a major comedian. This comedian is a physical comedy guy, though. The director who is making the movie really wants to cast this comedian. The style of humor in the movie is going to change, and the story will change to accommodate it.

OR:

The way the director envisions the final project involves a particularly way of shooting, of editing, of music. Jennifer's family drama becomes a dark comedy.

OR:

The script is a screwball comedy involving a kidnapping. There's recently been a tragic kidnapping in the news. Even though the film will not be finished and in the marketplace for more than a year, there is the concern that what was once funny will now be seen as tasteless—so maybe the crime should be a robbery, and the subplot should be changed accordingly.

OR:

The script is made as written. During production it becomes clear that there is not enough chemistry between the two leads, or one of the actors who must be sympathetic is not. Or once actually filmed the ending feels flat and the payoff is just not there. Or the funny lines, once spoken, are not funny enough. Or it's decided that what is needed is a happier ending.

Or, or . . . things happen, and these changes sometimes take on a life of their own. A cast member isn't convincing as a poor Midwestern insurance salesman, or as a steamy femme fatale. Everyone thought it would work but it doesn't, and it's too late to walk away. Too much has been invested.

CREATIVE CONTROL AND FINAL CUT

Occasionally a director will lose confidence and do take after take, and that uses up so much time and money (more about that coming up) that critical scenes must be cut or combined, and somehow that throws off the balance of the film.

When there are problems with a script or in production, often those problems are the result of the lack of a strong, dominant voice—a leader. Without a leader, there is often a void, and people and their opinions rush to fill it. Filmmaking by committee has been the downfall of many projects. Part of being a good director, producer, or executive is the ability to unite and focus a diverse group of people, many with conflicting personal and professional agendas. They must sign on and be prepared to support the actual project and not the version of the project each person thinks would be better. Films often come out of the starting gate strong and original but are weakened along the way because too many opinions were permitted into the mix. That's why you often hear about *creative control*. Everybody wants creative control. Usually the source of the funding of the film gets it for the simple reason that if there is no money, there is no movie.

Sometimes a director's attorney or agent is able to negotiate *final cut* as part of the director's deal. Final cut is the ultimate creative control, meaning that the director has the final, indisputable say as to the content, editing, and delivered version of the film. Although the term is often bandied about, contractual final cut is quite rare. That's because the entity writing the check wants to be sure that the film is what they intend it to be. If it's a work of art *and* commercial, great. But the only directors who get final cut as part of their deals are those with a history of artistic and commercial achievement. Everyone else relies on their powers of persuasion, the idea that once they make their script revisions, or screen their version of the film, the group holding the purse strings will agree that it's best. Even with final cut, most directors have little control over how the film is presented and marketed, and usually no control over the trailer, or the publicity. If there is a disagreement and there is no resolution, a production company can bury a film through lackluster distribution and a meager marketing budget. You probably should not worry too much about creative control, especially early on. For the first-time filmmaker there is very little real control, there is only the ability of one person to convince another.

Chapter 11

Protecting Yourself and Your Movie

SETTING UP A PRODUCTION COMPANY

Look at the opening few minutes of most films these days and you will see a veritable laundry list of proprietary credits. Sony Pictures Entertainment presents a Beach Glass Entertainment Production of a Laughing Lamb film, starring. . . etc., etc. What is this all about? Well, usually the studio is the distributor (and possibly at least partially the financier). Beach Glass Entertainment may be the production company that brought the project to the distributor and often will be the company that developed and actually produced the movie. And Laughing Lamb? Could be the director's company. Could be the star's company. Could be the company that was created just for the production of this one film.

When a production company makes a movie, more often than not, a corporation, specifically an LLC (Limited Liability Corporation), is set up just for that film. Let's say that Beach Glass Entertainment is a company run by a major producer. Over the course of a year Beach Glass makes one to three films, all with budgets of $40 to $60million, all distributed by major studios. Beach Glass sets up a separate company for each film. Film A, *Straw Man*, may be produced by Straw Man, Inc. The officers of Straw Man, Inc. might be the president of production for Beach Glass, the producer of *Straw Man*. The treasurer of Straw Man, Inc. may be the head of accounting of Beach Glass. Film B, *Once Upon a Time*, may be produced by Tidal Wave, Inc. Again, the president of Beach Glass might be the CEO of Tidal Wave, the line producer may be the CFO (chief financial officer), and the treasurer may be the accountant. The assets of Beach Glass Entertainment may be abundant: BGE may own an office building, all the scripts they've purchased for development, and profits from past films. The only assets of Tidal Wave, Inc. or Straw Man, Inc. are the production budgets. Creating separate production entities can serve to limiting the liability of the parent company. It can also simplify accounting that must take into consideration the profits and losses of individual films. Also, if each project is a separate legal entity, the production company has the option of picking and choosing among union signatory agreements. (More about that coming up.)

PAYROLL COMPANIES

Part of the business of making a movie is paying people and one hopes, being paid yourself. A studio or a production company, however large or small, assembles a team of technicians and artists to work on a film—but as discussed in Chapter 10, they are all working on a freelance basis.

The production company is coming up with the cash, but they are not actually writing the checks. Almost always, the production company has contracted with a third party, a *payroll company*. That payroll company becomes the *employer of record*. What does that mean, exactly? Most obviously, it means that when the weekly paychecks are issued, the production company doesn't issue them, the payroll company does. Every week the production staff and crew fill out time cards: what time they started work, when they broke for lunch, when they were back on the clock, what time they finished. The time cards are sent to the production accountant, who verifies the hours. He or she then tallies the amount each person is due and sends the list to the payroll company. The payroll company assigns a representative called a *paymaster* to each production. This representative rechecks the accountant's totals, then adds on the payroll company fee (a percentage of the amount) and notifies the production account, who then issues a check to the payroll company. Once the payroll company has that check, they release the crew member's paychecks back to the accountant, who either delivers or has an assistant deliver the checks to the set. This goes on every week for everyone on the project, except the big stars (who are usually paid in several lump sums rather than weekly) and the producer and director (same reason.) If a film is backed by a studio or an established production company, the studio or company might not have to front the money before the payroll checks are released, but that's really the only difference between how it works for them and how it would work for a small independent.

Why Go Through All This?

It's a lot less work to outsource all this. You'd need a huge accounting staff to handle all this *and* to take care of the much more important cost analyses and tracking that are necessary to keep a production budget on course.

Also, the payroll companies are signatories to the unions. They have signed contracts and have ongoing relationships with each film union, and part of what they do when they add up the paychecks is to split off the amounts that must be funneled into the union crew members' health and accounts.

The payroll companies also do the same thing with all the government required payroll taxes, whether an employee is union or non-union. They deposit the appropriate amount into each employee's Social Security account, Unemployment insurance account, and Medicare account. And as employers of record for thousands of crew members, for a price, the payroll company supplies Workers

Compensation. Workers Comp contributes towards the medical expenses of crew members who are injured on the job. The production could buy their own Workers Comp policy, but it would be much, much more expensive, because there are savings in the volume of employees that the payroll company covers.

So although the production company budgets for all of this, and pays for all of it, the payroll company is the ongoing employer. When crew members receive W-4 forms for their taxes at the end of the year, they receive those forms from the payroll company. When they wrap a show, if there is not another project in their immediate future, they file for Unemployment compensation. All the people on the production have scattered to the winds. The payroll company is the company that has all their information on file and that has been paying into their State and Federal Unemployment accounts.

Finally, the companies that are created just for single productions are eventually just ghost companies. There is no one who works there once the film is done. But the payroll companies are here to stay.

PRODUCTION INSURANCE

Anyone who has ever owned a car knows all about insurance. You find a broker, and the broker comes up with a policy that best suits your needs and your budget. You purchase the policy, and cross your fingers that you won't have to use it. The idea of insurance is that you have to have it but you hope you won't need it. Insurance is intended to cover major losses not small ones, and there is always that annoying deductible. Sometimes it seems as if they've got you coming and going. You're parked in a lot and someone dents your fender. The repair shop quotes you $1200 to make it as good as new. Your deductible is $1000. All this time you've been forking out a couple thousand dollars a year for your policy, and now it's time to collect and you're only getting $200. How is that fair? Let's say you grudgingly get the fender fixed, you're parked in the same lot two weeks later, and it happens again. Same story—you're out the $1000 and the insurance pays only $200. And to add insult to injury, if you're doing business with the wrong company, they'll even raise your rates—because now you're officially accident prone!

Insurance is a game of odds. What's the chance something will happen? Insurance companies play the odds, figuring that there is safety in numbers. You and thousands of other car owners pay in thousands of dollars but proportionately few of you will actually have claims that the insurance company will have to pay out. Even if the company does have to pay out, they won't usually have to pay out anywhere near as much as they take in, and deductibles protect them even more.

Insurance for films is in some ways no different than car insurance. The production company buys a policy from one of the special brokers that serve the industry. The policy is expensive, because the potential losses are higher, and because these companies don't sell fifty or seventy-five thousand of these policies a year. The risk is higher, and the odds are worse. On film sets, things happen. Accidents happen. Equipment is broken. Cameras jam.

A typical ***Producers Package*** of insurance includes:

General Liability—This covers the production if anyone is injured or if property is accidentally damaged as a result of the production. For example: Someone is crossing the street and trips over the cables that the electric department ran from the generator. When your location manager goes to get permits to shoot on city, town, or state property, this is the type of insurance the local Film Permit Office or Film Commission wants to see.

Third Party Loss and Damage—This covers the production for damage done to property that a production does not own, such as the storefront or office building or private residence you're renting as a location. You don't own it, but you're using it.

When your location manager is confirming the location agreement with the owner of the property, he or she will give them a "Proof of Insurance Certificate" issued by the insurance company. The certificate will name the property owner as an *additional insured* and state the limits of the policy's coverage. "Additional insured" means that in addition to the production company being insured, the party listed as "additional insured" will be also be covered. A city or state government might be tagged on as insured. Or a city or landlord may stipulate that they must be named as a *loss payee*. This means that if there is a claim, the insurance company will pay them directly rather than the payment going first to the production and then the production writing the check to the payee.

Faulty Stock and Negative Film and Video—This covers damage to your actual film or tape stock, whether it is faulty to begin with or is damaged in transit, or whether it is damaged during processing and/or developing at the lab.

Equipment—This covers camera, grip, electric, and sound equipment in case of theft, breakage, fire, water damage, everything but *negligence* (deliberate carelessness or destruction) and normal wear and tear.

Vehicles—These policies vary, but the production should be certain that there is coverage for hired (rented) vehicles, like trucks and nonowned vehicles; that is, damage to a vehicle that is not part of the production, caused by someone who is part of the production. Sometimes people on the crew will use their own vehicles as part of their job. The production manager determines whether or not that person's car is listed as covered or whether it will be taken care of in another way. Will the production rent this person a car so that his car is covered under the general vehicle policy? This kind of thing might be handled by giving the person who uses his own car a *car allowance*, an amount that is negotiated as part of his overall deal and that is meant to offset insurance expenses and cover the wear and tear (*depreciation*) on someone's personal vehicle.

Props, Sets, and Wardrobe—This covers purchased and rented props, sets, and wardrobe for theft, breakage, fire, water damage, etc. Again, a claim can be refused if it is determined that the reason for the problem is negligence.

Extra Expense—This covers the production for whatever additional expenses are incurred as a result of any of these claims. If a set burns down there will be delays as it is rebuilt. Extra Expense insurance will cover the "down" time and the expenses it caused because of the change that must be made in the schedule. A day of shooting is lost due to a problem with the camera. The camera damage is covered by the equipment part of the policy, but the extra expense of the reshoot will be covered by this part of the policy.

Union Travel Insurance—If your film is either SAG (Screen Actors Guild), DGA (Directors Guild of America), IATSE (International Alliance of Theatrical Stage Employees), or Teamster (International Brotherhood of Teamsters, or IBT), part of the deal the production company signs with the union dictates that there must be travel insurance coverage.

Cast Insurance—This is an interesting one. When you purchase production insurance, you are given a number of slots for cast insurance, usually about five. The producer and/or production manager have to choose which people will be insured. The decision is based on the damage and loss to the production if the cast member gets sick, is hurt, or even worse. Often (although he or she is not cast) the director gets one of the slots for the simple reason that if something happens to the director the film generally is shut down, at least for awhile.

The other slots should be filled by actors who are essential to the financing and distribution of the film and according to an analysis of the problems the production would face if an actor (due to his or her shooting schedule spread) is established in the film early on, but then has to work again during the last part of the schedule. An example of this: Charles is playing the small but inciting role of the brother who taunts the star into an action that sets the rest of the film into motion. For whatever production reasons—possibly location availability, possibly Charles' availability—two of Charles' four scenes must be shot during Week 1 of production. The other two of his four scenes are scheduled for Week 5. If during Charles' off time something prevents him from being able to complete his final scenes, the production will have only a few choices: recast and reshoot the first two scenes, which is expensive and sometimes not even possible, or rewrite the script. Doing that on the run, in the middle of shooting, is usually not the best way to solve a problem. If Charles is one of the named insured, the money will be there to shift the schedule to make it work, or to recast and reshoot. Charles is not a major star, but his schedule makes insuring him a viable option.

There is also ***E&O*** (***Errors and Omissions***) insurance. This insurance protects the production from lawsuits that arise when things fall through the cracks. You thought you had the proper clearances for the use of a song. You went through all the correct channels, have signed license agreements. The song is in the movie, and out of nowhere, the composer's brother turns up, and it turns out that they wrote the song together. Now you have an invalid license agreement and you're being sued.

Or it comes out that although the screenwriter said that the script was entirely a product of his imagination, his ex-girlfriend is suing you because she and the community where she lives recognize that she is the murderer in the film and she is now traumatized. Or a search was done for you and didn't turn up the corporate logo that you used as the symbol for the futuristic evil empire and now the lawyer for a company that manufactures kids products in Great Britain has contacted you.

E&O does not cover negligence. Anyone dealing with legal or intellectual property issues must be sure that the research, the homework, has been done ahead of time so that these mistakes truly could not have been helped if more attention had been paid to the problems.

The price of an E&O policy goes up if the script is based on a true story or on true events, particularly if these events were in the recent past. Even if everyone does exactly what they are supposed to do, there's always something that can slip through and cripple the distribution, sales, and/or profit for a film.

Finally, there is additional insurance available for films with boats (Marine insurance), planes, major visual effects, etc. When the production manager approaches a production insurance broker, the broker reads the script, asks some questions, and decides if any special insurance is necessary. The broker quotes a price for the overall package. There is no single formula that is used, but you can count on anywhere from 2 to 5 percent of the production budget. Insurance is expensive, but without it, you will not be able to rent equipment, rent locations, obtain your shooting permits, use SAG actors, or get distribution. That's why you need protection.

Chapter 12

What People Do, and Who They Do It With

Making a movie is collaborative but not democratic. Collaboration means working with everyone to get the best out of them, all for the sake of the movie. There must be one vision. That vision is almost always best served when it is the director's vision, as the director controls what is shot, how it is shot, and how it is put together. Once the producer finds the material and the financing, his or her job is to do whatever it takes to support the project. This can include finding the right director, interesting the best cast, and creating an atmosphere on set where the vision is supported by an organized and productive cast, staff, and crew. In postproduction the producer's job is to be sure that the vision is maintained. The producer interfaces with nervous financiers, fields problems in the editing room, helps find and contract for the best possible score and music buys, and usually is completely immersed in the distribution and marketing process. The producer must keep the buzz of the opinions and political maneuvering away from the director so that the director can concentrate on directing.

For the director, collaboration means assuming the creative leadership role, working with the team in prep, production, and post. Collaboration means that the director is able to form and articulate his or her plan so that the crew can do their jobs, creatively and technically supporting that plan. A director must be a communicator. The director's vision must be consistent, and it must be worked out ahead of time, not made up as the shooting of the film goes along. There is nothing less effective than a director who doesn't know what he or she wants, or is not prepared. The team is there to serve the project, but the project can only be well served if everyone knows the plan. Without that the director loses authority and even the production assistants can sense when no one seems to be captain of the ship. Once that happens, it is difficult for a film to recover. It is human nature that when there is no defined order to things, we try to fix it. The trouble is that there are so many people involved in the making of a film that when they each try to fix things in their own way, the result is chaotic and directionless. The imprint of the single driving creative force behind the film is lost.

ABOVE AND BELOW THE LINE

There are two categories of production personnel; those above and those below the line. What is this line? Believe it or not, it is a real line that appears on a film budget. *Above the Line* includes those who are seen as truly impacting the creative direction of the project: the screenwriter, producer, director, and the cast. *Below the Line* is everyone else. Although almost everyone on a film is involved in some kind of creative capacity, the Above the Line personnel are considered to be the key creative contributors. That said, filmmaking is a group effort, and in the end, a project is only as good as its collaborators.

Examining the structure of most departments, you will notice that there is a pattern that illustrates both the hierarchy and the lines of collaboration. The Department Head is the key creative chief or creative problem-solver. The second tier position serves as the right-hand to the Department Head and is the manager of documentation and organization. The third tier positions are filled by helpers, who are important contributors but not decision-makers. Many crew members start their careers at the bottom of the ladder, perfecting their technical and organizational skills. After years on the set they combine that experience with creative expertise and rise to the level of Department Head.

THE TEAM

On shorts, student films, or very low-budget films, in part because the crew is small, there is overlap of job responsibilities. You might work on a project where the production designer is the construction coordinator, the prop master, and the costume designer. Or the cinematographer helps tie cables and drives the camera truck. Once you move into the professional world it is important to understand how a set works and what the jobs really are. Everyone on a professional set knows exactly what everyone else's job is, and they know whether or not they do it well. You may have already experienced how it all comes together or doesn't, when you're short personnel and funding.

If you aspire to make a living directing, producing, or working on set, you must know how things are run when a set functions at the most sophisticated level. If you plan to be an executive, an agent, or to work in public relations and marketing, you must be at least conversant in the way a movie is made. If you want to direct or be a "creative producer" and assume that other people will be dealing with the nuts and bolts of production and you'll be ideating and delegating, be assured that the more you know about every aspect of production, the more credibility you will have with your investors, your cast, and your crew. No one on a set will respect you if you don't master the environment. You must make it your mission to know who people are and what they do. Remember, these are the people who are actually making the movie!

The Director

Arguably the most sought after and significant position on a movie, the Director's job can be summed up in a single sentence: the Director must find a way to bring the script to life utilizing visuals, performance, and sound to create a bond between the film and the audience.

The stress of the position is enormous. Most participants in the making of a movie are responsible for one area. The Director must carry the entire schematic of the film in his or her head. As the creative decision maker, the Director is the final arbiter of the big questions—"This actor or the other one"—and the small ones—"should this character drive an Audi or a Saab." A film is a compilation of a million details that fit together to form a dramatic whole, and the Director may be the only one who has a precise sense of the ultimate intention.

The Producer

The Producer's job is to do what must be done in order to come away with a fully realized movie of the highest dramatic or comedic quality possible.

Some seemingly but not actually similar titles that you see in the credits are: Executive Producer, Co-Producer, Associate Producer. In the television world these credits are very specific, with clear responsibilities and tasks attached, but in the world of film, the recipient of one these credits can be someone who found the material, helped put together the money for the project, someone who is owed a contractual payoff for developing the original project with the writer and then selling the script, or someone who was on the film from idea to market. One of these credits may be awarded to the manager of the actor who was enough of a star to move the project from yellow to green light. By the time a film is actually in production, the person receiving the credit might be around set all the time working with the Producer, or he or she might be sent a check and have nothing at all to do with the project.

The Line Producer and UPM

The ***UPM*** (Unit Production Manager) might sometimes receive an Associate Producer or Line Producer credit as a way of augmenting his or her status. It serves to acknowledge the contribution this person makes to the project while not necessarily paying him or her more money. **The Production Manager's job is to structure, monitor, and control the logistics of the production.** It is an organizational position. The Production Manager finds and sets up the production offices, controls the budget, hires the crew, negotiates agreements with unions, works with vendors of equipment and facilities, negotiates and approves production and financial arrangements. The creative part of the job is creative problem-solving. The Production Manager must be someone who can supervise and unify the multitude of talents and egos involved in the making of a film and coax them into working as a smoothly cohesive team who can work magic within the confines of the schedule and budget. At the same time, the Production Manager works with the preproduction and production schedule to plan the flow of cash, and to find a way to get the most bang for the bucks available.

Every film has a Unit Production Manager. Sometimes there may also be a separate Line Producer, the idea being that the Line Producer straddles the gap between the creative and the logistical sides. But as mentioned, the Line Producer and UPM title are often given to one person, and that seems to work just as well. The UPM is the intermediary between the funders of the production and the production; and he or she must look after the investment of the project while ensuring a well-run production that results in a film that will satisfy everyone's artistic and commercial intentions.

The Production Coordinator is the assistant to the Production Manager, runs the Production Office, is the chief communications facilitator, and the distributor and keeper of production paperwork. The Coordinator is the contact for the equipment houses and insurance companies, and organizes all travel and housing arrangements. The Coordinator is also the contact person for all of the production crew and cast members and works with every department to be sure that everyone has the most up-to-date information about anything involving production logistics.

The Production Accountant tracks expenditures, calculates crew weekly paychecks, pays the bills (the Production Manager approves them), and keeps a running tally of how much is spent, and how much is left to spend. Depending on the scale of the film, accounting may be a one-person department or there may be a sizable staff of Assistants and Payroll Clerks. The Accountant works with the Production Manager, who actually manages the money. The Accountant is in close contact with all departments to be sure that all reimbursements and payments are timely and correct.

The First Assistant Director

The responsibility of the First Assistant Director (First AD) is first and foremost to create and maintain an achievable production schedule. The ideal schedule is one where there is ample time to shoot the film but no leisure time. This means that although no one is loafing around, neither is the director under constant pressure to move on to the next scene before he or she feels that the lighting, framing, and performances are right. A production schedule is not about grinding out the work. An expert schedule allows the filmmakers sufficient time to shoot something that will have value in the editing room. A schedule should take into consideration not only the basics of "how many days have we bought in this location," but "wouldn't it be better to shoot the most emotional scenes later in the day," and "wouldn't it be better to finish up this sequence rather than jump into another sequence and then return to this one."

An experienced First AD knows the difference between shooting at an efficient, brisk clip and a foolhardy, breakneck speed that can result in injuries or unusable footage. Each director has a different shooting style, and a competent First deals with reality rather than deciding that they can change the director. If a director likes to spend time on intimate talking head scenes and shoots lots of *takes* (attempts at filming useable shots) so that there will be an abundance of choices in the editing room, the AD will not decide, "this is just two actors talking in a room, we'll get it done in an hour." Time will be allotted according to the way a particular director works.

The First AD not only schedules *principal photography*, which is the main shooting period with actors, but also any *second unit* photography that may be necessary. Second unit photography may be stunts and effects shooting, crowd scenes, establishing shots of buildings—any shooting that is scheduled outside the main shooting period and where no actors with speaking roles are present.

While preparing a film, the First Assistant Director acts as the liaison between the director and the rest of the crew, sitting in on most meetings, listening to and formulating the actual hour by hour, day by day shooting blueprint of who and what should be where and when. The First AD must be intimately familiar with the director's intention for each scene. This information is needed in order to create the final *shooting schedule* and *day out of days*. These documents form the basis for the Casting Director's negotiations with agents for actors, and the Location Manager's negotiations for contracts with property owners. The First AD consults every department and collaborates with all of them. There must be a strategy that allows everyone to accomplish what they need to in order to support the director's vision of how the film will look, feel, and sound.

The Second Assistant Director is the Assistant to the First AD. Like the relationship of the Production Coordinator to the Production Manager, the job of the Second AD is to support the First. The Second distributes production paperwork to all on-set personnel; tracks *in and out times* (arrival and departure times) of personnel; coordinates the process of moving the cast through *the works* (hair, makeup, and costume) so they are camera ready once the set is lit; manages the *background actors* (extras) to be sure that they are ready when needed; collects whatever paperwork is needed from each department at the end of the day, and does whatever is needed to help prevent slow-downs or stoppages during the shooting day.

THE LOOK OF THE MOVIE

The ***Production Designer*** and ***Location Manager*** are two of the first people hired on a film. As preproduction begins and casting is completed the focus shifts to the macro decision of where the film is going to be shot. Will it be shot in New York, Los Angeles, a different state, a different country? Once that is determined, the questions become micro. Will the project be shot on a sound stage with locations that are built, on actual locations that are rented and altered for shooting, or on a combination of both? These decisions must be made right away, because locations and settings determine so much about what has to happen in preproduction that until everyone knows where the shooting is going to take place, it's difficult to move ahead.

Once the decision as to geography has been answered, there is the question of build or find. Are the scenes set in modern structures? Do old buildings of the type needed still exist? Will using *practical* locations (locations that are still functioning buildings—schools, jails, hospitals, homes) lend realism to the project? Is the story a period piece or a fantasy, set in a different time or a different world. There is the question of how "shootable" a location is. Are we talking about a 1900s working-class urban apartment? Any number of those apartments can be found, but how large are the rooms? Old buildings tend to have small rooms. Might the director and cinematographer prefer to have a room built on a sound stage so that walls can be *wild* (constructed so they are movable). This would create a situation where the possible shooting angles quadruple, because now there's space for a variety of lighting setups or camera moves. What action takes place in each scene? Is there a house set on fire, a building exploding? You're looking at some construction.

The Production Designer's job is to create the look of the film, whether it is set in contemporary suburbia or the old West. The Designer reads the script, presents his or her ideas to the Director, then works with a team to come up with a visual and logistical plan and a budget for the Art Department, Construction, Greens, and Set Decorating. The Production Designer meets with the Line Producer and/or Production Manager. This version of the budget will be much more detailed than the theoretical budget that the Production Manager made weeks or months before when everything was hypothetical. It may be lower or higher than originally estimated. The Production Designer and Production Manager work to reconcile the two estimates.

Although the Designer is usually the choice of the Director, the Producer has input, and the studio or production company often holds veto power. When looking at a prospective Production Designer, it is not a case of "whoever does the most beautiful work wins." The Production Manager calls the UPM or the Producer from the Designer's last several films to see if the work was completed on schedule, and if the department stayed on budget. The Production Manager asks those listed as references and anyone else he or she may know who has worked with the Designer in the past. A listed reference is going to say great things. It's the other people who might give a less biased report.

Note: Often the Production Manager will hear that the Department Head was wonderful but there were weak links within the department. Then the Producer and Production Manager are faced with the problem of what to do. Splitting up an established team in any department can cause problems. When someone is hired to do the job he usually does but then is told that he can't use his team, there had better be a strong justification. From then on the person who broke up the team will be seen as the enemy. That's a terrible way to start a project. And anytime something doesn't happen the way it should, there is a built in rationalization—it's because so-and-so isn't there to take care of it.

The Production Designer creates the visual design of the world of the film. This world helps to tell the story in the same way that dialogue, casting, and lighting do. What is the mood and theme of the film? Who are the characters? How do they live? How does the visual environment support the emotional effect of the story? The Designer is expected to lead, and however much delegation goes on, the Designer is responsible for the artistic, financial and logistical areas of the department.

Depending upon the size of the project, the Production Designer may have an assistant, the ***Art Director***. If the project is small, the Production Designer may take on the responsibilities of the Art Director. This means dealing with the administrative side of running a department and interfacing with the Construction Department, the Set Designer, Illustrators, and the Set Decorating department. The Art Director is often the person who tracks Art Department spending and communicates about both what is spent and what has been saved to the Production Accountant.

Sometimes the Art Department has a ***Coordinator***, whose job is to help out with the office, with the set, and with making runs to pick up materials, supplies, and sometimes lunch for the department. On some films there will be a ***Researcher*** to help answer specific creative questions. What did English signage during WWII look like? What are the details of the baggage area in the belly of an airplane? How will the materials used in the construction of a space capsule react when subjected to overheating by the sun? What does it really look like when a house is flattened by a tornado?

The Set Designer generates the plans and blueprints necessary to construct the sets. Depending upon the number of sets or renovations to existing structures planned, this person may work for anywhere from a few days to the entire preproduction and production schedule.

Once the Production Designer approves the blueprints, the ***Construction Coordinator*** works with a crew, sometimes consisting of a couple of people, and sometimes made up of what may seem like an entire army. There are carpenters, plasterers, and painters. Unlike the building of any type of structure intended to last or be lived in, construction for a film set is largely cosmetic: building fronts with nothing behind them, rooms with ceilings that can be removed to make space for hanging lights or cameras. Film construction is meant to be erected and dismantled quickly and economically.

Greens men are responsible for the plants, trees, flowers, and other "green" elements that are seen on screen.

The ***Set Decorator*** uses flooring, furnishings, draperies, décor, and color to enhance the visual world of the film. Assisting the Set Decorator is the ***Lead person***, who schedules the Set Decorator's crew and coordinates the logistics of the pick-up and delivery of set dressing. Also assisting is the ***Swing Gang,*** actually not a gang at all but three or four people. The Swing Gang work under the management of the Lead person to do the physical work of picking up and returning furniture and all kinds of set dressing. Under the creative direction of the Set Decorator, the Swing Gang would place the dressing, hang the curtains, even write the $2 + 2 = 3$ equation on the blackboard in the schoolhouse scene.

There is also often an ***On-Set Dresser.*** By logistical necessity, the Construction, Art, and Set Decorating departments work ahead of the shooting crew. The set for Tuesday has to be ready by Monday so there is no delay when the crew arrives to shoot. The Art Department almost always works off production. This means that the Production Designer and Set Decorator appear on set for the first shot of the day until they are sure that the Director is happy with the way the set looks. Then they leave to work on the set scheduled for the following day's shoot. The On-Set Dresser stays behind. The On-Set Dresser works on the continuity of the placement of the dressing, re-setting and freshening the flowers in the pots, making certain that at the start of take 10, the books and carelessly strewn papers called for in the script are exactly where and in the condition they were at the start of take 1—even though each take requires the actor to tear them up and dump them all onto the floor.

Locations

The Location Manager and her assistants collaborate closely with everyone, as she is responsible for finding, securing, negotiating for, and managing every location on a film. The Location Manager starts early on a film, *breaking down* the locations cited in the script by interior, exterior, and description. The Location Manager meets with the Production Designer, who will decide which locations must be found and which will be constructed. Construction is expensive in terms of labor and materials. The lower the film's budget is, the more likely that the locations will be found then *dressed* to suit the visual needs of the project. The Production Designer will indicate the look the project requires. The Location Manager will begin the search, driving for hours, pouring through Film Commission photo libraries, speaking with companies that represent properties for filming, and knocking on the doors of strangers if a house happens to look right for the film.

The Location Manager must balance the dramatic demands of the film with the schedule and budget. She is sometimes on the hunt for a house or a hallway that the director can't quite explain, just "I'll know it when I see it." There will be *show and tells*—presentations of photos, and *scouts* (searches and visits) to potentially suitable locations. Finding the correct location is an essential element in effective storytelling. The quest can take months. A street front café may look perfect, but the early morning hours planned to shoot the scene may be just when the city garbage trucks go barreling down the street. Because the director wants to shoot on restaurant row, the racket of the trucks may go on for hours, potentially causing production delays. The chapel may be exactly what everyone wants, but shooting in that location is scheduled for the day of the annual Sisterhood luncheon. The neighborhood may look right, but the neighbors aren't willing to be disturbed by night filming. Or everything may be just right but is too expensive. Possibly the owner just doesn't want to rent out her house to a film company, even though the Location Manager is offering a substantial fee and a first-class hotel room. The discussions go on between the Location Manager, the Director, the Producer, the UPM, the Production Designer, and the First AD, and the final question is always, how much do we want this place? Is it worth changing the schedule and facing possible financial consequences?

Production is like a line of dominoes. Topple one and there is a chain reaction. A neat, workable structure can become an illogical heap. Once that happens, each piece has to be repositioned. That happens repeatedly, at all stages of production. Everyone working on the project must learn to roll with it, and recover quickly as if the new plan has always been in place.

Once the locations have been chosen, the Location Manager must negotiate the contracts for the location rentals; find convenient parking for trucks and crew; hire any necessary security, police, and fire personnel; and obtain *shooting permits*, which are licenses issued by a city or town, granting permission to shoot there. The Location Manager must communicate any restrictions to the AD and UPM. For example, perhaps it's been specified that there can be no crew arrivals until after 7:00 am. The Location Manager must also communicate any requirements—street closures and police on motorcycles for a driving shot. The Location Manager stands between the property owners, neighborhood groups, government agencies, and the production. When the actual shooting is taking place, the Location Manager or someone in the Location Department "babysits" the set and is the go-to person if there is a question or a disturbance that occurs as a result of the shoot. Once shooting has been completed, the Location Manager is the clean-up person, visiting property owners to be sure that everything has been restored to the way it was before filming, and checking and resolving any damages that might have been the result of filming.

A Location Manager must be a politician, serving several masters. The Director and Production Designer want to feel that the Location Manager is on their side, the Producer and UPM want to know that the Location Manager is their guy (even when the Location Manager is a woman), and the studio or production company want to be sure that the Location Manager is looking out for their interests. Location Managers are ambassadors, adept at navigating those political waters and remaining diplomatic and helpful as the public face of the production.

Camera

The Cinematographer (or Director of Photography, or DP) supervises photography and lighting for the camera. With the director the cinematographer determines film stock, lens size, camera angles, and the composition and framing of the shots. In post production, the cinematographer collaborates with the director on color grading or color timing sessions. Traditionally color timing sessions have been where the determination is made regarding the final overall intensity and color temperature (warm or cool) of the project. Now though, digital processes allow for a much broader spectrum of possibilities, from adding shadows and highlights, to a re-conceptualization of the entire look of the project.

A Cinematographer uses light—or the lack of it or the shape of it—to support the script and the way the Director chooses to tell the story. The Cinematographer is familiar with the different effects of the various films stocks and lenses. Working with the Director and Production Designer, the DP comes up with a visual plan that will seamlessly support the story.

Directors begin to lock on to the style of shooting and the look of the film fairly early in the preparation, so the Cinematographer will come in for meetings and participate in the production several weeks before the beginning of the shooting period. Once the Location Manager is closing in on final choices, the Cinematographer will be present on scouting expeditions, pointing out the opportunities and challenges a particular location might present.

The Camera Operator deals with camera movement and frame composition. The Cinematographer is the Operator's supervisor. Together they determine what is actually seen, and how it's photographed.

The First Assistant Cameraman is in charge of focus. Outside the United States, this person's job title is ***Focus Puller,*** and the responsibility of the position is to maintain a sharp image, working with light, distance, and lens capacity to be certain that everything is precise and distinct, not *soft* (blurry). The job can be nerve-racking because the stakes are so high. If the project is shooting on film, there is a time lag of sending shot footage into the lab for developing, so it may not be obvious that something is out of focus for a full day. Anything out of focus might have to be reshot, which may entail a great deal of expense if the shooting company has moved on to the next location or if the out of focus scene was complex, with crowds, stunts, extra personnel, etc. A First AC is often given the benefit of the doubt with one mistake and fired from the film with a second.

The Second Assistant Cameraman is responsible for loading the film into the camera; for maintaining and operating the identifying slate that appears at the start of each take, so that the footage is can be easily recognized and sorted by the assistant editor and synched by the sound house or assistant editor; and for working with the Production Office to maintain a count of how much film is used each day, and whether or not the inventory of film on the truck is sufficient or more must be ordered. The Second AC is also responsible for the department's paperwork. There are camera reports that accompany the film when it is sent into the lab for processing and developing. If the project is digital, then film is not sent to a lab, but the camera reports, along with the script supervisors notes, serve as a guide for the editor as to which takes are meant to be saved and which disregarded.

The Operator, First AC, and Second AC don't begin work on a picture until a few days before shooting, when they arrive at the *camera house* (rental facility) to test, inventory, and check out the equipment package they will be using during production. Occasionally the First AC will be called in early to work with the DP on camera, hair, makeup, and wardrobe tests, but unless the film has a hefty budget, these tests are often scheduled to occur as late into the schedule as possible in order to avoid starting the AC earlier than necessary and then keeping him or her on salary for a week or more of down time.

On digital productions, there is a technical position called a ***DIT*** (Digital Imaging Technician). This person works with the Director of Photography to assist in managing the complicated data and systems that are necessary in order to achieve the best images.

Although not a member of the Camera Department, the ***Video Assist*** person operates a video monitor that is linked to the camera, so that the Director can view the scene on camera as it is being filmed. There is the tendency for so many crew members to crowd around the monitor to check details in the shot, that the area around the monitor is often referred to as *video village*.

Grip and Electric

Using stands, ropes, dollies, and cranes, the Grip department is responsible for the physical mounting and securing of the lights and camera. ***The Key Grip*** is the department head, and the ***Best Boy Grip*** is the second in command. Part of the Best Boy's job is keeping the truck, equipment, and personnel organized. The ***Dolly Grip*** rigs and pushes the camera dolly. This may not sound like much of a responsibility, but it requires a great deal of skill. Anything less than smooth movement of the camera will call attention to itself and pull the audience away from their emotional involvement in the movie. ***Company Grips*** assist in the rigging or building of any piece of equipment that supports lights or the camera.

The Gaffer is the chief electrician, responsible for safely delivering and executing the lighting plan that the Cinematographer has designed. The *second electrician* is ***the Best Boy***. The Best Boy Electric is also responsible for the ordering and inventorying of equipment, and the management of outside Electrical personnel and equipment (someone with a specialized skill who may not be on for the entire film, or a specific piece of equipment needed for a particular scene). The ***electricians*** are technicians who work under the Gaffer's direction.

The Pretty Committee—Costume, Hair, and Makeup

The Costume Designer finds, designs, or assembles the wardrobe for the cast. This is a creative and administrative position. The wardrobe must serve the storytelling effort. If the film takes place in 1862, the Costume Designer will research that period, not only to explore the design options but to be historically correct with the colors and fabrics used in the "new" old clothing. If the script calls for "sometime in the future" the Designer will meet with the Director to discuss just how much in the future—five years, ten years, fifty years? The answer will inform decisions as to the shape and materials involved in the wardrobe. What is the socioeconomic status of the characters? What about ethnicity? What is their *back story*? All of this will determine the purchases or designs.

The Costume Designer's position can be politically precarious. He works intimately with the actors and actresses, and in addition to serving the story, the Designer also must keep in mind that the actors want to feel comfortable in front of the camera. That means that in almost all instances the wardrobe must be flattering. It may seem counterintuitive for authenticity to take a back seat to vanity, but given the choice, the Designer will almost always agree to be less accurate rather than unflattering, finding wardrobe with a style and fit that will suit the actor. ***No matter how stunning or brilliant a design is, the Costume Designer must forever bear in mind that an actor cannot for a minute wonder, "does this make me look fat/old/foolish."*** An actor who does not feel at ease is not going to be secure enough to let go and give an unself-conscious performance. That will hurt the film.

The Costume Designer must know how an outfit moves, drapes, and functions in various lighting and physical conditions, in addition to being capable of managing a staff of Costumers, Dressers, Seamstresses, and Tailors so that every costume is clean, ironed and ready for 7:00 am Wednesday, even if it was used in the final scene of the day before and wrap wasn't until 8:00 pm Tuesday. Like all crew members, he must keep up a pleasant, reassuring demeanor standing outside the wardrobe trailer alongside the actors at midnight in the rain, helping them to feel attractive and appropriate, while simultaneously maintaining contact with the ADs and communicating how much time it will take to get the cast camera ready.

Hair and Makeup

The job of the Hair and Makeup department is self-explanatory. The responsibilities are to create a hair and makeup look for each actor, and then to maintain the continuity of that look throughout the shooting period. Easy? The Hair and Makeup department work some of the longest hours on a production and deal with some of the toughest politics.

Sometimes the star of a film will have his or her own makeup artist or hair stylist, someone who works on all his or her films. It may not be that this person is any more talented than others, but either due to personal chemistry or through luck, this person has established a close relationship with the star, and one of the star's contractual demands is that this person is hired whenever he or she is hired. This person has the ear of the star and therefore should be treated with kid gloves. The Star Makeup or Star Hair person often earns a higher rate than even the Department Heads (***Key Hair*** and ***Key Makeup***), while working on only one person while the Keys are working on everyone else. This can lead to bruised egos and backbiting. Not a good idea. The department members must make it a congenial relationship, or they are likely to find themselves branded as difficult to work with. If a conflict arises, you must realize that Production will do almost anything to keep the star happy.

Unless the film is a huge extravaganza, there are usually only a few department members who are hired for the entire shoot. There are the two Keys, each has one or two Assistants, and all other members come and go, depending upon the scheduled scenes each day. If the script calls for a day of crowds, shoppers, courtroom jurors, then there will be ***background actors***. These are players who have no dialogue and whose purpose is to create atmosphere for the scene. There may be a Hair and Makeup person called in to work just on them. If there is a nude scene there will be a ***Body Makeup*** artist, and if there is a Stunt or Special Effects scene there may be an ***Effects*** or ***Prosthetics*** specialist.

In most situations, Hair and Makeup artists have small departments and are given a very brief prep. They are interviewed and chosen weeks before production starts. Depending on the world of the film, they may spend some time researching, ordering specific makeup or wigs for individual cast members, but they don't usually begin work until late in the preproduction schedule. Often they are put on payroll only a day or two before shooting begins. Once shooting starts, however, there is very little leisure time for the Hair and Makeup team. Their *call time* (the time when they are told to be present at work) is often hours before the rest of the crew. They are there working on the cast so that the minute the Assistant Director asks for actors to appear on set, the actors will be there and ready. They are on set or in the Hair/Makeup trailer or dressing rooms, watching for any break in filming so that they can run in and *touch up* (refresh) the actors' hair and makeup, making sure that it matches from shot to shot but also from scene to scene. They are there at the end of the day to help the actor go through a reverse process, removing the makeup, undoing the hair from however it was done, and preparing everything for the following day.

The Hair, Makeup and Costume trailers are often information central. There is something about sitting in those chairs or being fussed over for hours that seems to invite gossip.

It is critically important to remember that along with the Costume crew, these are the people the actors see first thing in the morning and last thing at night. A calm and cheerful team can do wonders for the actors' state of mind. If there are discussions of trouble on the set or behind the scenes, this can come out in small ways that can undermine the actors' confidence in the production.

THE ALL IMPORTANT CREW MEMBERS NOT ALREADY ACCOUNTED FOR

Sound

The Production Sound department is comprised of the ***Mixer***, whose job it is to record as much usable dialogue as possible while the film is shooting, and the ***Boom Operator***, who controls the boom pole that holds the microphones that record the sound. It is necessary to record clear dialogue while shooting. There are techniques in postproduction for fixing inaudible or distorted dialogue, but using production sound lends a feeling of immediacy to actors' performances that is hard to duplicate after the fact. Dialogue re-recording and replacement (also known as *ADR* for *automated dialogue replacement*) is time-consuming and can be costly. Actors who give fine performances on set may be less natural sitting in a booth months after shooting, re-voicing their lines. Emotionally and financially, production sound is almost always more satisfying.

With so much emphasis on the visual side of filming, audio is sometimes neglected. Inexperienced filmmakers fall in love with locations under an airport flight path or want to shoot on bridges at rush hour to make the most of the sunset. Generators are parked for convenience, rather than behind a wall to muffle sound. An inexperienced Location Manager will negotiate a contract for a house in a quiet neighborhood that he's scouted on a Saturday afternoon, forgetting to visit the place on a Thursday evening, which is when the scene is scheduled to be shot. The day of shooting, there's a bustling farmers market a block away. Market goers park right in front of the shooting location. The constant flow of vehicle and pedestrian traffic is distracting and involves lots of waiting for windows of quiet.

To save money, the Sound Mixer is sometimes not put on payroll until a day before shooting begins. Rather than work something out financially, the Sound Mixer is often left off the list of invitees for the ***Tech Scout***, the final tour of locations. The Mixer is the ears of the production and would undoubtedly point out any areas of concern and then be prepared to deal with them properly through equipment and microphone selection. Once production is wrapped and the Director and Editor are reviewing usable footage and sound, the lesson is learned: the more input from the Sound Mixer, the better.

Script

The Script Supervisor is the conduit of information between the set and the Editor. His or her notes serve as a written record of everything that is shot and how it is shot (focal length, duration, master shot, over-the-shoulder, etc.), and which of the takes are good and which are not. The Script Supervisor also works with *continuity*—in the last shot, did the actor light his cigarette with his right hand or his left?

The Script Supervisor works with the Director to be sure that she has gotten everything needed before moving on to the next shot or scene, and with the Second Assistant Cameraperson, to be sure that the notes and slates are in accord so that there is no confusion in the editing room. The Script Supervisor is the Director's choice and usually is given a week or less of preparation time.

This prep period is used to do a continuity breakdown of the script, sometimes to attend rehearsals if there are any, and to do a *timing*—a mental walk through of the script with a stop watch to try to estimate the true length the film will run when completed. Sometimes there is a contractual obligation that a film will run between 89 and 120 minutes. Right now, the trend leans towards the shorter run time. Audiences have less patience, shorter attention spans these days, but they feel cheated if they've paid for tickets for a movie that runs less than an hour and a half. The other side of the coin is that unless we're talking about blockbusters where the expectation is that the theatre seats will be filled for the first several weeks, anything longer than two hours limits the opportunities for the theatres to screen by limiting the number of times per day a picture can be exhibited. The theatres want to make money. Think about the show times at your local cineplex. There are usually about five screenings per day. If a film is extra long, the last screening of the day will be so late and the theatre will be empty. This is why a timing can be important. The usual time/page rule is one page equals one minute of screen time, but sometimes dialogue-heavy scripts read short or long. A Script Supervisor will time it out and make the Producer and Director aware of where the script sits on the time continuum. Adjustments will be made, either during shooting or during editing. As you might imagine, this is particularly important when working in television, where a program can't screen a second less or a second more than the allotted time slot.

Props

The Prop Master and his assistants find, purchase, rent, or fashion every item that is touched or handled by an actor. If the script calls for the actor to pick up a pencil, the Prop Master searches for the right pencil. The Prop Master deals with certain accessories—eyeglasses, wristwatches. If the scene calls for a wedding or a gala event of some kind and the actors will be eating, the Prop Master may call in a ***Food Stylist*** who will work with a caterer to stage the swanky, sumptuous spread. If there is a scene with gunplay, the Prop Master will bring a ***Weapons Specialist*** on for the day.

The Prop Master usually has several weeks or months of preparation and many, many meetings with the Director so that he is positive that the look of what is found coincides with the Director's concept. The Prop Master has another traditional and highly political function—the moving and placement of the canvas director's chairs on set. Believe it or not, there is a protocol to the chairs. Woe be unto the innocent newcomer on set who mistakenly plops down in a chair that is not earmarked for him. (And even though the Prop Master is in charge of the chairs, he isn't officially expected to have one.)

Food

Food is a hot-button topic on set. The crew sees the quality and abundance of food as an indication of whether the Producer and Production Manager care about their well-being. Special movie catering companies are contracted to feed movie crews. The chefs and cooks are charged with consistently producing and presenting tasty, varied, fresh meals to a hungry, tired crowd.

When the crew arrives each day, they are served what is called a *walking breakfast*. This is food meant to be eaten while the crew sets up for the start of the day. Easily toted around, it is still substantial. It is easy to forget how physical set work is. For the most part, crew members spend the day on their feet, climbing and carrying. The intention of the walking breakfast is to get everyone off to an energetic start. Labor law dictates that workers must be permitted a lunch break every six hours. The first sit-down meal of the day on set is called *lunch*—even if it's a night shoot and lunch is served at 2:00 am.

Members of the crew usually have thirty minutes to make their way to the catering truck or table, be served, sit down, eat, relax a minute, then get back up and shoot for the next six hours. Lunch for anywhere from 50 to 150 cast and crew members must be prepared, hot, and ready to eat. If the first part of the day goes slowly and the crew isn't broken for lunch until six and a half hours, the expectation is that the meal will be just as appetizing as if it were served when it was scheduled.

Caterers usually start their day early with the breakfast, stay until lunch has been served and completed, then leave set to shop and prepare for the following day.

The ***Craft Service*** person deals with food in a different way. The Craft Service person is a member of the crew and is often the first person to arrive on set and the last one to leave. Craft Services manages the snack table or truck. Visit a film set and there is an array of fruits, sweets, coffee brewing, bottles of water, and sandwich fixings available. On big-budget films, the Craft Service spread can be lavish—an ongoing feast of hot and cold treats. No one goes hungry on a film set.

Transportation

If everyone arrives on set but there are no trucks filled with equipment, no trailers, and no dressing rooms, there will no filming. The job of the ***Transportation Coordinator*** is to supervise and manage a fleet of vehicles and a crew of drivers so that everyone gets where they belong and everything is where it should be in time for the start of the shooting day. At the end of the day, the ***Coordinator***, the ***Captain***, and the ***Drivers*** make sure that everyone is returned to where they started and everything is parked somewhere safely for the night.

All this can be a logistical nightmare. The Transportation portion of a feature film is often one of the most expensive segments of the budget. It is not unusual for there to be at least fifteen trucks, a couple of vans, star trailers, multiroom mobile dressing rooms for actors, a mobile hair and makeup trailer, a car carrier, and a fueler that gasses up all of the trucks—not to mention any *picture vehicles*, cars or trucks that are seen on camera. The drivers have the longest days of any department, as they must get to set before anyone else arrives so that the equipment trucks and other vehicles are ready to be opened by the other departments. A Transportation Coordinator juggles crew members so that the hours are not horribly abusive but it is not unusual for a driver to work 16-hour days.

Animals

Is there a kitten in your movie? Is there an elephant? No matter how large or how small, if there is an animal in your movie there will be a ***Wrangler*** (animal trainer). Professionals will never cast a household pet for use in a film.

Animal actors are trained to be around strangers and bustling activity, to focus unwaveringly on their trainer, who is usually standing behind or off to the side of the actor who is in the scene. These animals are trained to react in specific ways to signals. It may require several lookalike Golden Retrievers, all doubling for each other, to play one dog. Each dog may excel at a single task. One dog may be great at jumping up and nearly drowning an actor with enthusiastic face licks, one may be accomplished at mournfully moping, paws over his face, or better at digging holes in the garden on cue.

A production will usually contract out with an animal actor company. These companies work or own a variety of animals and will interface between the animal and the production, analyzing what actions are needed then training one or several animals to do what is needed. They look after the well-being of the animals, making sure that they are being treated well and will leave as healthy and as happy as when they arrived. The fee for animal actors usually includes both the time it takes to train them to do whatever special thing they must do (unless it's already in the animals' repertoire, in which case it means the training that must be done to accustom the animals to their co-starring actors). On the shoot days animal actors are on the clock from the time they leave their home (usually the trainer's home) to the time they return, plus their food. If it's a horse or an elephant, the cost of their hay, their feed, and possibly a special clean-up person, must be added.

Scheduling the time it takes to shoot a scene with even the best trained animal can be a guessing game. Sometimes an animal will be brought onto set, do his thing perfectly the first time, and you're done. Sometimes it will be take after take, and the AD will be trying to figure out ways to shoot around him. Animal actors can have bad days, but I've personally worked on films where some days the animals were the most professional actors on set.

Stunts

We all know what stunts are, right? Maybe. In a film, a stunt is any physical activity that a cast member would not normally (intentionally) do. A trip and fall is a stunt, but so is walking a high wire. Is riding a horse a stunt? Not necessarily. If the actor is trained to ride and is trotting along, it's not a stunt. If the actor is jumping off the moving horse, it's a stunt.

Stunt Coordinators are hired to manage the stunt aspects of a film by performing stunts themselves or by hiring the stuntmen and stuntwomen. A Stunt Coordinator works with the Director and Cinematographer to help orchestrate and stage stunt work so that the stunts can be performed safely while selling intense peril on screen. The Stunt Coordinator works in tandem with all the other departments involved in a scene. The Art Department and Construction have to understand the plan in order to design and build a set where a fight scene takes place. The Costume Designer has to be sure that there are four identical shirts made of the correct material so that the blood packets are concealed until the gun goes off and the blood splatters. The Special Effects person who is working with the Prop Master and the Armourer may work with the Stunt Coordinator to create a rig that will jerk the body of the stunt performer so that the "hit" looks hyperdisturbing and realistic.

There are ***Stunt Performers*** who have expertise in types of stunts—pilots, crash drivers, martial arts. On a film, Stunt performers are either *ND* (non-descript), or *doubles*. ND stunt players drive the cars swerving around the lead actors during the chase scene, or the guys who join the bar fight, the shootout, the prison riot. They drive the stage coach and jump out windows. If they are doubling (descript as opposed to non-descript), they are dressed, made up, positioned, and photographed in such a way that the audience doesn't know they're stuntmen or stuntwomen, but thinks that the actor is performing the dangerous, daring deed.

Special Effects

There are several types of Effects. The ***Special Effects Supervisor*** on set deals with *mechanical* or *pyrotechnic effects*. Mechanical effects are achieved through the physical rigging of special equipment. Wind and rain, for instance, are mechanical effects. Pyrotechnics are the effects involving projectiles, explosions, fires. Effects people are highly trained and most are specially licensed. They are expert in making something look spectacular while maintaining safety.

CGI (Computer Generated Images) are the type of effects that are usually designed, photographed, and edited in after shooting has been completed. CGI effects often involve intricate combinations of several types of computer technology. Your film might require blowing up a galaxy, or a tidal wave cresting and sweeping the city of Los Angeles under water. Maybe a talking dog, a dancing penguin. It can take months of planning, hordes of technicians, and a lot of money to make these effects look convincing.

Editing

The Editor starts working before the first day of filming. She sets up the editing room, hires an ***Assistant Editor***, learns the script backwards and forwards, and meets with the Director, getting a sense of where the director wants to go with the tone of the story. From the first day of shooting, the Editor is waiting to get her hands on the footage and sound, to begin shaping the *editor's cut* or assembly of the footage from beginning to end, in script order.

Using the Script Supervisor's notes and continuity logs, the Assistant Editor does the so-called clerical work, sorting, logging, and organizing the footage so that the Editor knows what shots and takes are available and where they all are. During filming, the Editor and the Director speak about the footage daily. At times during filming, the Director might suspect that a scene is just not working and will ask the Editor to do some preliminary cuts of that scene so the decision can be made whether to continue shooting an alternate version of the scene or move on. Or the Editor might tactfully make a suggestion regarding an additional shot that could improve the drama or flow. In order for the Director/Editor relationship to succeed, each must trust the judgment of the other implicitly.

The Editor is rarely seen on set. She is busy assembling and cutting. Also, the Editor wants to maintain a dispassionate view so that the film is being cut with only the footage in mind. If an Editor sees how much time has been invested in getting a big setup or a delicate emotional performance, how will she have the heart to cut it out of the film? You want cold, tough objectivity from an Editor, not sympathy.

Once shooting is done the Editor has an assembly that is usually much too long and doesn't play particularly well, because everything is in it. Then the Editor and director get to work, sculpting the movie, shaping and sharpening the narrative, polishing the story. Some people are experienced enough to view an early cut and understand the direction it's headed. Most are not. This is when the politics begin. The Producer and the investors or the studio are anxious to see what's been shot, but the Editor and the Director don't want them to see the film in this early stage, because it is so rough it in no way resembles a well-made movie.

Once someone has seen a bad version of something it takes a lot of effort to woo them back to have a fresh look at a newer and much improved version. If the Director is a member of the Directors Guild of America (DGA), there are rules in place to protect the creative progress of the *director's cut*, so that no one is standing over his or her shoulder, kibitzing, undermining confidence in the work. The Guild rules state that the Director gets ten weeks before he or she has to screen the film for anyone. After that ten weeks the people with power begin to weigh in. Sometimes their input is valuable. A Director can become too close to the film. An Editor can show the Director alternative versions of a scene that may be better, but at a certain point, it's the Director's call. A Producer, on the other hand, especially a Producer with a good creative relationship with the Director, can help the cause.

Chapter 13

A Producer's Life

Walter Coblenz

Walter Coblenz has been a Producer, a Unit Production Manager, an Assistant Director, the Senior Vice President of Worldwide Production at Tri-Star Pictures, and Vice President of Feature and Television Production at Carolco Pictures. *All The President's Men, The Candidate,* and *The Onion Field* are among the many projects he has produced.

Part of what you have to do as a producer, you've got to be a diplomat, and you've got to find ways to get everything that you need out of people. The business is volatile—not just the business, but the people are volatile, too. There is no security. A lot of it has to do with keeping everyone comfortable—keeping the performers comfortable, and also keeping the people you work with comfortable that you are properly representing them, because that is really what you are doing. And keeping in mind at all times that the end result has to be a successful and entertaining project. No matter how smooth a production may be, it is forgotten if the end product didn't come out the way you wanted it to come out.

You are constantly dealing with the politics, and the politics in the business are very extreme. There is a lot of money involved. There are times when you can't do something again. You've got one shot. In the type of work that I've done over the years, I'm the one who coordinates, who smooths these things over, who finds another way of doing something. And along with all of that, [to do]all of it within money parameters. What I've learned very quickly is that there was always a lot that I had to learn. I knew quite a bit about scripts, about producing, about directing, but I had to learn about law. I had to learn about accounting. I had to learn about public relations. Because there are very few guides. There are very few examples. No two projects are the same. Each one has a different set of problems.

There are always politics, and the politics are about the project, and the politics always revolve around money. So, whatever the politics are, they ultimately lead back to money. If you can't deal with the politics, then you can't play the game. You can't be in this business.

If you have to get it down to what should someone know so that they are not ambushed . . . if you were going to start out today knowing what you know, what

Continued

Walter Coblenz—cont'd

would you make it your business to know about any situation, project before you got involved?

First of all, I'd make every effort to get along with all of the people. Second, I would have no secrets and be upfront with everything. There is too much going on and too much happening. The easiest way for you to be and the only honorable way to be is completely open and completely upfront. If you are not, you are going to lose respect, and without respect, no one is going to trust you. No one is going to permit you to function. It has always been important[to me] that people know that when they deal with me, they are going to get straight answers whether they like them or not. If you're in a management position, people look to you to have the answers. As you develop more and more experience, you find that you can come up with the answers because there are similarities to all of the answers with all of the different projects.

Is there a political decision that you have made at any point in your life that you look back and say, "If I knew what I know now, I would not have made that decision"?

You can't do that. You can't look back. You can learn from the mistakes. You can say, "OK. I'm not going to do it that way again." But I like to think that at the time, I made the decision after careful consideration, and at that time it seemed to be the logical decision. Now, if I knew then what I know now, I would tell you a lot of stocks I would have bought, but you can't look back.

There are ways to avoid making huge mistakes. For one, something that I learned a long time ago is that I do not like to lose. Most people don't like to lose, but I have found a way never to lose. The way never to lose is never get into an argument unless you know you're going to win it. I've been in many situations where a star wanted something. The star did not deserve it, should not have gotten it, but I knew that if I didn't give it to the star, the studio would give it to the star. So I'm not going to get into this battle that I'm going to lose no matter how right I am. Instead, I will accommodate the actor in the hope of having more leverage the next time around. Just don't get into that fight.

If you are a producer, everything is your business, and you are expected to run an operation. If there is something going on that is shady, somewhat dishonest, you put a stop to it. You're never going to be wrong. The chances are that if you approach people and say, "This is unethical. Let's make it go away," it will. If it continues, I'd have to go to the studio. It has always been my experience in the many, many times that I've been in a situation like that, that I was always able to get the proper backing when it was necessary. Every situation is dealt with on its own basis. You cannot say, "Well, this is just like that." No, nothing is just like anything. I find that if you can set ground rules that are reasonably fair, people will go along and people will cooperate

Having been around the world, having seen people come and go in various positions, assuming that, yes, one has to have talent, but in terms of peoples skills, personability, that sort of thing, what do you think works for people in any position in terms of having a lasting career?

Walter Coblenz—cont'd

A career is based first on the quality of your work, how good are you and the relationships you establish, and on timing and luck, because along with everything else, you have to have timing and luck. So, you find that the cinematographer, the art director, who is extremely talented and ends up working with [a major director], are able to make a very long career for themselves. People hire you because they know that they can depend on you. Even though I say I always want to hire the best people, there are times when I had to put a crew together, and I would hire someone who has worked with me before even though there may have been someone else out there who had more talent, who was better, but who was unproven to me. I knew that these people who have worked with me in the past were very good and could also work on the team, and it would make things work very smoothly. Many times, these are also the people who are the busiest.

A little bit more about relationships. I think there is a hesitation by a lot of people to stay in touch. What do you think is the right way to go about networking, as opposed to the annoying way to do that?

I think people know when they're annoying. One suggestion that I have that can prove very profitable over a period of time is not to let people know when you are out of work, but to let people know when you are working—because then you say, "Hey, I just want to keep in touch, and I'm working on such and such movie." You're not putting them under any pressure. You're not looking for work. You are just updating them on what you are doing. Maybe when that project is finished, and you are looking, you can say, "Hey, I just finished on this." You make it informative. Most people who work in the business don't object to getting calls from people who are between jobs, because they've all been between jobs. I never objected to someone calling me. I can't blame them for looking for work.

I've tried to do whatever I do with a degree of humor. One of the things that I told people who work as assistants is that I try to treat them reasonably. I said, "You know why I'm being nice to you? Because I want you to be nice to me when I'm on my way down."

In this business, you are working from project to project. You're going to be out of work, maybe every year, maybe a couple of times every year, so you have to network. That is what it is all about. You have to establish the relationships. I've always wanted to work with assistants who are ambitious, whose job with me was just a steppingstone, and so that any assistant that I had, I tried to assist in getting the next move up. I would be disappointed if an assistant didn't have that sort of ambition. I always tried to get people who were smart; if they are smarter than I am, great. I was asked what is a sign of a good producer. I said when I can sit on my chair on the set and happily look around, because I hired all the right people and they are taking care of all the problems!

Travis Knox

Travis Knox has worked his way up from assistant, to Production Associate, to Producer. He was the Executive Producer of *The Bucket List* starring Jack Nicholson and Morgan Freeman, and Co-Producer of *Hairspray*, with John Travolta and Michele Pfeiffer.

I graduated from college in 1993 with a pretty broad Film and TV Production degree. Thanks to a professor, I'd had a brief conversation with an executive at Fox who gave me some basic job hunting advice. [I] found an apartment and I packed up and moved up to Los Angeles. With no real contacts, it probably took me a year, constantly looking for a job, meeting new people wherever I could...

I joined the IFP [now Film Independent]. I started going to their mixers. On one day, I had three job offers. One was not in the business, I disregarded that. One was to be a set PA for a new cable channel called Science Fiction Channel, which of course is now the *SyFy*. And the one that paid the least amount of money was the receptionist with a movie star's production company, which was probably the least glamorous, but it was the closest to what I wanted to be doing. And like every job in Hollywood, that one came from a personal contact—my former roommate's girlfriend was leaving her job and put me up for it.

So, you got the job through a contact . . .

You've got to constantly be meeting new people and maintaining those relationships. You have to pick up the phone at least once a week and just keep bugging the people that are trying to help you, because people do want to help you. But find that balance between friendly and annoying. You'll know who's going to help you and who won't.

I took that first [receptionist] job. At the time, the producing partner was looking for an assistant, but she wouldn't meet me for it because I had no experience. So I took that first job, and the smartest thing I could do was just to pretend that I was the producer's assistant. I would never leave before she did at night, make sure she was aware of my presence and ability, basically always see to it that she was taken care of as if I were her assistant. And it took about six weeks, but she came out finally and told me to switch desks because I was coming to work for her. Again, that's just being in the environment, and knowing what you're going to go after. Create the job you want to do within the job you have, but not at the expense of not doing your job.

There are plenty of assistants out there who have... overstepped their boundaries. They let the desk they're [actually] working for turn to shit while they are on the hunt for something better. So you have to do your job first. Fortunately, my first boss finally promoted me off that desk, and her words to me were, "You've got to go find somebody who's as good as you are." It didn't happen. I fired the next four people in the next couple of months.

It's more than likely that the all-important first job is going to be an assistant, and there's a good chance a lot of it won't be glamorous. I spent my first job picking up birth control, managing the beach house—even bailing the boyfriend out of jail once—all sorts of crazy stuff. There were plenty of moments I couldn't believe that I had a four-year degree, but I always knew that there was an upside to it. I was able

Travis Knox—cont'd

to participate in the development and production of some pretty cool projects, and I always knew that job had an expiration date—something better was coming.

You said that you fired the first four people you hired as your replacements. Why?

The big one that I'll never forget. There was a guy that we had hired who came in, and he was one of those guys who knew it all on day one, but in reality he couldn't figure it out. Despite the fact that after day four I had corrected him countless times, he very much just wanted to be in charge. Our office at that time was in Santa Monica, and on just about every day, my boss would eat at The Ivy (a restaurant), which was near the office. She wanted to eat at the one in Santa Monica, not the one in West Hollywood. When she said "Lunch at The Ivy today," I knew what she meant. So when she says it to the new fish, I tried to help out—"Just make sure..." And he shut me up. "No, I got it." At this point the writing was on the wall, so I let him dig his own grave. Knowing that it would take about half an hour to get to the restaurant in West Hollywood, I waited 'til about 20 minutes before the scheduled time before grabbing him and saying, "Did you tell her lunch date The Ivy at the Shore or The Ivy on Robertson, because she's thinking she's about to walk to lunch?" He knew he was screwed as I sent him into her office to fix this. I expected a huge explosion, but instead it was silence as she emerged with her purse and keys. Walking by she looked me in the eye and said, "I don't want him here when I get back." The point is, I don't care what level of job you're taking, if on day three you think you know all there is to know you should probably just pack your bags.

You said this guy was getting trained on the desk. That's a real industry expression. Someone comes into a job, they're brand-new as an assistant, what is the training on the desk?

It sounds deceptively simple. You run the phones and you manage the calendar. But I can tell you from personal experience, having worked for a couple of different producers, everyone has different ways they want things handled. I've worked with people who you could give a phone message to once, and I knew they would pick up the phone on their own and return the call. On the other hand, I know of producers who need constant reminders and perhaps don't think they know how to dial a phone—that's the assistant's job. Every boss has different things that are important to them. Some bosses want the assistant involved in every aspect of their lives, from driving kids to piano lessons to picking out presents for their wives [or husbands]. Others don't want you anywhere near their personal lives. When I made my first career move, I think I almost lost my job in the first week. I didn't have anyone to train me, and my new bosses were the polar opposite in needs and wants from my previous one, and I made a crucial mistake and assumed that I could just run the office (which is really their lives) the same way I'd been doing for a year. But the system that had been incredibly efficient for the previous position was a near-disaster in this new office. Everyone is going to have their own way. You're their go-to person. They rely on you for everything, and any mistake is catastrophic.

Continued

Travis Knox—cont'd

You were an assistant and moved up. How did you do it?

You need to find a way to quietly do the job you want to do, just not at the expense of the job you were hired to do. During what were to be the final weeks of my assistant career, we were in a position where we'd brought on a second assistant to help out. We were shooting several projects at once. One of which was a very high-profile, expensive television event movie. Because we had a first-time director (who didn't yet have a go-to crew), I knew we were going to have to bring in a lot of department heads for him to meet. I handed off the phone and calendar duties to the second assistant and started calling and introducing myself to below-the-line agents. Next thing you know, I was able to present everyone with a stack of resumes of potential candidates, and then while my bosses were out of town they asked me to bring the director in and start interviewing. A week prior my job was to handle a lunch order, and suddenly I'm choosing a production designer on a $13 million movie.

I continued working in physical production for a year or so, but then I noticed another need within the company. We were coming to the end of a two-year deal with a major studio. We hadn't set up one project during the previous eighteen months, and we were looking for someone to run the feature development side of the company. My bosses didn't see me as a development person and didn't want to give me the job. I knew that the studio wanted us to be bringing high-concept family material for them, so I spent a Saturday afternoon at a huge children's book shop, just reading all the synopses. I bought ten or so books that sounded promising, figured out that the film and TV rights were available for a few, and convinced a studio exec to get on the phone. She loved the idea I pitched her, and the next day while the studio was on the phone with the book agent, I was moving into my new office.

Of course, that was just the start of development hell. In other words, you've got a project—it might be a script, but more than likely it's a book, an article, or even just an idea. You don't get to make a movie, you don't have a green light yet. I had a book, I didn't have a script. So the long process of hiring a writer, waiting for a draft, then the painful rewriting was underway. But just getting a project set-up at a studio was a big victory for me and was reason to celebrate.

Setting it up is starting the development process. There's a studio backing you and they're going to put real money into it. But that can be a long painful process. You end up spending way to much time developing projects, sending them down this long dark path to nowhere. The next challenge is to get the movie made. Later in my career I was submitted a script called *The Bucket List*. No studio would touch it. I loved it, met the writer, and together we started brainstorming ideas for a director, hoping that if we could secure one we could package the script and take it back to the studios. The idea of Rob Reiner came up. I've been a longtime fan, and at that point in time he was in my world a bit. I'd had a meeting with him the month before and just had drinks with his agent. It seemed like a good first shot, so I submitted the script to him and within a year we were rolling film. The irony is, if I'd been able to set that script up with a studio development deal, odds are it never would have been made. Instead, I was able to pull together my experience, my confidence in my taste, and my expanding rolodex, and go make a movie.

Jawal Nga

Jawal Nga received his first credit as Associate Producer on *The Clearing,* starring Robert Redford, while he was still at film school. His first credit as a Producer was on *Forty Shades of Blue,* which won the Grand Prize for Best Dramatic Feature at the Sundance Film Festival in 2005. He has since produced *Married Life* with Pierce Brosnan, Patricia Clarkson, Chris Cooper, and Rachel McAdams, and was Executive Producer on *Last Chance Harvey,* with Dustin Hoffman and Emma Thompson, and *Howl,* starring James Franco.

Can you talk about getting independent film projects set up? You're going in to meet agents and people at production companies and talk about projects you have, and other than it helping you fund the project, or helping you attach someone to the project—what is your goal?

Other than that they decide to green light my picture right away . . . somebody that you can call up later that you sort of have rapport with, that you feel that you can sort of talk to and show material to again . . .you basically try to put your best foot forward.

What does that mean?

Just show that you know you're somebody that they would like to be in business with. You try to leave them with the impression, "You know what, he's smart. He knows what he's talking about. He's getting movies made. I would want to show my clients his material if he sent it."

Backtracking a little, you went to two film schools, both undergrad and grad. What is the value? What did you learn that was worthwhile, and what do you wish you'd learned? What If someone called you and said, "Should I go to film school. . ."

I'll answer your second question first. If someone asks me if they should go to film school, I'd say, "Great. But really, spend some time, and is this something you want to dedicate your time in life with." Really, be sure about it, because it's so hard. You know, I'm young in the business, and it's not like I've achieved anything huge, but I've only done what I have because it's something I do every single day. And you meet a lot of people who are out here and sort of washout, and they go home. So that's my long-winded way of saying, "Before you go to film school and spend all that money or beg, borrow, and steal and work really hard, be sure." It's hard to be sure if you want to do it the rest of your life and you're 18.

I was very fortunate that I did. What I got out of film school, besides liking hard work, you work really hard on these films, you achieve a basic understanding of optioning material, and you know equipment and stuff like that. [At film school] you learn about short films, and you learn all about budgets—not that thoroughly—but you never actually get to make [a feature], and so it's all theory. It's extremely scary. It's extremely daunting, and the feature is just this big mystery, and one of the first and most profound lessons I learned on *Forty Shades of Blue* was that it's just a short film with more zeroes.

But I think there's only so much you can teach. They teach the basics, but when you get out there and you start making films, immediately there's something you've never covered in film school. I guess at school you're covering just the basics. And some of them you're going more in depth, but I don't know if they could really

Continued

Jawal Nga—cont'd

teach as much as they needed to, because eventually you have to get out of there. So I think ultimately what I wish I'd gotten from school, no school could give me. But I'm a believer in film school. But at the end of the day, it's how well you play the game, how well you can talk to people, how smart you are. And you know, even these people that we consider idiots out there and who are in positions of power, they're smart in some way because they've managed to get to that position—or at least they've managed to stay there.

What did you learn on your first projects? Were there specific things you learned on* The Clearing *and* Forty Shades of Blue*?

With *The Clearing* I learned a lot about development. It took a few years. I had developed stuff before, but that was the first thing that I had seen actually go to screen. *Forty Shades of Blue,* I guess having that illusion burst and realizing that it's just people standing around like it was on a short film, you know same thing, there's no difference. That was a huge realization. On *Married Life,* probably navigating through more people, and we have the studio and we have the executives. I handled relationships in one way when we started shooting because I didn't get it. I handle them differently now.

On one film, everything was open. I just didn't realize it. You know, one of the lessons I've learned on the first day of [another film] was, we had our chairs lined up, right, and I was sitting in one of the actresses' chairs. There are three chairs beside me that were open, and so when she walked over, she just sat in the chair next to me and started chatting. Anyway, one of the other producers said, "Listen, whenever the person comes you need to get up from their chair." It was not like anything happened. It was just like one of those moments. A lot of little things like that. You know, there are 30 chairs on either side of you open, but if you're sitting in that person's chair, then you've got to get up and move. It takes a little getting used to. On our film, everybody really got along so it was never a big deal. But you know, it's just amazing—this thing is made of cloth and wood and is so much more than just cloth and wood with your name stitched on the back. You've earned that place, you've earned that right to have it. I think outside of the film industry, it must just seem completely insane.

One last question: Talk about the Sundance festival, and winning the Grand Jury Prize. Do you feel it changed your career as a producer?

It certainly didn't hurt it. Yeah, it changed it, but. . .if *Forty Shades of Blue* had come out and made $50 million or $100 million, that probably would have changed my career a lot more than winning the Prize. I made a film that won the Grand Jury Prize but that nobody saw. But at the end of the day you have this thing . . . it's in the books and it's official. It's such a well-known thing, yes it helps, I just don't know how much.

Do you think it helps get actors for your next project?

No. I think the film that you make helps get the actors. The performances you got help get the actors, not winning some award. They don't care. If the actor watches the film, talks to [the director], and sees that he's really serious and really smart and really cared, that's what got them, and the material. Sundance is a great thing, and that was so exciting, it was great that we won. But it's about the body of work, it's not about sort of this prize. Again, it was great on the market; don't get me wrong, it was a high point. Winning is good, don't let anybody ever tell you different.

Chapter 14

The Director, the First AD, and the UPM

THE DIRECTOR

Shana Feste

Shana Feste has been named one of *Variety's* ten directors to watch. Her directorial debut was *The Greatest*, with Pierce Brosnan and Susan Sarandon. Her second film was *Country Strong*, starring Gwyneth Paltrow. She is currently working on a retelling of *The Little Mermaid*.

Before I made *The Greatest* I was working as a nanny, a tutor, an assistant—whatever would give me enough cash to allow me to keep writing.

The contacts that I made really paid off later in my career. *Country Strong* was produced by someone I worked as a nanny for. I am signed at CAA [Creative Artists Agency], and I worked as an assistant for an agent there before I made *The Greatest*. I knew that I wanted to be creative and work as a director, but I was also really broke and couldn't support myself, so I looked for domestic jobs (something I was really good at) working for people that were involved in the business. I never thought I would use them as contacts initially. I just thought I could observe their lifestyle and see how it intersected with their work. At the most I thought I could pick their brain or get career advice if it ever came up. *The Greatest* was made because of my producer Lynette Howell—my agents at WME [William Morris Endeavor] gave her the script, and once she was on board, we found financing and we got our cast. I think working for celebrities helped me when I went on meetings with actors. I knew how to talk to people and how to connect with actors from all my experience working in their homes.

Looking back now, what do you wish you'd known as someone trying to get her first film made?

I spent years trying to get my first script made, which was called *Love Easy*. Every day my life was either great or horrible depending on how close I was to getting it made. After two years of this I realized that I needed to have more than one project out in the world, so I wrote *The Greatest*, which ended up getting made first. I really believe you should have a few things out there——not just one script that you are investing everything in.

Continued

Shana Feste—cont'd

Once you got the green light, is there anything you wished you'd known then that you know now?

Hmmm … I wish I had known that if an editor isn't working out you replace them quickly and immediately. I wish I had known that as a director you should meet and interview your line producer before they are hired. I wish I had gone through the script with an editor's eye and made sure I had transitions written into the ends of scenes, so they would cut together better, and I wish I had held longer before I called cut. There's also a lot of things that I'm glad I didn't know, because if I knew them I would have been too scared to make the film! I went into work every day thinking, "Of course we can shoot eight pages with a company move today," and "This water scene will be no big deal, my actors told me they knew how to swim," and "Six-day weeks sound fun!" Things like that—I needed to be naïve, or I would have never gotten through it.

Jacob Chase

Jacob Chase started on the other side of the camera. He did theater, film, and TV from the age of 7 until he was 14. Now he is successfully navigating the indie scene. He has directed several short films, including *After School Special* written by Neil LaBute, and *Patient Zero.* His first feature is *The Four-Faced Liar.*

I always loved storytelling and being a part of the creative process—I'd put on stunt shows and magic shows for my family in the backyard. Being an actor at such a young age gave me an upper hand with a basic understanding of how a set works, and the good and bad ways to tell a story. I asked for Movie Magic Screenwriter for Hanukah one year when I was in middle school, and I wrote my first screenplay.

I finally wrote a feature in my first year of high school that I tried to shoot with some friends, but I never could get enough people together. So I started smaller—I made my first short film in Junior year, and it won a few awards at a film festival, which was an honor and helped me realize I wasn't wasting my time with a hobby. I kept making shorts, and one of my teachers in school asked me to come in for a job interview on this feature she and her friends were putting together on the side. I got hired as the DP, and we shot during my month off between graduating high school and starting film school.

While at school, I started getting a lot of freelance editing jobs. It started from that feature I shot, which was a Christian-themed film. One of the producers worked for a church and hired me to edit all their video content. There is a lot more video content for a church than I would have imagined. I started building my resume and getting gigs editing small commercials and short films, etc. All the while, I was writing and directing short films in film school.

Jacob Chase—cont'd

A bunch of my short films played the festival circuit, and I tried to go to as many as possible, and I just kept meeting people. Most folks at festivals are just other filmmakers like you trying to make it, but every once in a while, you meet someone that can really help your career.

One of my teachers at film school recommended me for an editing job on a commercial for this startup company. The owner of that company liked my work a lot and offered to finance my thesis film. This was my first time working with someone else paying for me to direct, essentially, so it was a good learning experience for things to come. He was happy with how things turned out, and one day he was getting a massage and he met someone there who was a writer trying to put together his first feature. My work came up in the conversation, and I ended up meeting with this writer and working with him to make a movie!

It was a big rock opera musical that he was writing and starring in. We got a ton of Broadway names for the movie, both from his connections and mine (from my theater acting days), and we shot in 18 days. We shot it for super-low budget and didn't pay anyone. Most of the crew were people I went to film school with. I had the foresight (I'm not sure how) to invite this producer I knew to the set. I knew him from when I was a kid. I used to do the sets and lighting for this youth theater company when I was about 13, and he was a friend of one of the parents that came to the shows. He had hired me once as a kid to do the lighting for an awards ceremony he produced. Anyway, I always kept in contact, knowing he had produced some decent-sized movies.

So I asked him to set on one of our biggest days on the musical. The day with the crane, 50 extras, shooting on the CBS back lot . . . He ended up bringing a few other producers who were looking for a director on a $2 million movie they were putting together. Luckily, that day went really smoothly, and I think it just looked impressive that I was able to command a crew of that size and still get all the shots I wanted and get out on time (give or take.) I wasn't that good every day, but I tried to show off a bit for them, if I'm being honest.

A few weeks later, I got a call from one of the producers offering me the job to rewrite and direct their movie. It was to shoot in North Carolina, and they flew me out to rewrite and start preproduction. I got paid for two or three months of work, rewrote the script, hired the key crew members, and then the rest of the financing didn't come through. So I was heartbroken.

That feature didn't happen, and the rock opera feature never got finished. We got it to a locked cut, but the producer never found the rest of the money to finish postproduction costs—and frankly, I'm quite pleased it will never see the light of day. For me, it turned out to be a very lucky opportunity to learn how to manage a long shooting schedule and an ensemble of actors.

While continuing to work as a freelance editor on bigger and bigger projects, I applied for a directing job on Mandy.com. It was a low-budget feature with first-time producers. I ended up meeting with them multiple times—the script was fabulous—and got really attached to the project. I didn't get the job, however. So I went back to my daily grind, and about six weeks later I got the call that they fired the director they hired, and wanted to go with me instead. So this is what I

Continued

Jacob Chase—cont'd

would consider my real big break. Even though it was a low-budget film, it was with a group of people that were as passionate as I was, and together we made a film [*The Four-Faced Liar*] we were all really proud of.

It was not a totally easy process, however. Having this many passionate people in one room made for some very passionate arguments. I did not have final cut on the film, so every cut ended up being an argument in the end, it seems. At the time, it was frustrating, and I remember feeling like, "This is low-budget filmmaking, where the director is supposed to have full control!" 'Cause I know that's not how it is when you start working on the studio level. But I can honestly say now that that amount of arguing went to good use. I really am glad the producers hired an outside editor to re-cut the film without me for a few weeks, and I'm really glad the movie is shorter in places where I see now it ought to be. All that massaging of the edit really did make the best film.

We premiered at Slamdance and hired a great publicist and sold the majority of our rights over the next few months on the festival circuit. We got broadcast, DVD, and VOD deals, and even theatrical in some territories (outside of the U.S.). Two years later, [*The Four-Face Liar* is] still playing in festivals around the world, and one of my favorite things to do is go on Netflix and see how many people have rated it. (I figure if X amount of people rate it a week, at LEAST that many people are watching it.)

To delve into this a bit more, the selling of this film was not the easiest process. It's a mainstream movie, but the main characters are girls who fall in love. So naturally, we had that built-in LGBT audience. We didn't want to sell to that market, however, since we felt that market would come to us if the movie was good enough and was successful in the mainstream market. It's so hard to look at this with hindsight, but I worry our sales agent didn't push quite hard enough for those mainstream buyers to attend our festival screenings and distribution screenings. Did we hire the right guy? Who knows ... Regardless of what was promised, and how much they claim on the backend, there was no publicity done in the mainstream market for the release of the film. This was hard for me, and I tried to get all the producers to agree to four-wall a movie theatre with me so we could get those big reviews and get some much needed publicity. But having been on this film for so many years I think left everyone drained. In the end, I don't think the film will ever get noticed as much as it could have.

It screened to a sold-out crowd at the Ford Amphitheatre during its festival run, and a producer there really responded to the film. He recently had a major box office/critical smash hit film released and was in post on his next film. He was looking to replace the current editor after a few less than desirable test screenings. He asked me to take a look at the film and give my notes and tell him what I would do differently. Needless to say, since filmmaking is so subjective, I had a ton of suggestions. He ended up hiring me to re-cut the film, and that took up the next six months of my life.

He was very happy after the next few test screenings sent the audience ratings way up. We worked well together, and I showed him a few more of my recent shorts. (By recent, I mean shorts that I made while my feature was playing the festivals. I didn't want to get rusty, and I had an amazing opportunity to work with an A-list

Jacob Chase—cont'd

writer on one of them. That short is currently playing the circuit.) He had another film he was gearing up to hire a writer/director for and asked me to come in and pitch on it. Through a few months of pitches, I finally got the job. I'm writing the film on spec, but it has big producers attached with a major studio attached to distribute.

That is currently what I'm doing, and I'm still editing to pay the bills.

This book is about the soft skills a person has to have to survive in the Industry—people skills, political skills. Can you think of any do's and don'ts for someone starting out? Can you think of any examples?

I think it's all common sense. Return people's calls and emails promptly, arrive to meetings on time, and just be nice. It sounds simple, but I'm always surprised how many people fail to do all three. Also, always check your BCC field! A big thing for me, is if you get recommended for a job by someone, realize that that person's reputation is on the line as well as yours. So do your best to maintain both.

How did you get the jobs you've had—recommendations and contacts, cold interviews?

With the exception of my feature, everything has been through recommendation. Nine times out of ten there is still an interview process, but coming highly recommended is the most important part. I've found that as I've been working on more and more larger-scale studio films as an editor, people care less about my work and resume, and more about other people's praise and my personality in the room. For instance, I'm currently editing a very high-profile project, and I got that job based on a recommendation from a friend and one sit-down interview. The director never saw any of my previous work.

What have you learned about the film industry that you did not/could not have learned at school?

Really just how important networking is. You always hear it and I thought I understood it, but because I'm a very antisocial personality, the hardest part of my job is going out to the parties and drinks and dinners that help shape your career.

I wish I could have learned more about selling your first independent feature in school. I think that's something that could be taught. Even though every film is different and requires a unique selling strategy, there are some basics that would have been great to know going into hiring a sales rep and choosing the best deal from competing distribution offers.

What has surprised you about the industry?

As cliché as this may be, just how small the industry is. I literally can't go on a set or to a company now without having some, sometimes small, but some connection to someone working there. Everyone really does know anyone. And if you screw up, it will get around. I promise.

What advice would you give someone just starting out in the industry who wanted to be (a) a director, (b) a producer, or someone with an independent project who is just looking for funding?

Align yourself with people that add something to the project that you can't do yourself. For instance, one of the producers I've worked with has an incredible gift

Continued

Jacob Chase—cont'd

at working with A-list talent and getting them to sign on to projects. Then there's another producer that has extensive postproduction resources and knowledge of the film-selling process. Everyone is sort of what they bring to the table.

Then there are the obvious things, like make sure you have a script you are passionate enough about to spend the next two to three years of your life with. And mainly, I would say it is very important to write your own first film. I made the mistake of directing someone else's script first, and agents find it tough to figure out how to make money off of you solely as a director. If you are a writer as well, agents can see making money off you by having you do rewrites, sell specs, etc. It's much harder to get work as just a director.

What would you have liked someone to have told you, any lessons that you've learned that you could have learned an easier way?

People did tell me this but I didn't listen: have tons of material ready for when you start getting some heat. After my film premiered, won some awards, and sold, I got some good meetings at agencies but didn't have anything I was really passionate about to do next. I always heard that you should, and always thought I would, but you get so involved with just getting your film done in time that you don't have time to write anything new. So I would say write, write, write, no matter what, every night, so you can have enough material ready that you can really take advantage of the opportunities you get when they finally arrive.

THE UPM

Christopher Cronyn

Christopher Cronyn worked his way up from Production Assistant to Location Manager to UPM and Line Producer. His credits range from bigger studio films such as *Heat,* with Al Pacino and Robert De Niro, and *Bad Boys,* starring Will Smith, to smaller, independent films, including *The Slaughter Rule,* starring Ryan Gosling.

My first job in the film business happened almost by accident. A family friend called me and asked if I would like to work on a low-budget feature that his wife was making. While working on that job I met a cameraman who took my phone number and offered me employment on commercials. Slowly I expanded my circle of professional acquaintances and spent several years working on commercials in New York City. Most of my work during this time was as a crew member, usually an electrician or gaffer.

After several years of making commercials I wanted to work on a feature film. I was much more attracted to the narrative form. I was finally able to get a job on a studio feature film that was shooting in New York City, and I went to work as a PA, but within a few weeks I was elevated to location manager. I went from that film to other films, always due to some connection I had made, or my reputation. For a few

Christopher Cronyn—cont'd

years I was usually a production assistant or a location assistant, then I became a location manager, and finally an assistant to the production manager. Eventually I got into the Directors Guild as an assistant director. Eventually I was asked to production manage a film. Line producing is really an extension of production management. When I first started out, in the mid-1970s, there weren't really line producers; there were producers who knew how to produce, and there were the production managers who managed daily operations for them. Today's films are, generally speaking, more complex than the dramas and comedies of the mid-1970s and the 1980s. The digital revolution, made possible by computers, has allowed filmmakers to attempt much more extravagant narratives. As the making of films has become more complicated, so too has the job of producing or managing those productions.

Unit Production Managers [UPMs] are responsible for the day-to-day operation of a motion picture company. That is to say, they oversee the hiring of the crew, the preparation of the schedule and the budget, the rental of equipment, the purchase of goods and services, and they are responsible for tracking and reporting the expenses for all of the above. They report directly to the producer and the studio (if there is one), and they must have a good understanding of the intentions of the director and his vision for the picture.

This book is about the soft skills a person has to have to survive in the industry—can you think of any do's and don'ts for someone starting out?

Don't speak before you think. Know what you are talking about—or else shut up! Know who you're talking to or about, and don't underestimate who they may become. Courtesy is always important. Listening carefully is twice as important as speaking. As a matter of fact, you should always, always be listening. Some people may call this eavesdropping, so be it. Make sure you understand the difference between eavesdropping (learning, or gathering information) and gossiping about what you have heard (spreading false or unsubstantiated rumor).

Always be on the lookout for friends and mentors. They will be with you a long time, if you're lucky.

THE ASSISTANT DIRECTOR

Linda Montanti

Linda Montanti studied film at Columbia University in New York. She completed the Assistant Director Training Program, and then worked as a Second Assistant Director for four years before moving to Los Angeles. She has worked as a First Assistant Director on numerous features, television, and commercial productions, including *L.A. Confidential* and *Righteous Kill.* Linda's work has taken

Continued

Linda Montanti—cont'd

her on location to Canada, Australia, and across the United States. Her latest project is Mitch Albom's *Have a Little Faith* for ABC.

There is a hierarchy on a film set. There is a producer who put the deal together—initiated the project, got the funding, hired the cast and crew. He (or she) usually has the power, in addition to the Studio. The director tells the story, and is the king of the set. That is his domain. He sometimes is a producer as well, which gives him more power. The director has been hired for his particular skills and expertise in storytelling. The person who puts it all together on the set and gets it ready for the director is the assistant director. The assistant directors are managers. It's a putting-the-puzzle-together type of skill, as well as a motivational skill. The assistant director schedules the day's work, informs the departments of what is needed for the day, and runs the set, keeping the set moving in order to accomplish that day's work. Over the years, a system of separate crafts has been developed into departments like camera, sound, grip, electric, etc.

A film crew does basically the same thing every day. It's the locations, actors, costumes, makeup, and words that change. Actors rehearse, get ready in makeup and wardrobe; the crew lights the set and readies the cameras and sound; you shoot the scene, and move on to the next scene or location, and do it all again. We as a film crew are basically a traveling circus, loading everything onto trucks to go to the next location and shoot the next scene. The overall task of the assistant director is to figure out how to make the best movie you can make with the amount of money you have, in the shortest amount of time possible, following all the union contracts and safety rules. That's basically what the job is.

It's a very political job. If there's a studio, if there's a production company, there's the production manager whose job is the overall financial logistics of the show, but as a First AD your job is to manage what's happening on the set to fit in with the budget. The director has the vision of what they want to do, and your job is also to facilitate what the director wants to do. How do you approach working with the director? How do you approach your job when you're actually on the set?

As a First AD, I am contractually hired by the director per the DGA contract. My main allegiance and responsibility is to help the director to film his vision of the script. It's to the director's advantage to get the project made on time on budget. For a TV movie or a series, there are a predetermined number of days allowed; it doesn't matter what's in the script. If a TV movie is budgeted for 25 days, that's what the pattern is, and it doesn't matter that you're shooting five different time periods and three different cities with rain or snow in the middle of summer and it's 100 degrees. The pattern is for 25 days, and the AD must fit the schedule into that pattern. Directors know what the budgets are. They know what they have to do.

The best way you can get the script into some sort of manageable piece of work is by doing a good schedule. Directors don't necessarily know how to schedule, but they know what's important to them. One of the reasons directors like to choose their First AD is because they build a relationship with this person. The First AD needs to determine how the director likes to work. Some directors like to do a really big scene

Linda Montanti—cont'd

on the first day. Some like to be very small. Some like to shoot in continuity. Generally, I think the best plan for the first day is to find a scene which introduces the characters but that is doable. The director has to make [achieve what is scheduled] the first day. If the director does not make the first day, the studio will rightfully become concerned and will become a presence on the set. The studio has invested a large amount of money into the film, and they fear this production is going to be over budget before they've got everything in the script shot. So making a good schedule is very important to the outcome on the set, and to the director's ability to get his movie shot.

Scheduling can make or break the budget. Usually, the story will tell you how it should be told. I don't know how that happens, it's just over the years, your experience of making stories will guide you . . . First, I read the script. I read it as a reader and as a viewer. I just read the story. And then, I read it again and start to break it down. After that, I enter it into the Movie Magic program on the computer and start to move strips around. By the time I actually get to scheduling the scenes, I've been through that script three times.

There is an art to scheduling. Breaking down a script is a process that takes a lot of concentration. I try to do the first breakdown at home, where it is quiet, not at the production office. The office is full of interruptions. Someone will come in to ask a question, or more likely, 45 emails come in which need your attention. When this happens, it is easy to lose your place in breaking down the scene. For example, you could forget to include a character in the scene you were just breaking down. This could affect the actor's schedule, which could affect the money paid the actor. It could be an expensive mistake, and it could be a disaster on the set if you don't have all the actors in the scene on set and ready to work. I've seen this happen, which is why I always hire people smarter than I am who are obsessive, who go through my breakdown to make sure that everything is included.

When you're scheduling, you need to determine how many scenes the company can shoot in a day. You have a certain number of characters who speak, and they usually have to be *covered* (shot from several angles). I try to imagine how I would direct the scene. My years of experience give me an innate ability to sense how much time it will take to shoot.

Let's talk about people who want to break into the business by being a set PA.

There are so many things to learn as a set PA. First, you have to do what you are told. You are not really allowed to have an opinion, unless you see something that is unsafe. You are there to help out, to assist the directors in mostly menial jobs. However, if you want to learn how to make movies, you should try to get as close to the camera as possible so you can see what's going on. You will learn how a set is run, how close to be, what to do, and what not to do. You will be noticed and will get better assignments. If you're not eager to learn, or if you're on the phone or texting instead of paying attention, then you are not going to be noticed in a positive way and will soon find your days are numbered on that project. I tell the PAs who come to work for me to make themselves indispensable, to read and know the script, read the call sheet to know what we're doing every day, and to know where the cast [members] are at any moment.

Continued

Linda Montanti—cont'd

The most important thing a PA can have is common sense, which is not so common, and a feeling about people, a sensitivity to people's feelings. And they need to know that time is money. Here is something I teach my brand new PAs. When I first came up with this, the numbers were right and they might be a little off now. If the production cost of a film is $80,000 a day, you divide the $80,000 into 12 hours. Divide those hours into 60 minutes. You find out how much per minute the production is costing, let's say $100 per minute. It's like a meter in a taxi. We have a number of minutes per day, and we need to be able to spend those minutes wisely. So, when a PA doesn't know where the actors are and then looks for them for five minutes, you just spent $500 because he didn't know where the actors were. If somebody won't come to the set, we're all waiting 20 minutes, we wasted a lot of minutes, a lot of money, because the meter starts when the company's in and the meter stops when we wrap and the meter doesn't stop during the day. It just keeps ticking off that money. That analogy usually gets the PAs to at least understand that filmmaking is very expensive, and they can have an effect on the budget.

Linda's Cautionary Tale:

On one show, the scene was about a teenage boy, 15 years old, who was very depressed, and commits suicide. His family has all gone to his sister's recital, but he doesn't go. He stays home. The teen walks outside to the garage, attaches a hose to the tailpipe of his father's car, gets in, and starts the car. It's raining for dramatic effect in the story. And then, of course, his parents come back and find him dead.

We set up the scene to shoot with two cameras. We rehearsed the teen actor coming out of the house, walking to the garage, getting in the car, putting the hose in the car, starting the car. We rehearsed without the rain, mainly for the cameras, but also for the actor to prepare. The cameras were then ready. For emotional scenes like this one, the First AD normally keeps everything quiet on the set. You try not to have unnecessary people around to distract an actor who has to give that kind of difficult performance. I cleared the set, including a very tall trainee AD who was always getting in the way, always standing in front of me to block my view, always getting too close to the director's video monitor.

After the rehearsal, we called for makeup, hair, and wardrobe to do touchups and get the actor ready for camera. Once he was ready to go, we rolled the cameras, turned on the rain, the director called action. The kid comes out, starts to walk towards the garage, throws his hands up in the air like he's praying, then walks to the garage and gets in the car. The director is standing next to me freaking out. "Cut! Cut!" The director turned to me and said, "What the hell did he do? Why did he do that with his arms? He didn't do that in rehearsal. We've got to do it again!" Now the actor is wet and we've got to dry him off to get him ready for take 2.

The director goes in to talk to the actor, and the kid says, "Oh, well, that other director came over and told me that I should do that. That it would be really cool if I put my hands up like, 'No, please, God, forgive me.' So, I did it. I thought that was what you wanted." He pointed to the "other director," and the other director was the trainee!

The director was understandably furious, and asked the trainee, a guy in his early 20s, if he gave the actor direction. The trainee said, "Yeah, I talked to him.

Linda Montanti—cont'd

I thought it would be good if he put his hands up. I thought it would be better." The director screamed, "How dare you talk to him! You don't talk to actors! You're a trainee!" The trainee thought he was there to help direct a movie, as opposed to doing his job which usually was keeping people out of shot.

We then had to spend another 20 minutes to get the actor dressed and dry his T-shirt and dry his hair and redo his makeup. We lost about 30 minutes of shooting time. The trainee said he just thought he was helping out, but he never really understood that what he did was wrong. I told him, "Your job is to be a trainee, not a director. You don't have anything to do with what happens in front of the camera." But he would always be right there, right next to the director. There is a certain hierarchy of concentric circles where everybody on set stays, near the director's space. You don't get in his way, you don't make noise near the video. There are a lot of little rules. Everybody has to learn those rules and use common sense. The trainee was fired that day, and that was the end of his career. We found out that he had been fired on the last three jobs he had been on.

Chapter 15

Decisions, Decisions

When a company has a script and is thinking about beginning production, the first order of business is almost always a discussion of cost—as in, how much do the investors want to spend, and how much will it cost to make the film they want to make. The script is given to a Unit Production Manager, with the expectation that in about a week that person will generate a realistic, well-considered budget. The person creating this "first pass" budget is working with very little information. The producer or production company may tell the UPM that there is a deal in place with Actor A for X amount of dollars, Director A for Y amount of dollars, and the screenwriter has been paid Z. There will be a tentative *start date*, the day film is supposed to begin running through the camera. This date depends upon:

1. the readiness of the script,
2. the availability of key cast members, and
3. the marketing and distribution department's input as to when the film will be released most effectively. What is scheduled by the competition? Is this a summer movie, best seen when kids are on vacation from school? Is it a winter-but-not-holiday movie—maybe a drama? Who is the audience, and when are they most likely to go (or in the case of children, be taken) to the movies? If there is a target *release date* (often as much as a year and a half after the start of production), the start date is figured by counting back from the planned release of the film.

That's often it as far as what the UPM has in the way of hard information.

The first budget is merely a highly educated guess. In order to create a budget that is somewhat real, a first pass shooting schedule also needs to be created. This schedule is vague due to the scarcity of information. There is an intrinsic relationship between time and money on a film, and you must have a sense of how long the film will take to make in order to predict how much it will cost. The person or people creating the schedule and budget usually have years of experience. There are certain fixed aspects to production rules and costs, so these "guesstimates" can be amazingly accurate. At this stage, it's not necessary to know exactly which scene will be shot on a particular day, the question is how many days in total will the production need.

HOW MUCH, HOW LONG? THE SCHEDULE AND THE BUDGET

How Long Does It Take to Make a Movie?

Here's something to think about. It usually takes between 20 and 100 days to shoot a 90- to 120-minute feature film, between 18 and 20 days to make a television movie that runs approximately 94 minutes, and a little more than a week to shoot an episode of a dramatic TV series that runs an hour (including commercials). Assuming that the crews on these shows are all professionals and experienced, why such a difference?

First, there are the requirements of the script. If you look at those \$100-million, 100-day-shoot blockbusters, the scope of the story is usually larger. Lots of costly stunts and effects. Numerous acting parts and scenes that call for boatloads of background actors. Possibly the story takes place way in the past or in the future. Virtual cities and forts must be created or recreated. A big movie is like an ocean liner. It takes a lot of people to make it work, and steering is complicated.

Second, there is the money. Every film has what is called a *day cost*—a rough estimate of what it costs per day to shoot the movie. A film can cost about \$100,000 per day or \$30,000 per day, depending upon what is involved in the work of each day in terms of personnel, equipment, housing (if shot on location), etc.

Finally, there is *page count*. Although the rule of thumb is that one script page equals one minute of screen *running time*, it can take anywhere from a couple of hours to several days to shoot a page. A page could be a single scene of back and forth dialogue between two people, or it could read "they fight the Battle of Gettysburg."

The Assistant Director first takes the script and breaks it down into scenes. (If this is for a preliminary budget, the UPM will do this.)

Let's say the script opens with the following:

INT. Living Room—Night

An upscale room in an upscale house circa 1975. Christmas Eve. A fire is roaring. Beautifully framed photographs on the walls. More photos in frames on the mantelpiece and propped up on the grand piano. The photos show Kathy and Ben as twenty-something bride and groom, progressing to thirtyish suburbanites standing with rakes next to a pile of leaves, then with baby Andy, then Andy as a toddler, then at a high school graduation. This is the all-American family, well-dressed, smiling, they've got the world on a string.

If the AD is creating the schedule, he or she is going to number this scene and then decide upon the page count. This scene, Scene 1, runs for about two-eighths of a page. You notate 2/8, next to the scene number (usually in the right hand margin, next to the logline, *INT. Living Room, Night*). *INT.* stands for Interior and *EXT.* for exterior.

On to the next scene. The AD would say it's the next scene because the location has changed. The script reads *INT. Kitchen—Night*. When there is a change of location (the kitchen rather than the living room) or a change of time (for instance, *INT. Living Room—Morning)* the scene number changes. This scene reads:

CUT TO:

INT. Living Room—Morning

BENJAMIN

(Late 40s, still attractive but a little out of shape)

I can't stand this. The waiting is killing me.

KATHY

(A little younger than Ben and a little more well-preserved)

He said he'd call. If he said he'd call, he'll call.

CUT TO:

EXT. Major Metropolitan Airport, Taxi Lane

ANDY, 20s, weighed down with luggage, frantically hailing a cab. He is overwhelmed by the frenzied mob of holiday travelers. Cabs pull up, drop passengers, other travelers shove their way to the front of the cab line, sneaking in ahead.

The Assistant Director will number these scenes 1, 2, and 3. Scene 2 is one-eighth of a page. Scene 3 is one-eighth of a page. The AD will continue to break down the script, number the scenes, and notate the page count of each scene until the very last scene in the script (could be ninety scenes, could be one hundred and ninety). Each speaking role in the script will be marked, no matter how major or minor the character.

Once this process is completed, the Assistant Director will begin to assemble the shooting schedule by sorting and grouping scenes with the same location together, grouping scenes with the same characters together, and linking clusters of Interior and Exterior, Day or Night. This is the beginning of the process of creating a shooting schedule. The schedule becomes the foundation for the production.

After an analysis of the type of action in the script, and with an eye towards the work habits and speed of both the director and the cinematographer, the AD may decide that a realistic per day average page count for production will be two pages per day. If the script is relatively simple and the director is known to work quickly, the page count to aim for might be four pages per day. If the scenes are elaborate, maybe it's one page a day, and if there are effects and stunts, maybe even fewer than that.

The Assistant Director will build achievable days using the following principles:

1. There are approximately 12 hours in a shooting day, but most of the crew has both setup and wrap time in addition to that 12 hours, therefore a workable schedule must take into consideration not only the length of the scenes scheduled but what must be done technically in order to set up and properly shoot the scenes.

2. The most efficient schedule is the one where the downtime between setting up shots and scenes is minimized
3. Every time the shooting company moves from one location to another, a great deal of time is lost as the company packs everything and everybody up, deals with traffic in transit, then unpacks everything and sets it up again. Therefore, if possible, mid-day location moves should be minimized.
4. Actors are hired on either a daily, weekly, or *run of show* basis. Unless the actor is a star and is contracted for the entire run of production, it is important to spread the actors' work days over the shortest period of time possible, scheduling their scenes as closely together as possible. This means you usually don't want an actor scheduled to work day 1, be off day 2 and 3, then come back day 4, then be off day 5, etc. Depending on the individual contracts, in keeping with the Screen Actors Guild regulations, you may find that you are paying an actor not to work.
5. Per Screen Actors Guild, the actors must have a 12-hour rest period between their wrap time one day and their call time the next. If the crew is union, their rest period is also regulated. This rest period, called *turnaround,* weighs heavily into the sequence of days. If there is a night shoot on Monday, you can't begin to shoot for twelve hours after wrapping on Monday, so you won't be shooting a full day of exteriors on Tuesday. You won't have time before it gets dark.

   Because of turnaround requirements, a shooting week will usually begin with a very early call (6:00 am on a Monday, possibly), and exterior scenes will often be scheduled for the beginning of the week. The Assistant Director usually pushes the call back a little each day (Tuesday's call may be 7:30 am, Wednesday's may be 9:00 am) so that any night exteriors can be scheduled towards the end of the week—by Friday the call might be for noon, and shooting may last until past midnight. This gives the cast and crew the weekend to turn around and start early again the next week.

Once there are achievable days, the AD will begin to organize them into clusters of weeks that work together. The priorities in scheduling are usually location, cast availability (or sometimes the other way around if you're dealing with stars), and finally dramatic content. Although it may seem more comfortable creatively to shoot a movie in script sequence, it rarely happens. The director and actors are expected to adapt to working out of order, shooting the wedding scene before the scene where the characters meet.

Looking at Scene 1 of our hypothetical movie, you can assume that the scene—an establishing shot, no cast—will probably not take long to shoot. The AD will meet with the director and will want to know the plan—will the camera be moving through the room on a dolly track? That will take a little more time to light and shoot. Will the camera be handheld? If this is a thriller, a handheld or steadicam shot might signify that someone who shouldn't be there is prowling through the house. The Assistant Director might decide that as long as there is nothing much going on in the scene, this would be a good scene to save for the end of the day. The cast could be released before the scene is shot, some of the crew could be wrapping equipment, and it's a night interior. If the house is being built on stage, there will be no problem, and if the house is a real house, it won't be necessary to hang heavy black fabric outside the house to cover the windows.

Scene 2. There are two characters, and the director wants Benjamin sitting at the kitchen table and Kathy making coffee and toasting bread. If the kitchen is *practical*, meaning that it's an actual working kitchen, there is nothing special that has to be done in order for the actress to be able to run water into the coffee-maker, etc. If the scene is being shot on a stage, then a tube from a water tank will have to be rigged, and if we see the toaster oven light up when Kathy pushes the button, some kind of electrical connection will have to be wired to the toaster in advance. The scene takes place early in the morning, and the director would like sunlight pouring in through gauzy curtains at the window. That means lighting both outside and inside the room. How long will that take? The AD is going to schedule the scene to be shot during the day. Depending upon what other days the actors playing Kathy and Ben are scheduled, the AD will want to organize their work in such a way that their employment is consolidated in as few days as possible.

One consideration is that the actor cast as Benjamin is due to begin another film six weeks after the first day of production. He has to be done shooting his part before a specific drop dead date or a per-day penalty payment will kick in. The AD and Production Manager advised the director of this but no one else would do. Logistically the best schedule would call for Benjamin to work at the end of the schedule, but the Production Manager doesn't want to risk hitting a penalty date. The AD will want to schedule Benjamin's work in such a way that his employment is condensed in as few days as possible, but a film involves so many interdependent factors that this may not be possible.

Scene 3 is only an eighth of a page on paper, but there are lots of elements—background actors, vehicles, possibly *bits of business* (little scenarios) that the director wants to see behind the main action of Andy trying to get that taxi. It is expensive to shut down even a small section of a working airport. Usually all you can hope for is that the Location Manager has been able to negotiate control of a sizable chunk, maybe several yards of curbside and a specific traffic lane. The cast and crew will be dealing with pedestrian traffic, take-off and landing noise, orchestrating *picture cars* (on-screen vehicles) while not impeding normal airport business. It's an exterior so there is also the risk of the wrong kind of weather. The director feels that this scene is crucial, as it sets up the character and the basis for the comedy to come. This may take a while. Best to schedule it for early in the day. Which day? Whichever day is least busy at the airport.

On it goes. The goal of the Assistant Director is to juggle all of these factors and then to arrive at a grand compromise between art, time, and resources.

HOW MUCH WILL IT COST TO MAKE A MOVIE?

Time is money on a film set. The AD will organize the schedule with the knowledge that it is necessary to maintain a shooting pace that is appropriate to the project. Low-budget films can afford to shoot only a certain number of days, therefore the Assistant Director must craft a schedule that can work within those parameters. A script can be made for a lower budget with fewer shooting days if the number of locations is limited, the number of actors are limited, and the actual action is not terribly complex. That's why small independent films tend to be *walk and talk* films or domestic dramas.

Hour-long episodic television programs are able to average several pages a day because the same crew works together over and over again and they act as a fast-moving machine. There are standing sets, the police headquarters or doctor's office or hero's apartment that we see in each episode. Those sets can be pre-rigged and pre-lit, or because the crew is shooting those sets every week, they can light and block at an impressive clip. The actors who play ongoing characters in episodic television know their characters. There are few delays as they find their performance. The directors in episodic television are hyperaware of the schedule and know they have only so many days and absolutely no more. They can't slow things down in a quest for perfection the way a feature director often does.

Films that are large in scope with big names, major directors who are going for the gold, set pieces with crowds that take time to coordinate, lots of planes, trains and automobiles, stunts and effects—all of that takes time. If the budget is there, that's the way the shoot is scheduled. If not, it might not be possible to come up with a realistic schedule that will work.

Once this schedule is completed, the Production Manager must put a price tag on it. The Production Manager knows what things cost. There are the obvious costs of cast, crew, equipment, and food. But let's look at the three scenes again.

Scene 1. Not bad, as long as it doesn't cost too much to rent the house or build the room. The average per day cost of a location rental for film in Los Angeles is about $5000. This includes the permits, the location itself, and parking for crew vehicles, equipment trucks, and base camp. It can be much less or much more, depending on the actual shooting site, but nice houses can easily cost this much, so the Production Manager must compare the budget to the schedule. How many days are scheduled in the house? If it's more than one day, is there enough money in the budget to cover the homeowner's hotel and expenses for however many days it takes to prep, shoot, and restore the location?

Scene 2. More of the same.

Scene 3. Airport location. Could be $20,000 for one day. How many picture cabs, how many picture cars, and how many background actors driving? The crowds of people. How many of them have lines and will be paid as actors, and how many of them are silent and will be paid as background? How many police will be needed for this location? With security a concern at all airports now, will the film be able to shoot there at all? What kind of monitors will the company have to put on the payroll to liaise with the Transportation Authority? What kind of insurance rider might be required? If the scene can't be shot at a major airport, what will have to happen in order to find a smaller airport and make it look bustling and urban?

Three brief, uncomplicated scenes are not necessarily as simple as they appear. Once the analysis of each scene in the movie—its relationship to the film, each cast member and the constraints of his or her contract, and external factors such as weather, holidays, etc.-—is complete, the Assistant Director and Production Manager will have the answer to how much and how long it will take to make the movie. There are no shortcuts for the process.

Caution! When a filmmaker is looking to raise money for a project, often the first thing she does is hire someone to do a budget. IF that person does not insist on creating a production breakdown and a template schedule first, the budget is fairly worthless. Lately, lots of companies and individuals have popped up on the internet who are very willing to take your money, go away for a week, quickly tweak an already-existing budget for a film that has nothing in common with your particular script and production, and tell you that it's valid. Even worse, some of these people are willing to take money for creating a top sheet, a summary page with no details. They will tell you that a top sheet is all that is needed in order to meet with investors. Don't be taken in. It's not. As evidenced above, making a budget without a breakdown and at least a tentative shooting schedule is just pulling numbers out of the air. You don't have to know how to make a budget yourself, but you must understand how you've arrived at "20 days, $1 million," or "40 days, $4.5 million." You must be able to have that conversation with investors and executives. You want them to trust you to make your movie. How can that happen if you can't answer questions about the details of the plan?

Chapter 16

Union or Non?

Several important decisions must be made about the plan of the production before much else moves forward. One major decision is whether the film will be made under the auspices of all of the film-related unions and guilds, just some of them, or none of them.

A union is a collective bargaining group. In the case of film unions, the idea is that the union represents Labor, and negotiates or bargains with Management about working conditions (hours worked, benefits, grievance procedures, and salaries.)

Labor is:

1. the cast, stunt people, singers, dancers, and background actors, all represented by the ***Screen Actors Guild (SAG);***
2. the writer, represented by the Writers Guild of America ***(WGA);***
3. the director, production manager, and assistant directors, all represented by the ***Directors Guild of America (DGA);***
4. the production craftspeople—camera department, grip, electric, sound, hair, makeup, costume, art department, editors, and most postproduction personnel, craft service, special effects, and some office staff, all represented by a variety of offices, or *locals,* of the ***International Alliance of Stage and Theatrical Employees, or IATSE*** (e.g., Local 600 is the Camera Guild; on the West Coast Local 80 is for Grips; Local 706 is Hair and Makeup Artists, etc.—these are individual locals but are all chartered by the IATSE);
5. drivers, animal wranglers, locations department, and catering, represented by the ***Teamsters;*** and
6. musicians and composers, represented by the ***American Federation of Musicians (AFM).***

Management is the studio, the production company—the people who are spending the money to make the movie.

The underlying concept of a union is that one worker has no clout, but one hundred or one thousand workers have lots of clout. Let's say someone is working at a laborer level and feels that he is being mistreated; the hours he's working are too long, he's not getting enough of a break between quitting time one day and reporting time the next. He's exhausted, his health is suffering. What can he do? He can complain but to who? He doesn't have access to the people who can do anything about his situation. Even if he does speak to the people in charge, will they care? Will they act? He can quit, but there are lots of people who will be delighted to replace him. As one individual, he has no power. A proponent of unions will say that if a union is standing behind this guy, negotiating for specific pay and working conditions, he will be treated more fairly by management and won't have to fight the fight alone. There is strength in numbers, and a detailed contract outlining all terms and conditions of Labor has been negotiated, so the laborer doesn't have to stand up for himself, and doesn't have to negotiate his own deals with people who are much more powerful than he is.

HOW A FILM UNION WORKS

Once you apply and are accepted into a union, part of your agreement with your local is that you won't work for a company or on a film that is not signatory to your union. Film productions are either *signatory* (the officers of the company have signed an agreement between the company and the union, committing all parties to work in compliance with union regulations and working conditions) or not. If a film company has not signed the Screen Actors Guild Agreement it is not signatory to SAG. This means a member of SAG is not permitted to work on the film. If a SAG member is asked to work on a nonunion project they must turn it down. Some unions also ask that their members to inform them of any non-union projects that have been in contact with them. That way, a *union business agent* can find and try to *organize* the project (turn it union). In return for their allegiance and their payment of membership fees and dues, a union member—when working on a film with a company that is signatory—receives the benefits that have been negotiated between the union and the production company.

A big-budget studio film will hire only members of the WGA, SAG, the DGA, IATSE, and the Teamsters to work on crews. Studios have a standing history of signatory agreements with all the unions. Studios and television networks are considered the Producers. In fact, if you read about a potential strike or a new contract being negotiated, and the newspapers or blogs refer to "the Producers" they are actually speaking of the studios, not individual producers. The studios represent Management, just as the unions represent Labor. The only nonunion crew members on a studio film will be at the assistant level. (These production assistants to the director and assistant to the producer positions are coveted by anyone starting out in production.)

As discussed in Chapters 9 and 11, many production companies set up separate corporations or LLCs for each individual project. This allows a production company to avoid signing a blanket "all union all the time" deal, to tailor each agreement more specifically to the budget and shooting location of each picture, and to have more control over the individual contracts. Due to the budget level of the projects that major production companies produce, their films are almost always completely union, but sometimes they are able to negotiate concessions on a one-time basis to address the specific production concerns of each film.

Smaller Films

A company that is created for the production of a single low- or micro-budget film almost always chooses to become signatory to SAG. The sale and distribution of most low-budget films is dependent upon who is cast in the lead roles. We'll go into this in more detail in the chapter concerning casting (Chapter 18), but for now you should understand that for a small picture without a lot of resources in terms of marketing and publicity, casting is all important. Pretty much any actor you've ever heard of is a member of SAG, so almost every film you see is signatory to SAG. Fortunately for filmmakers, SAG has created a variety of contract levels. This means that whether your overall budget is less than $200,000 or whether it's $200,000,000 you can probably afford to become signatory to SAG.

Although there are several low-budget options for the DGA, whether or not to become signatory to the DGA can be a more difficult decision, especially if your director cannot afford to or doesn't want to join. There are many micro-budget and low-budget films that are signatory to SAG but not the DGA.

The decision becomes even more difficult when it comes to the IATSE and the Teamsters. Even their low-budget deals are often higher than filmmakers can afford at a micro-budget level. As someone just beginning in the film industry, you should be aware of all the options. Each union and guild has a website, and you can find not only the financial details of all the contracts but the production commitments that each contract requires.

The executives at production companies are usually dealing at a higher than micro-budget level, but as there are several tiers to each union agreement, they usually rely on the advice of a Line Producer or Production Manager to guide them through the decision as to which agreement best suits the needs of each film.

WHAT ARE UNION BENEFITS, AND WHY ARE THEY IMPORTANT?

The facts of life for union and nonunion crew members:

If you're a crew member, you are actually self-employed, working on a project-only basis. Most crew members hired on feature films prep for anywhere from one week to four months, shoot for four weeks to three months, then they're done and back in the unemployment line. You do not work twelve months of the year. On a feature film, the crew is usually paid fairly well, but the assumption is that your checks will have to stretch until the next job. That could be a week, two months, even a year down the road. You may have three good years during which you work six days a week, 14 hours a day for eleven months straight, bopping from a feature to TV series to commercials, but on year four you may work only three months total.

As a nonunion crewmember, there is no employer contributing to the cost of your health insurance policy, no retirement fund. As a self-employed worker, you do not reap the benefits of those who work for an ongoing business or corporation. You don't receive health insurance, and no company pays into a 401 K retirement account for you. As a nonunion crewmember, you shoulder the weighty expense of carrying your own health insurance. That can run into more than a thousand dollars a month. If you get hurt and can't work, you have no income. When you don't know how much money you'll be earning from day to day, or year to year, it is unlikely that you'll be putting aside and tying up a large sum of money to cover your own retirement fund. Retirement seems like a long way away when you're twenty and even when you're thirty, but there comes a time when you'll want that money to be there.

As a union crewmember, the employer (the signatory studio or production company, or a payroll company representing the studio or production company) pays your wages plus an additional percentage of those wages (on top of what you've earned). The additional percentage is paid to your union. The union has a health insurance and pension fund. The employer's contribution is noted. The idea is that when you need to access your health insurance or retirement fund, the money plus interest is there in your account.

The Good News... and the Bad News

When studios and production companies were making slates of ten movies per year and scripted television series production was booming, if you got into a union and worked regularly you could count on your benefits including great health care services and a great pension. The good news is, if you work several months a year on major films, that hasn't changed. The bad news is, as more and more companies have decided to make films in *right to work* states or out of the country (*runaway production* will be covered in the next chapter) there has been less and less work to spread around. Unions base their benefit payments on the hours the members have *banked* (a surplus accumulated and approved to be used later) in the past few months.

If you haven't worked from January to April but you get on a film that's shooting August through December, there is a chance that you will be operating without health insurance for several months until the required accumulation of hours worked kicks in. In order not to be working uninsured, most unions allow their members to self-pay, which means that you're doing what the nonunion crews do—carrying your own (albeit less expensive) health insurance expenses. If after a certain point you still aren't working, you may have no health benefits at all. Some unions and guilds have recently instituted different tiers of insurance—with X amount of hours you get the HMO (restricted doctors, hospitals, services, etc.), but with Y amount of hours you can have your pick.

Working Conditions

On a nonunion film, if you feel that you're being treated unfairly, as long as you're not physically in danger and no laws have been broken, you're on your own. You can speak up. Depending on what's happening the Production Manager or the First Assistant Director may be able to help with the situation, but there is no greater body to whom you can complain.

As a union crewmember you can approach your *steward* (the member of the crew elected to serve as the union representative on the film), and he or she may help you take action. If there is something untoward going on, you may file a *grievance* (an official complaint that must be promptly investigated and sometimes acted upon.)

On a nonunion film, there is no obligatory regulation of hours and pay. You can work a 15-hour day, wrap at 2:00 am, and be called back at 8:00 am. This short turnaround leads to unsafe working conditions, crew members falling asleep at the wheel on the way home, etc.

As a nonunion crewmember you are often expected to work for what is called *a flat*, meaning a flat fee with no overtime compensation.

As a union crewmember, working conditions and compensations are governed by the union agreement. You will receive an hourly rate that follows the formula of straight time for the first eight hours worked, time and a half for the next four hours worked, then double time for anything beyond. Your turnaround time is governed by rules. If your allotted rest period hours are *invaded* and you are called back before the contractual turnaround time has passed, you are receiving a *forced call,* which means the production company owes you and anyone else who is called back early a substantial fee. As a union crewmember you are still obligated to work the long hours. The union makes it more difficult (i.e., more expensive) for the employers, but if the schedule requires the short turnaround and the 15-hour day and the production company can afford to foot the bill, then you're in the same boat as the nonunion crews—you work now, sleep later. But you are paid at a higher rate for your discomfort.

Residuals

Some unions (the WGA, DGA, and SAG) ensure the paying of residuals as part of their contract. Residuals are payments that are tied to the type of exhibition of the film. An actor or director or writer will not receive residuals for a film in its initial release or when it is screened as it was originally intended (for example, there will be no residuals on a feature film when it is exhibited in a movie theatre.) But if the film has any sort of afterlife—DVD, network or cable or pay-per-view—the actor or director or writer will receive compensation. It may not be a lot, but it definitely adds up over the course of several years. You may hear someone refer to "mailbox money." They're talking about the lovely feeling they get when they receive a residual check.

THE SORT OF GOOD NEWS . . . AND THE NOT SO GOOD NEWS

Many nonunion projects are not abusive. Sometimes these projects are being managed by people who have less experience, the nonunion project is a labor of love, and there's just not a lot of money. Nonunion films tend to have lower budgets, smaller and younger crews, and they are almost always independent films. They are often financed by investors who might be the friends and families of the filmmakers, and they don't have the resources to pay the salaries and benefits of a union film. Most of the time the key creative people involved in the film are themselves not members of a guild or union. Usually they either aren't eligible or don't want to join and they are just starting out. They see their film as their opportunity to break in, and they assume that the crew feels the same way. The shooting schedules are usually shorter than the typical union film, and many of these films are considered steppingstones. The idea is that everyone will survive a month or two of low wages and endless days, and in the end they'll have a credit on a feature that will hopefully end up getting good buzz on the festival circuit and a distribution deal.

A film can have a micro-budget and still be run professionally, just as a big-budget film can be poorly managed and chaotic. On nonunion films, the best producers, directors, and production managers head off potential issues by coming up with the equivalent of a union agreement as part of the crew *deal memo*. The deal memo will clearly outline the terms and working conditions of the project, starting with your hourly rate and if and when overtime will be paid. A low budget doesn't mean that safety must be compromised, and a good production team knows where to skimp and when doing so would be dangerous. A film may be short on funds, but that doesn't mean that the producer, director and production manager don't appreciate the crew. They are often willing to do all they can afford to keep the crew happy. A smart production team will make sure that there is great food being served on set and plenty of it. Every effort will be made to keep the work day to a safe and sane length. For those days when the turnaround is going to be too short, producers and production managers who work at this budget level often purposely hold back a little pad of money to pay for a motel room for anyone who needs it.

The nonunion world is less structured than the union world, but many major filmmakers began their careers and flourished making nonunion films until they were able to or felt it was time to join a union. They had no family in the business to help pave their way, they didn't have the experience required to join, no one was banging down their door offering millions to produce or direct, shoot or design a big-budget film, and they weren't about to give up their dreams and go home. They saw their chance, and they made the most of it.

HOW YOU GET IN

Yet More Good News and Bad News . . .

Although the requirements for membership in each union vary, acquiring membership works in a fairly similar way. You must apply, and in order to be accepted, you must have a certain amount of qualifying experience in a specific job category. You must be able to prove your experience by presenting call sheets, crew lists, and paycheck stubs. This experience must be culled from films that the union membership office or business agent chooses to accept. They don't accept down and dirty guerilla films, or short films, or student films. Each union or guild has requirements regarding what counts and what does not. To obtain membership in the DGA as an Assistant Director, for example, you have to present proof of several hundred days worked on higher-level nonunion films or films that were shot in foreign countries. The membership committee can disallow work if the projects don't meet their standards. To get to the required number of days the membership committee is willing to count, you may need documentation of many more days because some may not qualify.

There is also a way to get in involving work you do in what the DGA calls "the third area"—meaning work outside of New York or Los Angeles. It's a complicated process, and the information is available through the DGA offices.

You can also apply to get into the highly competitive DGA Training Program. Getting in to the Training Program involves a series of aptitude tests and interviews, and it's a long process. Of the several hundred who apply each year very few are chosen. If you are chosen to be a Trainee, you will attend training seminars on safety and working with background actors—areas in which you will be expected to have expertise as an Assistant Director. You are paid low wages and are assigned to work on films and television series. Eventually you get your days—the qualifying number of days required to be listed officially as a Second Second Assistant Director. Getting your days can take anywhere from a year and a half to several years, because you are at the mercy of how many DGA signatory projects are being shot. There is usually one Trainee assigned to each DGA film or TV show. Once you are listed as a qualified Second Second AD you are no longer assigned work. You are freelance, and the hope is that all the Second and First ADs you worked with as a Trainee remember you fondly and will become a source of references and employment.

To qualify for one of the many IATSE Locals, you will have to prove that you worked on IATSE projects for a specific number of days or hours. Those days may have been acquired because every member was working and a general call was put out and qualified nonunion workers were allowed to join. This is unusual but it does happen. Your days may have been acquired working on commercials or major music videos. Depending upon how busy it is and how many of the current members of a union or guild are working or out of work, the requirements might be a bit elastic. Maybe you were *permitted* to work as an Assistant Makeup person on a location in Alabama, where there were no union members available, or you were *grandfathered* in for membership—a project you were working on was organized by the union and you automatically became a member as part of the deal. Joining a union is not easy. It can take years to qualify.

The good news is, union films have more money and pay better and the benefits are good. Unions negotiate the minimum a company can pay each member.

This is called union *scale*. The big films and most network narrative television shows are union. Being in a union gives you status.

The bad news is that you will not be able to work on a nonunion film, no matter how much you believe in the script or the talent of the people involved. You will also not be able to work on a nonunion film when you don't have a job. You not only can't do it, you may face a financial penalty from your union if you decide to work under the radar and you get caught.

Why Someone Might Not Join a Union

There are a few possibilities, all legitimate:

1. Your philosophical beliefs. You don't trust groups, don't want to be ruled by a group decision, and would rather take care of things like your health insurance and retirement on your own.
2. You prefer to work on the kind of independent films that are generally not union pictures. You wouldn't be able to continue working on them if you joined.
3. You're a writer-director who raises the money for your films through friends and family, and every penny counts. You're not making any money, and you don't want the production money to go to anything but minimal salaries and production items that will be visible on screen.
4. You can't join. You're not eligible. You don't have the days, and until you find a way to get those days, you're not going to get in.
5. You want to join—eventually. Right now your industry contacts and the folks who have kept you working are in the nonunion world. You're not making the big bucks, but you're working consistently. You're moving up to a higher rank in your chosen department, and you're being hired for more and more high-quality projects. Is this the right time to give that progress up and to start over at the bottom of the barrel? Or do you want to sit tight, track your days, accumulate your hours, but wait to apply for membership until (a) you are offered a great opportunity, or (b) the contacts who have been calling you have moved up and gotten into the union also? The one thing you know you don't want to do is to be accepted into the union but sit idle, unable to work in your old world but unknown and unemployed in your new one.

Should the situation arise, you'll want to think about all of the permutations and make an educated rather than a quick decision.

TO BE OR NOT TO BE

A production needs workers in order to make movies. Workers *need* the production in order to earn money. Each side needs the other, but it's sometimes a very uneasy alliance. As mentioned, studio movies and films budgeted above a couple of million dollars and shot in the United States are almost always completely union—WGA, SAG, DGA, IATSE, Teamster. They can afford to be. Because of the type of established and experienced personnel these films require, the tradeoff of the additional cost of making a union payroll is a proportionally small financial hit for them to take, and the feeling is that it is well worth it.

The costs of a full union crew are substantial. Even the lowest per hour or per day price of labor is set higher than it would be on most nonunion projects, and the benefits add up. Here's an example.

Let's say you are a nonunion crewmember whose rate is $200 per day. The first question for a nonunion project is, what constitutes a day? The norm for a shooting day on a feature film is 12 hours plus an unpaid half hour for lunch, which is supplied by the production. Is your hourly rate $200 divided by 12 hours? Is there a point where you go into overtime? If you do go into overtime, how is that overtime figured? Legally, you are supposed to hit some kind of overtime when you surpass eight hours per day. When you are working for a flat fee it is up to you to understand the particulars of your deal, and to get them on paper, on a deal memo—before you start work.

If the film is one of those labors of love mentioned earlier, you may be fine with "$200 for whatever it takes." That's the way most people start out. Everyone is working for experience and contacts and to pay the rent.

If you are the producer or production manager of this film, you are no doubt also working for very little money and committed to whatever it takes. What it takes is a capable crew who will work within the parameters of your budget while setting your production payroll up in a way that operates within the law. As an employer, the film is bound by law to pay certain taxes and make certain contributions to each employee's social security fund, federal unemployment fund, and state unemployment fund. You may think that the way to avoid paying this additional money is to have all freelance staff and crew bill the production company, rather than be added to the company payroll for a job that is short term, but that won't work. Every employer who pays an employee more than $600 per year must pay into these funds. The approximate cost of these taxes and contributions per employee totals about 19 percent over the actual salary you are paying. This means that your $200 per day grip will actually cost you about $238 dollars per day. The crew member won't receive that extra $38. The government will. But the per day cost of that person will still be about $238.

Multiply that $38 by 20 production days and you've got $760. Multiply that $760 times 30 cast and crew members and you've got $22,000. You've got to pay it, so you must plan for it. You don't have a choice. It's the cost of doing business—and as someone making a film, in addition to making art, you're doing business.

Suppose you're making a union film. Let's say we have a grip whose hourly rate is $26. This means that the production will be paying: $26 × 8 hours = $208, plus $39 (time and a half) × 4 hours = $156, so a total of $364 for the 12-hour day. Typical union *fringes* (fringe benefits) total between 14 and 17 percent, depending upon the union or guild (paid into the union funds, not to the actual crew member, who will access the money later, it is hoped, upon needing health insurance or with his or her retirement.) Let's say that is roughly $51. Now let's add in the payroll taxes of 19 percent, approximately $69. So the per day cost of this not particularly high-level union crew member is $484.

Even if the actual hourly rate of the union and nonunion crewmember is identical—let's say they each make $20 per hour, over the course of a lower-budget feature film with a schedule of four weeks prep, four weeks shoot, and a week of wrap—your union fringes for this crewmember could be $26 × 45 days = $1170. Multiply that $1170 times a crew of 30 and you've got union fringes of $35,100 in addition to your legally obligatory payroll taxes.

This is part of the reason why low-budget films may hire union crews. The hourly rates are lower, and overtime is negotiated, not a given. It's not necessarily that they wouldn't like to pay these benefits but with limited resources, there is often not enough money available to both make the movie and pay the salaries and benefits. They want to make the movie with the amount of money they have now, not the amount they may never be able to raise.

A cautionary note for all concerned: If the working conditions on a nonunion film are unpleasant (the hours are very long every single day, the meals are late and bad, conditions are unsafe) or inequitable enough (the director and producer are earning good money, but the camera crew is being paid minimum wage), the crew may decide to organize. This means that they will contact someone from a union and ask them to come on to the set and force the project to become union by threatening a work stoppage that would grind the production to a halt. This would presumably cost the project more money than a union wage and benefits would.

This kind of action can get complicated. Often the production doesn't have the money to go union and is forced to fold completely. Now the crewmembers have (a) burnt their bridges with this production group, (b) not achieved union status, and (c) maneuvered themselves out of a job. If a deal is made with the union, the crew members may be grandfathered in but could end up in a kind of a limbo. They may be technically union members and pay their dues, yet not know enough union people that they can work as often as they'd like. They definitely cannot fill in with nonunion jobs. Not only would it not be allowed by the union but word will get around to the nonunion people that they turned a show and they won't be offered the work. "Turned" here means they attempted to organize the project, to forcing it to become union by bringing union representative to the set and persuading non-union crew members to join a union mid-filming.

The point of this is, if you are trying to make a nonunion film and are on the management side, treat your crews with respect. They should know that you understand that they are talented professionals and that although you don't have money, you are taking pains to keep them as happy as possible. No 18-hour days. Really good meals every 6 hours. Air conditioning units in the heat. Extra rain gear. A real first aid person. Thank them. I know of a nonunion project where the business representative of the union came by and the crew declined to organize. The Key Grip told the rep, "We've been treated so well on this, we don't want to mess with them. They've been honest about the money, they've been consistent in how they're spending it, no one is getting a lot, and even the actors' trailers are pretty humble. We just want to leave them alone." Unusual, but it happens. In general, a crew will treat production—meaning the producer, the production manager, etc--in a way that directly reflects how they've been treated.

I have two former students, a director and producer, who were prepared to sacrifice for their passion project. They knew that they were not going to make money, and they were prepared to work very long hours. Their crew was not so passionate. After the second week of 16- and 18-hour days, someone on the crew called the business agent of the IATSE and invited him to visit and organize. The business agent arrived, the disgruntled crew was organized, and because they now had to pay union fringes or lose their crew and face the delay and expense of shutting down and finding an entirely different crew and starting up again, the filmmakers had no choice but to sign the union contract. This added approximately $35,000 to their already stretched budget. They finished the movie, barely, but they had no money for postproduction and music. They then had to spend the next several months raising that money, and the raise was harder this time because the original lenders/investors were not convinced that they wouldn't run out of funds for some other reason the second time around. Something to note: the crewmembers who called in the business agent from the union were not strangers—they had been friends and former classmates of the producer and director. They were just so overtired and had felt so used at that point that they didn't care. Thoughts of friendship went out the window. At the point that they organized, they were just an abused crew.

If you are a crewmember on a nonunion film, be sure that you get the terms of your deal in writing and that you understand what you're agreeing to. Once you make a deal, keep your side of the bargain. Don't make the mistake of thinking that you will get on a film and turn it. Don't try to use a production to get into the union. That backfires much more often than it works.

Chapter 17

Maybe We Should Go to Canada, or Someplace Else

WHERE TO SHOOT THE MOVIE

Your script is written for Wisconsin. It's a coming of age story. It's your story. Everything that happens in the script happened to you and taught you an important life lesson, and you are determined to replicate it all down to the last detail: that year, that town. It's your history.

But wait a minute. This is not a documentary. We're in the business of illusion here. We know that the dead bodies aren't really dead people. The talking animals can't really speak. Must you really shoot your movie in Oconomowoc, Wisconsin? I hope not, because it's probably not going to happen. Here are some reasons why:

There's no qualified local crew. You'd have to cover plane tickets, hotel, and per diem (daily expense money) for everyone, even the third company grip. You'd have to bring every piece of professional equipment in. You'd have to pay a great deal of money for all of the above, and that money would never show on screen but would reduce the available money to pay the actors and mount the movie, thus negatively affecting your *production value* (the visual quality of what is actually seen on screen). By insisting upon total veracity, you're undercutting the potential of your own film.

On the other hand, you want it to look like Wisconsin. What does Wisconsin look like? That depends on the town or city or neighborhood. Madison is a college town. There are areas of the state where dairy farms are rampant. The trick in deciding where to shoot a film is to have a strong sense of which visual elements sell the setting of your project, and to find those elements in a film-friendly location.

RUNAWAY PRODUCTION—WHY THEY WANT YOU THERE

Many countries, every state, and most major cities spend a lot of time and money trying to convince you to shoot on their turf. They have *Film Commissioners* (government representatives who interface with filmmakers and production companies). Why? Think of a block of forty otherwise vacant hotel rooms being rented for 30 to 70 days. Or a film cast and crew of approximately 50 people flush with spending money. Many of those people will direct deposit their weekly paycheck but spend all of their per diem at local restaurants, bars, and shops. Think of location rentals. Car and truck rentals. Film production is a clean (nonpolluting) industry, where a group of big spenders arrive and drop a bundle of cash. And how about the twenty locals who will be hired as assistants, carpenters, and sometimes as second- and third-tier crew labor. Since each trained local crewmember is one less person who must be transported and housed, the presence of trained locals can eventually attract other film companies to shoot there. In a matter of months the film people are gone, leaving a mini windfall of spending and possibilities behind them.

In this tough economic climate, states are looking for new sources of revenue, new services they can provide and employment opportunities for their residents. In the past few years states have created aggressive *incentive* programs—low-cost or no-cost shooting permits, discounts on each dollar spent, *rebate* programs, the ability to use public buildings and services for little or no charge, tax breaks tied to the number of local residents employed—to lure filmmakers away from the Los Angeles area. Some of these programs are simple. The production will get a certain percentage of cash back if they use qualifying local vendors, personnel, and accommodations. Some of them are more complicated. The productions get tax credits months after the project has been completed, and they can sell these credits to other productions in order to make money back for the film. These programs change frequently, some have *sunsets* (dates when they run out of money or cease entirely). *Runaway production* is the term used for projects (films, television series) that would ordinarily have shot in Southern California but have based themselves elsewhere because of the savings.

WHY YOU MIGHT WANT TO RUNAWAY

You want Wisconsin, but how about finding a place that looks and feels like Wisconsin yet where there is already experienced crew and equipment? The savings that result from shooting in a place that is economical in terms of local resources, access to crew and equipment, and general production conditions might buy you a higher-priced cast member, the location you love, a few additional shooting days. Let's say you find an extraordinary hotel deal for 30 crewmembers and 5 cast members—$40 per night including taxes. That's $1400 per night. If you have an average of 15 days of prep, a 20-day shoot, and an average of only 5 days wrap, we're talking 40 days. That's $56,000 on hotel. Airplane tickets? You get an amazing deal—$250 round trip for everyone. That's $8750. We won't even bother to figure out the per diem.

Now, if you find a location that looks or can be made to look right, and there is a local crew base, you will still bring your 5 cast members and pay their hotel and per diem (and if they are SAG members, you will have to travel them first class or *best available*). The Director, Producer, Production Manager, First AD,

Production Designer, and Cinematographer will also most likely travel, but they'll find their crews locally. That's 11 people traveling, being housed, and given per diem at a lot less expense than 30 people.

If you have limited funds, you may be able to avoid problems with unions if you shoot in states that are right to work (states that do not permit unions to run *closed shops*, or productions that shut out nonunion crewmembers) or that are just too far away from production centers for unions to bother to visit. Cities with heavy union affiliations are New York, Los Angeles, Boston, Chicago, Miami, San Francisco, and Las Vegas. Unless your budget is under $1,000,000, you will most likely not avoid unions in any of these locations.

Finally, when you shoot outside of the Los Angeles and New York area, the people you meet tend to be less jaded. They think having a movie made in their town is great, and they will often go out of their way to help.

WHY INVESTORS MIGHT WANT PROJECTS TO RUNAWAY

It's the money, honey. Say a film is budgeted for $5,000,000, but if you shoot it in Louisiana, it will cost $4,500,000 to make. That's a persuasive motivation to move production. If there is a competent crew available and an interesting visual landscape, your investors know that you can either save money or get more for your money by finding the right shooting location.

If a production is bringing a crew member or an actor to an out of town location, the production staff is minimally expected to supply a paid-for roundtrip plane ticket to and from location, and to find and pay for a safe, clean, pleasantly livable housing situation for each individual (no doubling up).The plane ticket will be economy class unless otherwise negotiated. (Production Designers and Cinematographers occasionally fly business or even first class. The Directors Guild contract requires that members—a DGA Director, UPM, First and Second ADs—are flown first class. The Screen Actors Guild requires productions to fly all SAG actors first class.)

If a crew or cast member is out of town for a project, they receive a per diem. Per diem is "per day" predetermined compensation for daily living expenses that would not be incurred if the person were working in his or her home city. Per diem is expected to cover any food other than the meals served on set, laundry, dry-cleaning, long-distance phone bills, etc. The actors and crew members are handed their per diem in cash, each week. The minimum per diem for members of the Screen Actors and Directors Guilds is set by the union contracts. The amount of the per diem for other staff and crew is dependent upon the cost of living in the location city. Crew members who are transported to shoot in Lincoln, Nebraska may receive $35 per day in spending money. Crew members sent to Manhattan may receive $75. Airfare, hotel, and per diem at the top end of the production food chain is a deal point. A major director or star may receive $500 per day in per diem, a suite at a luxury hotel, first class air tickets for themselves and their families, all in addition to their contractual acting or directing fee of $2 million. These details are worked out by a combination of the producer, lawyers for the studio or the production company, and the actor's or director's agent. Once determined and documented, these agreements are non-negotiable and become additional financial and scheduling factors in the preproduction plan.

Investors know all about this and how it mounts up. They may insist that a production shoots in a city with enough production resources that no one will have to be traveled, or they may want the script to be revised so that there is a way to make it work in a production center. Either way, it is all about seeing the investment up on the screen rather than in the pockets of the airlines and hotels. Financiers may want shooting to be near them, accessible for set visits. Anxious production executives may also want to be close so that they can keep an eye on what's going on. Filmmakers may not want that, because they want to avoid the added anxiety of working with "the suits" breathing down their necks.

If the film that was written for Philadelphia can be shot at less expense in another country, the filmmakers or financiers may come to the conclusion that due to the currency exchange rate, it may be worth it. If for every U.S dollar spent the production is receiving $1.20, this mounts up. On a million-dollar budget, you're looking at being able to afford an additional $20,000 of production value. On a $50,000,000 this obviously amounts to serious money.

Where to shoot can become a contentious issue. The creative camp will push the decision to shoot in the place written in the script, the argument being that the film will feel more genuine. The business camp usually pushes the production towards shooting wherever the film is likely to benefit by getting more value for the money.

Caution! You can't just jump head first into shooting in a place where there seems to be great savings. You must weigh the pros and cons. First and foremost, there is the story. What does the script call for? What do you actually see? If you're mostly interior, it may be more economical to shoot in Los Angeles. You won't have to travel anyone; you can pick up and drop off specialty equipment as needed rather than renting it all for an entire production; your cast is likely local, which makes scheduling easier. If the film takes place in an undefined location but you don't like the idea of everything looking like California, think about what California looks like. A good location manager can find areas where there are no freeways, Spanish architecture, palm trees, or agaves. You must use your imagination, rather than just accept "Southern California is the place," or "We absolutely have to shoot in Michigan because of the budget." There is never only one solution to a production problem.

If your film is set in the Arizona desert you're going to need at least some establishing shots that situate your story. If Connecticut or Louisiana works, go for it, but be sure that you know what you may be compromising. Shooting in Sacramento may be much more expensive than Los Angeles. You don't know until you've done the math.

The Pros and the Cons

Choices now exist that didn't before. At this moment, Michigan, Connecticut, Texas, Louisiana, and New Mexico all offer tempting financial incentives. The bad news is that many of these places have only one top shooting crew, and if there is more than one project shooting there you may get the B or even the C team. Also, although often Film Commissioners tout the resources of their state or city, unless you really investigate and speak to other filmmakers who have shot there before, you may be disappointed. You should keep in mind that incentive programs tend to change with each new incarnation of government, so the financial arrangement you are counting on can vanish with the next election. You must make sure the deal you're counting on is still in place.

At one time, due to the low cost of housing, labor, and individual situations with the unions, North Carolina, South Carolina, and Utah were all the "it" locations. Productions flocked to those states. Then other states began offering better deals, and productions looking for more for their dollars migrated to those new places.

SHOOTING OUTSIDE THE UNITED STATES

About twenty-five years ago, when a film was budgeted for a studio, the production manager who made the budget was usually asked to create two different financial plans. One was for the United States and one for Canada. The advantages of Canada were clear: English speaking, a favorable exchange rate (about $1.20 to every U.S. dollar), talented and experienced crews, a population of actors who could sound American, substantial provincial tax incentives, and union benefits less expensive than those in the United States.

Hundreds of films have been shot in Canada. Montreal plays Boston, Toronto doubles for New York, Vancouver is Seattle, parts of Calgary sub for the wide open spaces of the old West. Facilities in Canada are modern, and the style of filmmaking is the same as in the United States. It's easy, and there's little adaptation required. The catch is, you can't bring whoever you want to bring. The Canadian government wants U.S. productions but also wants employed Canadians. This means that in order to be a U.S. citizen and permitted to work on a film in Canada you must meet certain criteria: You must either have a unique talent (which covers the director and lead actors, and sometimes an award-winning production designer or DP), or be key management (i.e., the producer, and sometimes a line producer and accountant), or you must have a long-time history of a close working relationship with the U.S. director (i.e., a personal assistant, and sometimes a First Assistant Director who has worked with the director on several films). The Canadian government assumes that an incoming film production can find pretty much everybody else they need in Canada, and they are right. The producer and director may not be thrilled to have to break up teams and get used to people they don't know, but that's part of the deal and they do it. (The same thing happens in reverse. The United States is as tough or tougher on foreign filmmakers who want to bring their people in to shoot and will issue work visas for even fewer key personnel.)

As the global economic picture evolves, there are more countries that periodically become the hot spots for U.S. production. For a while everyone was shooting in the Czech Republic, then in Hungary, then Bulgaria. It's mostly but not all financial. There are some types of locations that are easier to find outside the United States. Need a medieval castle? They're all over Eastern Europe. Cape Cod 15 years ago? Nova Scotia. The style of working varies from one country to another. Canada is very similar to the United States, but in Bulgaria there are no unions, no child labor restrictions. Every country has different safety requirements and some have none. In France the crews work what we in the United States call (logically) *French hours*. The shoot day is 10 hours long, there is no overtime, and no one stops shooting to sit down and eat a meal. There is an ongoing buffet, and the crew eats and works at the same time. In some countries, it is necessary and expected that the Production Manager will set aside a thick packet of cash for *gratuities* (bribes).

Recently there has been a bit of a backlash. Runaway production has cut so substantially into the livelihoods of Hollywood workers that unions and production-dependent businesses have been actively lobbying for tax breaks and incentives for projects shooting in Los Angeles. Filming will go where the savings are, and that will in turn affect the crew employment picture. Production is always looking for the next great deal. Many crew people from Los Angeles bought property in Wilmington, Charlotte, and Salt Lake, hoping to be able to better their quality of life as the cost of living in those cities is far less expensive than in Los Angeles, and still work in their chosen field. A few years later, they had houses and lifestyles they loved but not as much work when the production boom moved on.

One More Thing You Should Know

Although it depends on the union and the particular agreement, on a union show that's shooting on location with non-local cast and crew, often the work day begins when the group leaves the hotel and ends when they return. This means that if you have brought a SAG actor from Los Angeles to Omaha and the actor is staying at the Holiday Inn, the actor is on the clock the minute his car or bus leaves the hotel, and stays on the clock until he is dropped off at the end of the day. If your location is an hour away, this means that you're paying for a lot of transportation (not acting) time. If your actor is being picked up at the hotel at 7:00 am to be in hair and makeup at 8:00, and if you break for lunch from 1:00 to 2:00 pm, the actor will reach his time and a half rate at 4:00 pm and his double time at 8:00 pm. So you will be paying for an hour each way of travel, not work. For films with lots of non-local cast and crew, this effectively transforms your 12-hour shoot day into a 10-hour day.

BUT I DON'T WANT TO LIVE IN A PRODUCTION CENTER

A Cautionary Tale: Mike was a film school grad. He wanted to be in the film business, but he also wanted to live in his hometown, Boston. He decided that he would watch for any film projects coming to shoot in the New England area, start at the bottom, work in any capacity he possibly could to get experience, and he would build his out-of-town (in this case, Los Angeles) contacts by working with incoming non-local productions at any level he could. Mike built a solid career as a production assistant, then as an Assistant Director. He worked on local commercials, music videos, even some locally made low-budget films. He got into the local union and made a decent living, but he found that jobs on the big films that came into town constantly eluded him.

The problem is this: Directors almost always insist on bringing their First Assistant Directors to location. A director wants someone he or she knows, someone who has dealt with big stars, egos, etc. The First AD starts work so early in the process (long before everyone leaves for location prep) that the studio rarely pushes the idea of hiring a local for the job. The cost of bringing someone in to Los Angeles from the distant location and housing and giving them a per diem so that they can work with the director to properly prepare the project, then traveling them back,would offset some of the potential savings. And a First AD from out-of-town might not want to hire a local First AD as a Second AD, even if the local First is willing, because they might then face resentment from the local crew for temporarily demoting one of their own. Either way, Mike was not an insider, and it was going to be difficult for him to find a way onto the inside track when it came to doing what he wanted to do.

On the other hand ... Tracey is from Atlanta. She moved to Los Angeles just out of school. She worked her way up from Production Assistant to Location Assistant, eventually becoming a highly paid and respected Location Manager. She worked on studio films, some of which shot in the South, where she worked as a local, staying with family and eventually renting an apartment when she needed to. The years passed and Tracey wanted to move home. She decided that she'd prefer to live where she had a close knit support network of old friends and family. She told everyone she knew in the business about her plan. She contacted Film Commissioners all over the region. She'd made a point of getting to know them well, keeping in touch even when she didn't need their help. She moved back home and became one of the "go to" people for locations throughout the South. She was able to have her cake and eat it too. Her secret was that she'd built her contacts in L.A., and she knew the directors, producers, production managers, and production designers. These are the folks who make the decisions about hiring the location manager. She became a major asset to productions headed South. She knew what they needed, knew the locals, and could recommend the best crew. She knew her locations inside and out, and had contacts all over. She ended up with a thriving film career in her hometown, but it took her twelve years to get it. She brought value added for the people who hired her. She was an L.A.-experienced location person who happened to live out of L.A.—an insider who lived outside.

A Second Cautionary Tale: Ali always worked with Pete. Ali was a Production Coordinator, Pete was a Production Manager/Line Producer. Ali had worked with Pete on 11 films and they were a great team. Then Pete got the call to work on a huge film, shooting in Russia and the Czech Republic. It would keep him busy for more than a year. The government would allow him to come in because he had an Associate Producer title and would be hiring local Production Managers to work under him in both countries. These Production Managers had their own Coordinators. The government of both countries would not give Ali a work permit. There were local Production Coordinators who were available. Pete couldn't turn the job down, and he couldn't bring Ali. Ali was in a situation where she had worked nonstop for Pete and didn't know other Production Managers. She spent the next six months out of work, looking for work, trying to meet other Production Managers. After half a year, she got a call to work on a television series and she grabbed it. She was still working on the series when Pete returned from his travels. He called her to say he had his next film, and he wanted her to leave the series and work on his movie. Ali had learned her lesson. She didn't leave the series, didn't burn those new bridges, and when the series wrapped, she called Pete along with the several other Production Managers she'd met during her period of unemployment. She sent them her updated resume and spent the next month trying to meet even more potential employers. Pete was disappointed but not upset. He understood. Ali continued to be his first call for every project he did. If she was available, she took the job.

As a freelance crew person, you often work in teams. You're a grip, and the DP likes you and hires you every time he can. You're a Production Coordinator who has such a good relationship with a Production Manager that you call him or her before you take a job with someone else, just to see if there's something coming up. You're a Set Decorator who has worked with the same Production Designer nonstop for three years. The PD tells you what an important part of her team you are and to call her before you even think of taking a picture with someone else. The upshot of all this devotion and admiration is that you wait or you turn down other offers in order to work with your favorite, and then you feel betrayed when they head off to Melbourne, Australia for six months to do a film. They're sorry but they can't take you.

It's not that they don't mean all that they say. They are making promises they can't keep. Often a department head will be hired but told that due to budgetary or government restrictions, they must hire a local crew. It's not negotiable. They love you but they've got to leave you. Were you a fool to believe in their loyalty? No. When they can, they'll bring you. Sometimes there are political reasons they can't hire you even locally. The Director insists on his girlfriend. An executive knows you from summer camp and doesn't like you. It can be that random, but unless the department head has a lot of weight to throw around and he or she is willing to wage this particular battle, you aren't going to get the job. What can you do? Work for a lot of people. Spread yourself around. Get to know as many potential employers as possible and dazzle them all with your competence. Don't sit around waiting for the phone to ring as if you're waiting for a date to call. Even if you're working as a Best Boy for your favorite Key and a job comes up as a Company Electrician, if you're not working, take it! That's one more contact, one more person who will think to call you—and maybe as a Best Boy next time his BB isn't available. You're self-employed, a free agent. If your regular person calls and you're not available, maybe you'll seem even more valuable. Or maybe he or she won't call again. Do you really want to be relying on only one person for your entire career? This person makes more money than you do. What if he or she decides to take a break from the business? What if your DP decides he's going to take the next year off to give a directing career a shot?

Get yourself out there.

Chapter 18

Who Is in Your Movie

The deciding factor as to whether or not a movie is funded is often the leading actors. With box office and DVD earnings down, casting is immensely important now more than ever. Outside of a few very successful and famous directors (Spielberg, Scorsese, Bay, Fincher, Cameron) only a tiny portion of the general movie-going public says, "I'm going to see the new [insert director's name here] film." Most everyone says, "I want to see Seth Rogan . . . Angelina Jolie . . . Matt Damon." In the independent world Ryan Gosling will probably get your movie made. He draws an audience. The marketers have something to market. There are no guarantees, but stars are as close as an investor or a distributor can get to being sure that there will be at least a sizeable population potentially interested in seeing your movie.

THE CASTING DIRECTOR

The Casting Director finds, secures, and negotiates for talent. A Casting Director is expected to be familiar with the work and ability of all actors, already known or still unknown, and to have the contacts to get a script to the actor's agent and/or manager for consideration. The Casting Director will hold countless auditions and readings to winnow down the list of "possibles," then arrange for the Director to see the few actors that most accurately reflect the quality of performance and appearance required for each role, no matter how minor.

These days, it is almost always necessary for one or two of the lead actors to be found and signed to a contract in order for preproduction cash to be released, so the Casting Director is often hired long before the film is officially green lit.

A Casting Director is a freelance employee and usually has his or her own company, offices, and staff. A Casting Director is hired for the run of production but is often working on more than one film at once. When casting a lead, the producer and director will generally want an actor with a name that means something at the box office but also who is someone capable of bringing something fresh and significant to the role. A Casting Director must not only have a sense of who is talented and recognized, but who is a good fit for the film, who is available, who will sell tickets, and who the production can afford. A Casting Director can't just show a list of the same old names. It is about having the instinct to see something new in an old standby or having the nerve to push a director to take a meeting with a phenomenal unknown who is perfect, then surrounding that unknown with talented veteran performers cast in roles they wouldn't normally play (*casting against type*). A great Casting Director is a creative partner to the director and can help make or break a movie.

Finding a Casting Director

You're a young director with just enough money to make your first project. You know it's of primary importance that you attract a great cast. You need the money to make the movie. How can you get your script to an actor who will mean something to your investors and help you get funding and distribution?

Find a casting director. Don't look in the phone book. Ask your contacts, get on line and see who has cast films of the same type and scale and budget as your film. You'd be surprised how many casting directors are willing to meet, read your script, and help out at a fraction of their normal rate. If they like the script, they may want to be a part of the project. They may want to meet an up-and-coming filmmaker who will have a rosy future and who will remember who came to their rescue before they were anybody.

A casting director will sometimes have enough faith in the director and the project that she will charge less than her usual fee but ask for a backend deal—a percentage of any profits. Or he may have producing aspirations and want to take the project on at a discounted rate in exchange for some kind of producing credit. Think of doing this only with an Associate Producer credit if you're giving one away. Donating a Co-Producer or Producer credit can undermine the real producer. You're going to have to rely on the producer to fight your battles, and to stick with you through discouraging times for not much financial reward. Tossing Producer credits around has lately become common, but it has come back to bite directors of small, independent films. They find out that they have given away a bit of control of their own project to someone who has more contacts and more clout then they do, and the real producer who got the project up to the starting line is too beat up and disappointed in the experience to help them get it back.

If you find a casting director who doesn't have the time to take on the project but who really likes the script, ask if he or she has an experienced assistant who might be ready to cast your film. Often an assistant will be thrilled to take a step up on a small film, and because the company will receive credit on the movie, the Casting Director will mentor or supervise the assistant to be sure that everything is kept on track.

CASTING FOR FUNDING AND DISTRIBUTION

Your script is original, exciting. You've managed to attract an experienced and well-respected Casting Director. The Casting Director wants to know how much you've budgeted for cast. You've budgeted little because you have little.

You're hoping that your cast, like your buddies on the crew, will work for free or for not much more than minimum wage. Here's the problem: your potential marketing and distribution people don't care if they recognize the name of the DP or the Editor or Sound Designer. Festival programmers don't care who the Costume Designer is. They can work for free or for minimum wages. No one is going to distribute your film based on those people. As for your actors . . . there should be at least one recognizable name in a major role. There should be one just-about-to-be-a-hot commodity that reviewers will mention and insiders will know. A familiar face and name. When people speak about your film you don't want to hear:

"Sounds interesting. Who's in it?"

"Nobody you've heard of."

Let's look at investors. You find someone with money. They read the script. It's a thriller with a twist. They like it. They tell you, "I might be interested." Their next question—or the next question after, "How much do you have so far?"—will be, "Who's going to be in it?" If you say, "Well . . . we don't know yet. Some really talented actors we've seen in showcases" or, "The actors we used in our student film that won all those awards," they will say, "Well, let us know when you've got someone good and we'll think about it." If you say, "We're in talks with So and So who cast *ABC* [successful indie film], and she says she wants to go for X or Y for the male lead and Z for the female, and maybe J for the mom—she's worked with them before and thinks they're available in our time frame and will like the script . . ."

See my point? Expecting to raise substantial funds to make an independent film with complete unknowns is rough going. The amazing thing about many mid-range working actors is that they love to act, and as long as they aren't turning down something that will pay them big money in order to be in your film, if they love the script and have confidence in the director, there's a good chance that they'll do it. The trick is to have a professional casting person with his or her finger on who may be willing and available, and the kind of relationships with agents and managers where he or she can persuade them to help rather than stand in the way of the cause. (Ten percent of a rock bottom salary is nothing. Unless the agent or manager falls in love with the script and sees it as an opportunity for their client to step outside the box and shine, why would they advise their client to make a super-low-budget film with an untested producer and director? How would that be good management?)

If you're lucky enough to attract interest from an agency that will package the film, you will be expected to cast your leads from an actor pool that they have approved. They will help you get your script to the actors they are interested in folding into the package. If you come to them with actors already attached (contractually committed) that can either benefit or be to the detriment of getting your project funded. If they like your attachments, they may be willing to put the considerable clout of the agency behind the project, helping with finding investors, working to involve more of their clients. If they don't like your attachments, they may be unwilling to move forward at all.

These days, with the international market bringing in about two thirds of a film's revenue, North American audiences are only one piece of the puzzle. An experienced Casting Director knows whose name means something in Europe, Asia, and Latin America. It's not always who you might think. Casting with the global picture in mind can help you with investors and may help entice actors who are established elsewhere in the world but want to make inroads into the U. S. market.

Distributors care about your cast. They want to be able to sell your movie. What can they tell people about it? Who can they get to attend a screening? How can they convince buyers to pay attention to the festival buzz? Which is better, "It won the Audience Award," or "It won the Audience Award and stars the guy who was in X independent film that made a lot of money"?

When you get to the bigger budgets, cast is still important. Cast is one of the elements that can transform a studio No into a Yes. It's not just a case of who is in your movie at that stage—it's who is in the movie, and are they playing a role audiences will want to see them play. The accepted wisdom at studios is sometimes that the public wants to see their favorite actors in one type of role only. That is until the actor breaks out and triumphs playing a completely different type of character—usually in a lower budget indie. This is good news for you. It only takes one Best Actor nomination to persuade lots of working actors who are trying to stretch their industry-imposed boundaries to give a smaller independent film a chance.

If you are a first-time director and your Casting Director is able to attract someone with a name, you may be concerned about whether you will be able to work effectively with someone who ranks higher up than you. You may be worried about the actor trying to take control of the film. That has happened occasionally. But if you are a director with a clear head and a dynamic vision, and if you don't pretend to be more than you are, the collaboration can be great. Don't worry about control. Worry about the film. Give the actor some space, plan to allow him time to let him try his ideas. Don't be stubborn, but know when to draw the line. If you have a veteran Producer, she can assist you in working through a potentially difficult situation. Most actors only try to fill a void of authority when there is no authority. After all, it is their name and face up there on the screen. Be calm, certain, and defer to what the film (not *you*, the film) needs, and usually it will be fine. In the end, the presence of the name actor will help you sell the film, and that's worth a lot of tact.

THE SCREEN ACTORS GUILD

The Screen Actors Guild is the union that covers actors, stunt people, on-camera musicians, singers, and dancers for film. Several years ago, SAG expanded its membership charter to also encompass *background actors* (extras). If a production is signatory to SAG, it commits the production to abiding by SAG compensation guidelines and working conditions. It also requires the production to pay benefits, provide Workers Compensation insurance for the actors, and to agree to pay *residuals* (compensation tied to the broadcasting and DVD rentals of the project when and if it is distributed and exhibited.)

Filmmakers with little money will look on the SAG website and panic when they see the minimum daily compensation for an eight-hour work day (and there are really no eight-hour days in production) and the benefits that add another 14 to 16 percent on to that amount. How can you possibly afford to hire SAG actors? How can you hope to cast a recognizable face and name?

Look further. At *sagindie.org* you will find the numerous agreements that SAG has developed for low-budget films. The compensation on those films ranges from *deferred* (no upfront money but fees to be paid later out of profits if any are forthcoming) to $504 for eight hours. Each *low-budget agreement* (signatory contract) is geared towards a different scale of production, from under $250,000 to under $2.5 million, and the wages, benefits, and working condition requirements are proportionate to each budget level. Every SAG member is permitted to work on any film that is signatory to any SAG Agreement. That doesn't mean that they will agree to work for the minimum, but it does mean that their union allows them to. Actors take their SAG membership and the protection it affords them very seriously. Many SAG actors will work for little pay if the circumstances are right, but they will not work on non-SAG signatory projects. Many reputable casting directors and talent agents would not dream of encouraging actors to work on a production that is not SAG signatory. Working under a SAG Agreement—it doesn't matter which one—is the credible way to go.

HOW DOES AN ACTOR GET INTO SAG?

Actors want to join SAG. If you work enough to earn the benefits, they are good. There are also informational seminars, workshops, and opportunities that are available only to SAG members. But an actor can't just join up. As is the case with the other unions, you must be *SAG-eligible*. You must be hired to work on a film or project that is signatory to SAG. Once you are hired, you must contact your local SAG office immediately and submit proof of this employment. You will sign an agreement, pay a membership fee, and from then on you will be responsible for paying your membership dues and for abiding by SAG rules.

Let's say you're not a SAG member and you happen to be working in a store where a SAG project is shooting. The director thinks that the scene is missing something. Maybe it needs a cashier who speaks a couple of lines about the purchase that the lead character is making. You're not an actor, and you have no intention of becoming one. Can you still speak the lines, have your moment of fun in the Hollywood sun and not join the union? Yes. You can do it once. You say your lines, have a good time, and the Second Assistant Director will help you fill out a form and ask you to sign it. This document is a *Taft-Hartley* form, which among other things, severs as a permit for a non-union worker to temporarily be hired in a position that is normally filled by a union actor. The Assistant Director will send the form to the production office. It will then be forwarded on to the film's SAG representative. The SAG rep will file the information in the SAG database, and you will be on record as having been Taft-Hartley-ed. If the chance to speak in a SAG project comes up again, you will be a *must join*, which means exactly what it says. You can't be Taft-Hartley-ed more than once, and you can no longer be in a SAG project unless you pay your fees and become a member.

DEALS

As stated, SAG actors work under a variety of contracts, depending upon the budget level of the film. Once your budget tops out of the low-budget realm, there are a variety of contract choices available. For instance, you might hire an actor as a *Day Player* (Schedule A) contract, a *Weekly Player* (Schedule C), or as a *Schedule F* (Contract) player. (Schedule F players generally earn much more than any of the other choices.) Schedule in this context means a schedule (list) of rates and conditions. These schedules reflect the parameters of a specific type of contract. (For example, Day Players go into overtime after 8 hours, Weekly Players hit overtime after 10 hours.)

Another casting deal term you should know is *pay or play*, as in, someone has a pay-or-play deal. This means that this person is guaranteed his salary even if the film is not made. Pay-or-play deals come up when an actor is hired for a film that does not have a firm start date. This serves to tie the actor to a project. It's reassuring for financiers and investors to see that a known name is committed even as all the other details of the film are being sorted out. A pay or play is a major financial commitment and helps the actor feel secure that the film is actually going to happen and that he they won't be badly off if he turns down other offers. If an actor is receiving a pay-or-play offer, he must be worth it. He must have enough name value that it will impact the funding or green-lighting of the film. Otherwise, why would a production risk the money? If the film isn't made or is postponed beyond a certain date, that actor must still be paid.

THE SAG BOND

If you are making an independent film with SAG actors, a condition of your film becoming a signatory and therefore enabling you to hire SAG actors will be that the production company puts up a SAG bond. This means that the production company must come up with a percentage of the total cost of the cast payroll plus health and pension benefits. That percentage is held in an account until the last SAG actor is paid the last penny she is owed for her role in the film, and until SAG has received all the required benefits payments. Once the film is completed and SAG verifies that the correct amount of money has been paid in, the percentage is released back to the production company. The requirement for this bond often comes as a shock to first-time filmmakers. Although they have budgeted to pay the actors and the fringes, they haven't counted on having this additional money sitting idle in an account until after production has finished. It can take months for a production to completely reconcile the account with SAG, so filmmakers should earmark the money that will finally be released for expenses that need to be covered months into postproduction.

BACKGROUND ACTORS

Background actors are also members of the Screen Actors Guild. A *background actor* speaks no lines. The minute a background actor has a line, he or she is upgraded to *actor* and is paid as such. Background action (a stadium full of cheering fans, a bar full of frat boys downing shots, school kids strolling behind the teenaged leads as they're falling in love) is intended to lend authenticity to a scene. If the action works, it is both effective and unobtrusive. If it's done poorly, it can throw off the feel of the scene. When background actors are used wisely, the action can enhance the look of the project. In an attempt to save money, many first-time filmmakers miss the point. They dismiss the production value of background actors. A scene that is supposed to take place in a downtown area at rush hour looks bare and unconvincing without a rush of pedestrians and traffic. The audience may not know why the scene looks phony and amateurish, but they do consciously register that something is not right and stop believing your movie.

There are nonunion background actors, and they make up the bulk of the crowds and the audience in the auditorium. Depending on the budget level of your film and whether it is a theatrical feature or a television series, the SAG Agreement dictates that a production must employ a certain number of SAG background actors before it hires nonunion actors. For example, for your stadium scene you may need five hundred screaming fans. The SAG Agreement may require that the first 50 of those fans are members of the union, to be paid SAG wages. The other 450 may be nonunion, working for minimum wage.

Background actors are paid through a voucher system. If only 49 of the 50 contracted background actors show up on set, the Assistant Director is permitted to make up the difference by upgrading a nonunion background to work as SAG background for the day. If a nonunion person collects three upgrade vouchers, he or she can apply for SAG membership.

How Are Background Actors Cast?

A casting person who casts speaking roles does not cast background actors. There are several background casting companies in Hollywood and New York, and background actors are their specialty. They have literally thousands of photos and contacts on file. After the Assistant Director breaks down the script, there is a discussion about how many if any background actors will be needed for each scene. A description of those background actors is sent to the extras casting company. For a Malibu beach scene, the Assistant Director may call the company and order 15 athletic-looking 20- to 40-year-old guys with tans, and 20 women ages 17 to 35 of varying ethnicities, 5 middle-aged privileged-looking couples, and a couple of kids. The AD will give a scene-by-scene list and a tentative schedule for the entire shoot to the casting company, and will let them know under which SAG Agreement the project is working so that the company will know how many SAG and how many non-SAG background to book. The company casting person will comb the files for potential background actors and make some preliminary calls. The costume designer will tell the AD what to tell the company regarding what people should be wearing and if they should bring more than one change of wardrobe. (Background actors receive a small salary *bump* for bringing extra changes of clothing.) A day or two before the actual scene is scheduled to shoot, the AD will confirm with the casting representative and let him or her know where and when the background actors are expected to show up.

On the day of the shoot, the background actors report to the Second Assistant Director who takes their vouchers, does a count, deals with whatever upgrades will happen if they are necessary. They are then usually ushered to an *extras holding area*, a space set aside for background. There is food, a place to sit. A costume person checks out their clothing, possibly makes some adjustments or chooses which of the two outfits they brought they are going to wear. Then they wait until they are needed on set.

Background actors are not given direction by the director, and in fact the director is not supposed to even speak to them. The AD positions them, tells them "walk here," "smile and wave," "cheer," and they are often timed to a signal—"when the guy in the red sweater crosses the street, group A should start walking the other way." The background is not supposed to be noticeable, just a backdrop to the main action. Background actors who call attention to themselves on camera are not rehired.

At the end of the day, the vouchers with the hours worked are sent into the Production Office. The Accountant tallies the money owed, adds in the casting company's fee, and a check is sent. The company pays the benefits into SAG for the SAG background actors, doesn't pay them for the non-union extras, and sends each background actor an individual check reflecting pay for the hours worked.

Kids

State labor laws governing the use of actors who are minors (under eighteen) are detailed and strict. The health and safety of a minor is the most important consideration and is emphasized above all concerns of production. A state licensed *studio teacher* or *welfare worker* (a teacher who has been specially trained and certified in the laws regarding minors in the entertainment industry) must be on set whenever a minor is present. A studio teacher is the final word regarding what is or is not appropriate for the minor to do and be around. The studio teacher on set has more power than the parent or guardian of the minor, and more power than the producer or director where the working conditions of a minor is concerned.

A minor must have a valid, up-to-date work permit, and the production company casting the minor must obtain a *permit to employ minors* from the Labor Board. This is the case even if your minor is a volunteer and not being compensated. Working a minor without a permit is against the law, and it is considered negligent and in some cases reckless endangerment of a minor. These are serious charges, and you shouldn't fool around and try to duck any of the responsibilities that accompany the use of minors in your projects.

A minor's work hours are strictly regulated and are dependent upon his or her age. The hours a minor can be on the set of a production is divided into working time (time actually on set), school time (when the studio teacher works with the minor in a separate, quiet area so that the minor keeps up with his or her schoolwork), and rest and recreation (play time). Even if the minor is not working on a school day, he or she must at all times be accompanied by a welfare worker, whose job it is to be sure that the minor is being treated well, not being subjected to anything that might be risky either physically, emotionally, or mentally.

Working with a minor can play havoc with your shooting schedule. It is difficult to predict how well the minor will do under the pressure of shooting or how long his or her attention span will hold up after several takes. For a director, working with a minor can be frustrating, because although many child actors are quite mature and professional, they are still kids who may or may not understand the nuances required for the scene. A director who is patient and can communicate well with kids will get a better performance than one who decides that the child actor is a miniature adult and does not modulate his or her way of working to adapt to the age and life experience of the child.

Cautionary Tale: Robert was a young, inexperienced director who sought a touching and genuine performance from his 12-year-old actor, Josh. The script called for the boy to steal something. Robert asked Josh if he had ever shoplifted anything. He said, "No, that's against the law." Robert asked him if he'd ever been tempted to shoplift something. Later that day, Robert asked his equally inexperienced producer to approach the manager of the store where they were going to shoot. The Producer said, "At the start of the day, I'm going to bring a little boy in and he's going to steal something. I'll pay you for it. We want him to get the feeling of what it would be like to want something so badly and not be able to afford it and then decide it would be OK to steal it." The store manager agreed. Josh was told to go in and steal something. He was told that the shopkeeper didn't know anything about it, but it would be OK because they would go back and pay for it right away. The boy stole a game and left the store. The Producer paid the shopkeeper. Then the boy's mother and the studio teacher heard about it. "You told him it would be OK to *steal*? What kind of idiot are you?" When the director explained that he wanted Josh to understand what it was like to feel the way the character did, the mom shouted, "He's an actor. He's got more experience acting than you have directing! He understands the difference between reality and acting! Do you?" Everyone was upset, angry, or embarrassed—except for Josh who thought the director was kind of dumb.

Another Cautionary Tale: Stephanie wanted her young actress to dissolve into frightened tears. She told her to pretend that her mom had died and was in a coffin. Enough said.

AN ACTOR'S LIFE

Imagine that you've discovered the thing you love doing more than anything else in the world. You know that your chances of succeeding are really low, that most actors are never able actually to support themselves as actors. You have a degree in Theatre or Film or Literature, you've taken workshops in voice and dance, invested in photos, studied with a teacher known as a guru and mentor to the greats. Now all you need is a shot. You're waiting tables or bartending or working at being a barista, doing whatever you can to be able to afford living in New York or L.A. so that you can be available for the audition that could set you on the path you desperately want to walk. Then after years of paying your dues, working on bad films for bad pay, scrimping and struggling, just when you feel that you're getting somewhere, you're seasoned and have polished your craft—you really get it—you're told that you are looking a little worn around the edges and audiences like their actors young and pretty.

It's not an easy life. Actors—not stars, mind you, but regular working-class actors—are not unlike all the other people out there trying to make a film. Why, then, do so many filmmakers who themselves are just starting out treat actors so badly? I've had actors tell me that they've been kept waiting at readings for hours, that they've missed a day of work to audition only to be told that the time had changed and no one called them. They've had their weight loudly commented on, been told that they weren't sexy/attractive/talented enough. They've been called in to read for something unpaid without having been told that in advance and given the choice as to whether or not to come. And on set they've been told in minute detail—down to a grimace—what they should do, how they should move. They've been scolded in front of the other cast and crew for blowing a line. Worst of all they've had directors say, "Do it this way," and ask them to repeat the words and tone exactly as they had before.

Here's the thing—actors are charming, canny, and insecure. They've committed to living a life in front of people on a screen several feet high and wide. They can tap into an emotion they felt when they were 10 years old, and it can bring tears to their eyes and to yours. To paraphrase a famous quote, "Actors are different. They're not like you and me." Actors must feel respected and safe, which means okay with being vulnerable—in order to emotionally and psychically go to wherever it is they have to go in order to bring a role to life. They have a skill in the same way your DP has a skill, but if your DP has a sleepless night, no one tells him, "You'd better watch it, you don't look like a kid anymore." An actor has to trust the script, the director, the hair, makeup, and costume department, and the DP, because his or her face and body is part of what he or she brings to the job. Actors can save you or ruin you. They are perhaps the most important element in the film.

A final cautionary tale about working with actors: Several years ago, a relatively unknown young actress (I can't tell you her name for reasons that will become evident) was cast in a supporting role on a film. The producer and director thought she was beautiful, talented, likable but overweight. (She was actually fairly slim but tall, big-boned, broad shouldered—not a dainty little thing.) When she got the part, they sent her the customary gift basket full of goodies, but all the treats were the diet versions. Imagine a beautiful girl in her very uncertain early twenties who's been cast in a pivotal role (hurray!); she opens the door expecting flowers, and instead sees diet soda and sugar-free candy. They set this woman up. She worried obsessively about unflattering camera angles, asked everyone on set and off, "How did I look?" and that insecurity colored what should have been an amazing experience. Even with all that, she did a wonderful job and about a year later she was offered the lead in what was soon to become a huge box office success. She became a star. I'm told that she never took a call from or spoke to either the producer or director again, even though they insisted to everyone who would listen that she would be nowhere without them.

Chapter 19

Prep

Now that you've got your lead cast, and you know where you're going to be shooting—and whether or not you'll be a union show—you have a lot more information than you did. As the *preproduction* (*prep*) period begins in earnest, more decisions about the film will be made. As more information comes in, the UPM will adjust the budget and the First Assistant Director will adjust the schedule. The final bottom line (total anticipated expenditure) of the budget can't end up radically different than the first pass, because the first pass is often the basis of the decision as to whether or not to go forward and make the film. If the production shoots many more days than anticipated, the cost goes up proportionally. Fewer days, and the cost is reduced. The UPM and the First AD are hired in part due to their expertise in managing time and money, and it is expected that a film will shoot for the amount of days originally scheduled and will cost very close to the original budget. One hears stories on DVD bonus features about projects going hugely over budget, and one reads gossip about films that are out of control, but you're hearing about these films because they are unusual. The people supervising projects with massive overages rarely get a chance to repeat their mistakes.

THE PROCESS

As hard as it may be to think this way, a film is the finished product of a physical manufacturing process. Imagine a company that makes luxury automobiles. The company goes through a development process, researches the market, decides which design is most likely to achieve success. What kind of car does the public want right now? Why do some models succeed while other perfectly functional designs fail? How much money does the company want to risk on this new automobile? When can it be previewed at car shows? Once the company decides to make a certain model, the powers that be figure out the most efficient, most economic way to do it while maintaining a high level of safety and quality. Then they begin production.

Before anyone gets too upset—you and I know it's not the same! A movie is an artistic enterprise. It's blood and guts and laughter and tears, not a car. If we didn't believe that, we wouldn't want to be filmmakers. The actual process, though, is a mashup of creative, business, and logistical concerns.

Everyone wants to make the best movie possible with the resources available. It is the Producer's and Unit Production Manager's jobs to make sure that happens.

There is no standing factory already set up for whichever model is coming down the line. Making a film is both a labor- and materials-intensive process. The requirements of producing every film vary, and the magnitude of the undertaking involves the management of millions of dollars. For all these reasons, once the decision is made to move ahead with production, the UPM is often the first person hired on the production side.

Regarding the creative side—what's become of the Screenwriter? The Screenwriter may or may not still be around at this point. If the script is ready to shoot, he or she may be completely done with the project. If there are revisions anticipated, a screenwriter will meet with the Producer and Director but will almost never be a presence during production. His or her job is done. The mantle of the vision for the project is passed to the Director, and it is unusual for the writer to be anywhere near prep, casting, or the set.

A slight digression: The writers in the feature film world work very differently from the episodic television world. In television, writers are often producers, and it is almost always their voice that holds sway. On episodic television shows, once the feel of the program is set, the directors are virtually hired hands. They come and go, one directing episode #1 while another is prepping episode #2. In television there is a producing position called a *Show Runner*. It's this person's responsibility to maintain a consistently effective show, and the Show Runner ultimately has both creative and financial responsibility. In feature films, though, it's the Director's vision all the way.

When preproduction starts up we have a core group: Producer, Director, UPM, First Assistant Director, the Production Accountant, the Production Coordinator.

THE FIRST HIRES

There was a time in the 1980s and 90s when box office receipts were so high, and sales to network and then cable television and profits from video and DVD rentals were so lucrative, that although there was studio and production company oversight on productions, there existed a little bit of a laissez-faire attitude of "ask the right questions, hire the right people, then give them the money and let them go make the movie."

As the profit picture has changed, the oversight of financiers has become more active than it ever was. These days, everyone working at a high level on a movie expects to be accountable not just when things go wrong but when things are working well. The people paying for the production expect to be listened to rather than humored, brought in to the mix rather than manipulated. They are often well schooled about who is supposed to do what and who is responsible for protecting their investment both creatively and financially.

Production offices are rented almost as soon as a project is green lit. The offices are ideally in a building or hotel on location with options for expandable and collapsible space so the production is only paying for the rooms it is actually using. A production may start out with five or six offices, and during the height of prep expand to ten offices, plus a Costume warehouse, an Art department space, and a Construction area. Once production begins, the Costume department will be working out of a trailer, so that office closes. Once the last set is built, the Construction department will often begin to downsize, because it takes fewer people and less space to *strike* (disassemble and dispose of) sets than construct and erect them.

When the decision has been made as to where the film will be shot and under which union agreements, the UPM will begin interviewing below-the-line crew. If the Director consistently works with a particular Production Designer, then the UPM will negotiate that contract. If the Director is hoping to work with someone new, the UPM will contact below-the-line agents or make calls to his or her contacts to compile a list of potential Designers for the Producer and Director to meet. The UPM will have already ascertained that these Designers are both available and have experience working on films within the budgetary range of the project. The UPM will go through the same process if the Director doesn't have a Cinematographer as a regular member of his or her crew, or if they are not available.

The UPM might also be negotiating with the various film unions and guilds, purchasing production insurance, hiring a caterer, and securing airfare and hotel deals if there is going to be any kind of travel during the production.

Once the Production Designer is hired, there will be meetings with the Location Manager, who will be searching for the shooting sites. The PD will choose his or her support crew, and the UPM will negotiate their deals. As locations are found, approved by the PD and the Director, the Art Department will begin to help to realize the Production Designer's fashioning of a design plan, a color palette, an overall visual style.

While this is all happening, the Casting Director is setting up meetings for the Director to meet the actors who are in serious contention for all of the roles not yet cast. The Casting Director is anxious for the First AD to produce a final production schedule, because without it, cast deals can not be finalized. The First AD is meeting with the Director, anxiously awaiting the results of scouts done by the Location Manager and approved by the Production Designer and the Director, because without locations it's impossible to create a locked schedule. The Location Manager is hoping for a locked schedule as soon as possible so that his or her deals can be made and contracts signed. It's a codependent system, and the ultimate decisions rest on the Director's priorities—this perfect configuration of the schedule, this perfect location, this perfect cast member. Sometimes it all works together, but when it doesn't, either the schedule, location choices, or (infrequently) the cast must be rethought.

HOW DEPARTMENTS PREP

The final shooting schedule can run over 50 pages. It is a detailed scene-by-scene plan of what is to be shot when, the actors and number of background required for each day, special equipment or personnel needed, the time of day of each scene (per the script, not per reality), and the place (per the script) where each scene takes place: Interior, Police Headquarters; Exterior, School; Interior, Gymnasium; and so on. The *day out of days* is a calendar grid listing all speaking roles and which days the actors playing those roles will be working. It's based on the shooting schedule. The Casting Director needs a day out of days in order to structure the cast deals properly and economically.

For months on a big-budget feature, and weeks on a low-budget feature, all departments prep. As each department starts working, more data is accumulated by the Production Manager and First AD. A detailed budget is created for each department. The Production Manager works with each department head to reconcile the preliminary budget that he or she made with more accurate detail. There are shifts in each department's needs as changes come in and the shooting style and plan are firmed up. The Accountant tracks all petty cash, rentals, purchases, and deposits against the now-revised budget. When there is a variance, the UPM meets with the department head and decides whether or not to approve that variance. The Production Coordinator makes sure that any script and schedule revisions are distributed to all personnel, and is in constant communication with the Casting Director so that each relevant department can be notified as each cast deal is finalized. The AD must know the details of each actor's deal so that anything that impacts the schedule can be dealt with. The Transportation Coordinator has to know if a rental car, a daily driver, or a special trailer is part of the contract. The Costume department has to know once someone has been cast so that they can meet, get their sizes, and start shopping or altering. Hair and Makeup want to speak with each cast member. The importance of this continuous cycle of communication is compounded if the movie is being shot on location, because when travel is involved, the Production Coordinator must be sure that whoever needs to get together for wardrobe, rehearsals, to scout locations, etc. is in the right city at the right time.

As prep continues and each actor's contracts are signed, costumes are purchased, rented, or sewn and fitted. The Transportation Coordinator meets with department heads and rents trucks and assigns drivers. Set Dressing may need a truck for several weeks during prep in order to pick up paintings and mirrors and large pieces of furniture. Props may need a truck for two weeks before shooting to collect items that have been found, tagged, and put on hold at shops, prop houses, and manufacturers. The Transportation Coordinator will meet with the Director so that picture vehicles can be selected.

Every department begins prep at a different point, and each has specific needs. Although Grip and Electric may not start picking up equipment until a few days before the start of production, the Transportation Coordinator will speak with the Best Boys to ask about their departmental needs. The trucks will be there waiting for them, waiting for the crew, the first scheduled day of equipment load in.

About a week before the scheduled start of *principal photography* (the day when work by the main production unit begins), the Producer, Director, Production Designer, Set Decorator, UPM, First Assistant Director, Location Manager, Cinematographer, Gaffer, Key Grip, Transportation Coordinator, and occasionally the Sound Mixer go on a technical scout. The First AD and Location Manager organize the expedition, which can last between one and three days and involves visiting every single location for the film. The purpose of this is for each of the departments to actually see where the scenes are being shot so that they can have the appropriate equipment ordered and be prepared for any problems that might arise, and so that the director can firm up his or her shot list while looking at the actual spaces that will be used.

When Camera, Grip, and Electric return to the production office, they create an equipment rental and expendables purchase list that is given to the Production Coordinator, who sends it out to vendors and rental houses for bid and, together with the Transportation Coordinator, organizes a load-in schedule.

A few days before shooting begins, there is a production meeting led by the First AD. All department heads and their seconds attend the meeting. They are handed an updated, highly detailed shooting schedule and a completely updated script with all revisions in place. The First AD reads through the script scene by scene, and as each scene comes up, there is a brief discussion about how the scene will be shot, what equipment, wardrobe, special arrangements, or personnel shooting that scene requires. Everyone hears what everyone else has planned, so that if there is any interface between departments or any questions as to who is handling what, the possibly conflicting responsibilities are settled and assigned. Resolving questions and conflicts in prep is cheap. Those same conflicts on set can run into thousands of dollars in shooting time lost.

Chapter 20

Production

Once shooting begins, the First AD is right there on set next to the director, controlling the schedule. This includes deciding actors' *call times*, the time each actor should report to work each day, planning the daily shot list, and working with the camera, grip, and lighting crew to assess the time required for each new camera setup.

THE CALL SHEET

The First AD is in charge of the daily Call Sheet, an advance plan for each day of work. The Call Sheet for Monday is created and distributed on Sunday. The Call Sheet for Tuesday is created and distributed on Monday, etc. The Call Sheet lists the scenes, cast, crew, and any special equipment required for the shoot each day.

The Call Sheet also lists the time each person is expected to report to the set, as not everyone arrives at the same time. A film typically has a cast and crew numbering from 35 to 100 people, and it is the First Assistant Director's task to arrange for them to arrive so that they are not waiting around to get started working (and being paid to wait), but in enough time so that they are available and ready when needed. In addition to the entire cast and crew receiving a Call Sheet, all production company executives or investors who expect to be kept in the loop as to what is happening on set and when, receives a Call Sheet. The Call Sheet is the prime method of communicating a plan to everyone all at once. The First AD doesn't leave the director's side, so the Second Assistant Director actually fills out the Call Sheet, but the plans and times are made under the direction of the First.

The Call Sheet is based on the shooting schedule that was distributed during the production meeting. The shooting schedule was based on everything going as planned. Once a film is in production, there will be changes. Shooting runs ahead of or behind schedule, for example, or weather conditions require a planned Exterior School Yard day to move to an Interior Office. The Call Sheet is the document that deals with the fluid reality of each shooting day, versus the plan that was made a month before when everything was laid out as if all things, conditions, and hours would fall perfectly neatly into place. Without the daily update of the Call Sheet, actors don't know which scenes to prepare, the art and set dressing departments aren't sure which locations to prep, that special lightweight camera body for the Steadicam operator doesn't get picked up at the equipment house, and no one is sure where to show up when they come to work.

THE PRODUCTION REPORT

Shrewd management of time is the Assistant Director's area of expertise. At every point, the First AD is hyperconscious of the time and where the production is in the day—how much of what was scheduled has been shot, and how much there is left to be shot before he or she calls that day's wrap.

The First AD is personally liable for safety on set. In part because he or she interacts with all on-set planning and personnel, it is the AD's job to be aware of all shooting plans and potential hazards, whether there are stunts, effects, children, animals, snakes in the woods, or merely potholes in the road. At least once a day, and sometimes more than once, the First AD holds a safety meeting with all on-set personnel. All activity stops as the First AD reviews the planned work and any possible dangers associated with the scenes, the locations, the weather, anything. This meeting is so important that a written record of when the meeting took place is noted on the *Production Report*, a form that documents each production day's activities.

If we look at the Call Sheet as the battle plan for each day, the Production Report is a review and analysis of the battle in the context of the war as a whole (the entire production schedule being the war). The Production Report is distributed only to the Producer, Director, Production Manager, Accountant, and the studio, production company, investors, and the Completion Guarantor if there is one.

The Production Report is a record of exactly what was accomplished the day before, and what was planned but not accomplished. It notes the Call Time of each person and what time he or she actually arrived on set. The Production Accountant uses the Production Report as a way to verify that cast and crew paychecks accurately reflect overtime, meal penalties (more on these in a moment), or any special one-time bonus fees (*adjustments* or bumps) that unions require. For example, if a smoke machine is used, background actors receive a *smoke bump*. This means that each extra receives a small bit of compensation for the unpleasant working conditions that day. The Production Accountant looks at the in and out times of the crew members to determine if any overtime pay is due. The Accountant uses the Production Report to put together a daily *hot costs* report that is an abbreviated tally of specific costs. The hot costs serve as indicators of the pattern of actual daily expenses, so that the UPM can make educated decisions and can quickly plan adjustments to spending if it seems necessary.

There is also a Comments section on the Production Report where anything out of the ordinary that occurred, or anything that must be legally documented, is described or explained. Comments would include insurance issues: "lens dropped and smashed"; injuries: "Sound mixer sliced hand on broken glass, was taken immediately to emergency room"; or problems: "Sam did not like wardrobe, refused to leave trailer—company delayed 45 minutes." The recording of the daily safety meeting, when it was held, and what was discussed is important, because the Production Report is a legal document and is used as proof that proper precautions were taken. It is signed by the First AD, the UPM and the Producer. It must be accurate.

WHY COMMUNICATION AND DOCUMENTATION MATTERS

Without clear communication and collaboration, delays occur. Delays are expensive. The average *day cost* for a low-budget film might be $25,000; for a mid-level budget film ($20 to 50 million), between $35,000 and $60,000; for a blockbuster film, easily $100,000 to $250,000. Once production begins and the cash spigot is turned on, the clock is ticking. The money is draining out of the bank account. Every hour spent waiting or discussing something that could have been decided before the cash began flowing can cost between $2000 and $8500. Every minute of delay costs. Personnel, equipment, and locations are paid for whether or not the camera is rolling. When the amount that was budgeted for the film is spent, it's gone. There is usually no going back for more. This is why avoiding delays is the be all and end all of production. It's why the First Assistant Director's job of keeping the project on schedule is so crucial. A First Assistant Director on a feature film makes a great deal of money, because the weight of time is on his or her shoulders, and it's a stressful load. When a film runs behind schedule, the First AD is often the first to be replaced (fired).

When more money than expected is spent, the only solution is to find ways to save a corresponding amount by taking it from other areas (*accounts*) in the budget. That's the Production Manager's responsibility. When a final production budget has been approved by whoever is financing the movie, the budget is signed by the Producer, Director, and Production Manager and that bottom line number is the number. It's what the film is expected to cost.

How are these millions of dollars tracked? Beginning in preproduction, all expenditures are monitored and recorded by the Production Accountant, who reports to the UPM and to the entity financing the film. The Accountant tracks all money spent and/or committed to be spent and compares it to the budget and to the amount of cash remaining, using a weekly document called a *weekly cost report*. The cost report lists the budgetary categories, the amount budgeted for those categories, the amount spent during the specific week of production, the amount spent to date, and the amount necessary to finish the film, the *estimate to complete*. It indicates which categories are over spent, which are under spent, and which are where they are supposed to be. Every week an updated cost report is given to the Producer, the Production Manager, and to whoever is paying for the film to be made. The Production Manager uses it to decide how to use whatever savings there are to offset the overages. The investors note the trouble spots and look to the Producer and Production Manager to explain what they will do in order to make sure that in the end, the figures will balance.

Lack of communication makes everyone nervous. When the Producer and Production Manager are not quickly forthcoming about both the problems and the solutions, investors and studios lose faith and begin to think that the people who are supposed to be watching over their money are negligent, dishonest, or incompetent. If the information and answers come before the investors have time to worry and ask, the trust will remain intact.

IT'S THE LITTLE THINGS . . .

Everyone is aware that seemingly insignificant unplanned costs can snowball and eventually cripple a project. That's why the Production Manager must be vigilant. Crew overtime is the cost of working beyond the customary 12½ hours per day. There are times when rather than shut down at exactly 12½ hours, the crew must work an extra hour or two, finishing up and ending the day at 13 or even 14 hours. When that occurs the crew is paid double time, or if the day lasts long enough, sometimes even double double time. That cost was not planned. Say a crew member is making $35 per hour, a relatively low wage for certain films. At double time, the crew member is now making $70 per hour. Multiply that single double-time hour by 50 crew members (and many crew members make much more than $35 per hour) and that 13th hour could cost the production a minimum of $3500, the 14th hour a minimum of $7000—and this is not counting Cast overtime. That $7000 plus will not be something that the audience can see on screen and will have to come from somewhere, usually from an account that holds money for what the audience *does* see on screen.

There is also the possibility that the single overtime hour threw the entire cast and crew into a *meal penalty*, a fee levied on the production when the cast and crew is not fed a real meal every six hours. Meal penalties are calculated in half-hour increments. For example: The crew call time is 6:00 am. At noon, the crew is still in the middle of a scene. The decision is made to not break for lunch until the scene is completed. The cast and crew don't break for lunch until 12:40. That means that the on-set crew has incurred two meal penalties. To get an idea of how those 40 minutes impact the day's budget, if there are 40 people involved the production:

For cast: approximately $25 for the first half hour, $35 for the second, therefore $60 for each cast member who didn't eat on time.

For crew: approximately $7.50 for the first half hour, $10 for the second, therefore $17.50 for each crew member who didn't eat on time.

This may not be a lot of money. If there were only three cast members, we're looking at $180. But what if you go into meal penalty 20 days out of your 40-day shoot? Now you're talking about $3600 spent on nothing that is ending up on the screen.

But the crew meal penalties? That paltry $17.50? Multiply that times 40 crew members and you've got $700. And if that happens 10 days of your 40-day shoot? About $7000 is gone from your budget, again, spent on something that makes no creative contribution to your movie.

The people scrutinizing the cost report will notice these expenses and wonder if it is likely that the crew will incur this extra hour or even more than an hour of overtime often. What will that mean for the overall budget? What or who is taking longer than anticipated? Was the schedule not correctly made in the first place? What is not going to be shot or what is going to be handled differently because now the money earmarked for building a particular set is going to be spent on overtime and meal penalties?

Even more complicated is the reality that although spending that money on something that doesn't end up on screen may feel wasteful, sometimes the smartest decision the First AD and Production Manager can make is to incur the expense but stay on schedule. Maybe the scene is an essential emotional moment in the movie and the actor has momentum going in his performance. Or the location is not available the next day. The Production Manager and First AD work together to figure the benefits and disadvantages and move ahead from there.

Another area where small acts can have big consequences is the actual cost of shooting film. We've entered the digital age, but many feature-length movies still shoot on film stock. On a typical feature film, there is a budget for about 5000 feet of film per day. When shooting film, there is an attendant film *processing* (developing) cost. Since most films are edited digitally on Avid or Final Cut Pro systems, every foot of film processed must be digitally captured via a telecine or datacine process. If the film is budgeted to shoot 5000 feet on Monday, but in actuality 6000 feet of film is shot, there is an extra thousand feet in costs of stock, developing, and digitizing. The $4000 that was budgeted as a per-day cost for stock, processing, and digital transfer will now be $4740 or $5000. If this happens on one or two days, it's no big deal. If this happens 30 days of the 40-day shoot, the film is now $40,000 over. Where will that money come from?

No capable Production Manager will decide that the solution is a knee-jerk "shoot less." The point of production is to end up with the best movie! If the footage shot each day is good, and it feels as if there is the correct amount of scene *coverage* (choices for the editor to work with), and if each take is different enough to warrant the amount of footage shot, then clearly the director has found his or her way of working effectively. It would be a mistake to try to restrict that.

The idea is to make a great film, not just to come in on budget. If the movie is no good, no one cares how financially responsible you were. But the problem must be solved, and quickly. The Production Manager has to make the assumption that the pattern is going to continue and revisit the funds other departments have been allotted, moving money to compensate. The people funding the film will want solutions, and those solutions must answer the question, "How can this be handled without negatively impacting the movie?"

The Production Manager approves or rejects expenditures that differ from the budgeted amount. He or she is constantly working the numbers. Ultimately the Producer and Production Manager work together, using the Production Accountant's reports and estimates to maintain the bottom line while not hurting the film. It's a juggling act. The making of a movie is not static. There are unforeseen events, and the Production Manager must manage the price tag that comes with these surprises. He or she will control whatever is possible, and will make sure that there is enough of a *pad* (wiggle room) in the original budget so that the picture is not in trouble when the inevitable changes occur.

Clearly, collaboration and communication is a key factor in the well-being of a movie. From the minute production begins until filming is completed, these people are under an enormous strain. To the observer in the production office, in prep these people may appear to be best buddies, laughing and joking and going for drinks or dinner at the end of the day. When production starts, it might seem to turn. People may become screamers or schemers working opposite sides of the fence and playing the fault game. In a business where everyone is a temporary employee—and as the saying goes, you're only as good as your last picture—people vie for credit when it goes well, and no one wants to be blamed when things fall apart. Once production is over, most everyone reverts to who they were in the beginning, and people decide whether or not they want to work together again. Ultimately when the drama comes to an end and the Producer, Production Manager, and First AD are evaluated regarding the job they did, the people who might hire them again want to know if they managed situations, cast, and crew well, kept everything safe, maintained their humanity at least a little, and most important of all, *were they effective*. In the long run, that's all that matters.

Chapter 21

A Day in the Life of a Production

There's a 7:00 am general crew call, so at 5:30 am the transportation department moves all the trucks and trailers in and parks them, forming a *base camp* in a parking area designated by the Location Manager. The catering truck will be there at 6:00 am, with the fixings for 75 breakfasts hot and ready, and a Medic will be on set from the first person's call until the last person's wrap.

Many of the crew members will have arrived earlier. The Second AD and her PAs call will be 6:00 am, so they can meet the actors and bring them to their dressing room or the Hair and Makeup trailer. The Hair and Makeup department people will be busy in their trailer working on the actors who are in the first scheduled scene. The Costume department will be alternating with them. If one actor is in the hair and makeup trailer, the other will be in wardrobe, and vice versa. The Grips and Electrics may have a call time of 6:00 am so that they can pre-rig the lights for the first lighting setup. The rest of the crew will arrive by 6:45, pick up a walking breakfast—breakfast burritos, egg and cheese sandwiches. They drink coffee, pick up a walkie-talkie, and head for their equipment or find their places on set.

The First AD, the Cinematographer, and the Director walk through the first couple of shots. The Grip and Electric department are watching so that they can make lighting adjustments. The sound mixer and boom person are watching so that they know where the camera will be, where the actors will be, so they can get good sound and keep the microphone from being visible in the frame.

The Production Designer and Set Decorator have already left the set. Once the Director saw and approved the set, they and their crew are off to ready the set scheduled for the next day.

Once everyone understands the first shot, the *first team* (the actors) are brought out to walk through the set-up, then they go back to Hair and Makeup for touchups. The *second team* (stand-ins who are roughly the same size, shape, and have the same coloring as the lead actors) are called in to stand in place for lighting. Once that's done, the First Assistant Director asks the DP for a time estimate—10 minutes, 20 minutes, however long it will take for everything to be properly lit. The First AD will be in communication with the Second AD (or the Second Second AD or the base camp PA) asking for an estimate from Hair, Makeup, and Costume. In an ideal world everyone will be ready at the same time, and there will be a brief rehearsal for *blocking* (camera and actor movement). Then the camera will roll on the first shot.

Make Your Movie: What You Need to Know About the Business and Politics of Filmmaking.

In between shots, the Hair, Makeup, and Costume people will quickly touch up the actors so that their look is consistent. The Script Supervisor will amend his or her notes. The Second AC will check the film magazine to be sure that there is enough film in the camera for the next shot. Everyone will take care of the dozens of minute details of their position, knowing that they must be ready to snap to as soon as they are needed. Waiting for a department is not a good thing. Each time the camera shifts, the lights will either also be shifted or tweaked to accommodate the move. This same process will be repeated again and again throughout the morning.

At 1:00 pm, the First AD calls lunch. (The first real meal of the day is referred to as *lunch*, even if it's served at 2:00 am.) It's a sit-down, full-course meal with a salad, usually a choice of two or three entrees, including a vegetarian selection, and dessert. During lunch the First AD and the Director may confer about the afternoon's work. The Production Manager and Producer may be part of the conversation, or they may be dealing with other issues. The Producer may be setting up a deal with a postproduction sound house. The Production Manager may be meeting with the Best Boy Electric to discuss the extra electricians who will be hired on as *day players* for a big lighting setup next week.

The Second AD will be starting on the next day's Call Sheet, filling in the blanks with all the information he or she can, with the exception of the times everyone is due back on set the next day. Since by SAG rules, actors receive a 12-hour rest period between their wrap time on one day and their call time on the next day, it's hard to fill in the times for the actors and the crew until mid or late afternoon, when there's a true sense of how the work is going and if the shooting will end on time—in this case, at 7:30 pm (12 hours plus a half hour for lunch)—or will run a half hour or more late, in which case the call might have to be *pushed* (moved later).

After lunch, the actors head back to Hair and Makeup for the ever-ongoing touchups, the crew heads back to set, and the process of prep, shoot, prep, shoot is repeated again, until the completion of the scheduled work. If for some reason the scheduled work is not completed that day, there will be a brief conference between the First AD, the Director, the Producer, the Production Manager, and whoever else needs to be in on the recovery plan. Will slopping into the next day involve a new negotiation with the location owner? Will the location that was scheduled for the following day still be available a day later? Will the actors, some of whom may have been contracted for one day only, be available to return the next day? What about the actors who are coming the next day? What does that do to their schedule? A new plan is formulated and a call is made to the Production Coordinator, who is probably in the office waiting to hear, and who may have to contact the Casting Director, the Art Department (who will be expecting the crew at the next set and location), and anyone who may need to know about the change.

Finally, the decision is made to go an hour later and finish up rather than carry the scene over into the next day. That means that the Production Manager will be calling the studio or production company the next day with an explanation, and the Accountant will be computing the overtime and adjusting the cost report accordingly.

The night wears on. The next-to-last shot of the day is nicknamed *the Abby* after the legendary First AD and UPM, Abby Singer. The last shot is called *the Martini* for more obvious reasons. Then the First AD says, "That's a wrap," and shooting is done for the day. The actors go to the Hair and Makeup and Costume trailers to get "undone." The Grip and Electric team pack up all the cables and lights and light stands and stow them carefully in their trucks. The Second AC unloads the film, packages it together with the camera reports, and hands it all to the Second AD. The Second AD fills in the blanks on the Production Report, which is expected to be signed and ready for distribution to the powers that be before noon the next day. Most everyone has something to do that keeps them busy for a half hour to an hour once shooting has ended for the day. The Script Supervisor takes his or her notes and reports and hands those also to the Second AD. A driver is standing by to drop the film and a copy of the camera reports at the lab, where it will be processed. The processed film will be picked up the next morning and brought to an editing assistant, who will begin to synch up the picture and sound so that *dailies* (a version of the work shot the previous day) will be ready for the editor and director to see by the end of the day. It is important that dailies are seen as soon as possible in case something is wrong, either with the film itself—a scratch, a focus that is too soft, a flare that renders the best take unusable—or with a performance, the look of a location, whatever. If a problem is caught immediately, the remedy is usually easier and less expensive than if it's discovered a week later.

An hour after wrap is called, the parking lot is empty. The trucks are on the road to a secure parking lot where they will spend the night, until the drivers, who have the longest work days, return to pick them up and bring them to a new base camp. The cast and crew are headed home. There may be phone calls to the Production Office about equipment orders that must be taken care of first thing the next morning, or dozens of other things that must be dealt with.

The next day the routine continues. The making of a movie can be a bit of an endurance event. The crew usually gets by on less sleep than usual, does not have much of a life outside of work while they're employed, but they keep moving ahead—for 20 days which is a short schedule or 120 days. Lots of physical activity, stress-because you don't want to be the malfunctioning cog in the machine, and adrenaline. Once the last day of filming comes around and the final \wrap\ is called, everyone goes home and sleeps, tries to readjust to the routine of their \real\ life, and gets ready for the wrap party, where they eat, drink, blow off steam—and try to find out where everyone else's next job is coming from, and if there's a chance they can get on the show too.

Production is grueling, but it's fun. You are always tired, stretched a little thin, but a year later when you see the finished film, there is a lot of satisfaction in knowing that you were there helping to make it all happen.

Section III

It's Just Beginning to Be a Movie

Postproduction

Chapter 22

After the Smoke Clears

THE POLITICS OF WRAP

It's the last day of production. The final scene has been shot. The Assistant Director shouts "Thanks for a great day!" for the final time. The actors are released, removing their makeup and costumes, and the crew is loading equipment onto trucks. Everybody is bone weary and happy to go hug their goodbyes and go home.

Most of them will be back the next day. Wrapping a production involves the returning of all rentals, which will presumably be intact. But if there are lost or damaged items, the production is obligated to repair or replace them. Anything that can be sold off is, even for ten cents on the dollar, unless there is the suspicion that additional *re-shoots* might be necessary once the editing starts. Set dressing and costumes are sold to consignment stores. Locations must be restored to their pre-shooting condition. The Location Manager may have to hire and supervise a crew of painters and landscapers to make things right. There may be insurance claims against the production. The Production Office staff usually finishes last, weeks after filming has wrapped. There are bills to pay. There are boxes of paperwork—contracts, license agreements, production and financial records. There are notes on where everything can be found and on any outstanding issues that cannot be resolved in a reasonable period of time. There are continuity photos in case anything has to be replicated later. It all must be accessible and complete. A company has been created, and all the documentation must be in order.

The freelance shooting crew is gone, but the company and the film lives on—first in postproduction, then in sales and distribution. On an independent film that does not yet have distribution, documentation is turned over to the producer who stays with the picture until the delivery of the project, or to the financiers of the project. On a studio film the boxes are delivered to the production and accounting departments, and the degree of detail evident in the wrap—or the sloppiness of the wrap—is noted. A Production Manager, a Coordinator, and Accountant can do a wonderful job in prep and during shooting but if there are a lot of loose ends, that's what the production company or studio remembers. The team is hired specifically to handle the production from beginning to end, and a careless wrap can diminish your chances of future employment.

A note of caution: The production team is expected to do this all in a relatively short period of time. Wrap time for many members of the staff and crew is part of the budget, but sometimes people without their next job milk their wrap, working more slowly than necessary to try to edge out a few additional paychecks. Bad idea. At best you seem incompetent, at worse chintzy and a bit of a con artist. Do what you have to do as efficiently as possible and move on.

WHO SEES THE CUT?

From the first day of shooting until the last day, the editor has been receiving and reviewing footage. He or she has been in meetings with the director about the good and the bad shots, what works and what is weak. While the shooting crew has been laboring away on set, the editor has been shaping the good takes into scenes, and by the time the actual shooting period is complete, the editor has put together an *assembly* or *editor's cut* in script order. A coherent story begins to emerge from the assembled bits of shots and scenes. The intention of the assembly is to have a first version of the entire film from beginning to end. The cut is usually much longer than the final edit because everything is in there.

As the editor refines this cut and works with the director to perfect the rhythm of the storytelling, scenes are moved—sometimes dropped—and pacing is improved. It's a painstakingly slow process, and while it's happening everyone wants to see the movie. If the director is a DGA member, he or she has ten weeks guaranteed to make his or her changes, to work with the editor, try shifting the scene order, cutting things short, letting drama play out, and in general crafting the film without screening it for anyone else. Anyone else includes the studio, the producer, the production company, and the financiers.

But just because the director can lock these people out, doesn't mean he or she should. It just means that as part of the union contract, the director has the right to get to a *director's cut* without comments or outside interference. After the ten weeks, the film must be screened. If the director is not a DGA member, there is no such right, and most likely the financial backers of the project will want to see what they've got immediately. Any attempt to dissuade them from seeing the film will indicate that the director isn't happy with the film, which is not a feeling that a director wants to convey, even if it's true.

So here's the dilemma: everyone involved is dying to see the film. However, the film as it exists as a rough cut doesn't really feel like a movie. It's choppy, and flat. There is no music. The transitions from scene to scene may still be ragged. The unmixed dialogue sounds hollow. Show this to a first-time viewer of a rough cut and you just know he or she is going to think, "Oh my God, why did I throw my money away?" Surprisingly, this is even the case with a lot of experienced audience members. Sometimes executives at studios have a hard time envisioning the result of the months of fussing and polishing still to come. Some of them can look at a rough cut and see the possibilities, and some can't.

A director knows that the first cut of a film is merely a starting point for what is to come. If he or she isn't pleased with the first cut, it means that there is a lot of work to be done. A smart director who has a good relationship with his or her producer will let the producer act as the middleman with the investors clamoring to see the results of production. A good producer can often allay any investor fears and still manage to save the director from the backseat driving of investors or executives, at least for a while. But sooner or later, you've got to screen the movie.

Once other people see the movie, it's the producer's job to help filter the comments and allow the director space and time to work with the editor and get the film to where it works. Inexperienced people or those with major ego, tend to think (a) they are welcome to drop by the editing room and express their opinion if they want to; or (b) that they are not welcome but since they're paying for the film, they don't care. They're going to do it. If they feel that the director is not being responsive to their ideas, they'll wait and catch the editor alone and try to convince him or her to try it. The editor is put in the position of one employer, the people paying for the film creating a situation where he or she must go behind the back of another employer, the director, who may not be paying the editor but who certainly has the power to get the editor fired. Not a good situation for anyone concerned, and it only serves to heighten the tension of an already inflammatory atmosphere. Believe me, when a film isn't working, an experienced director is usually all too aware and scrambling to fix it. Again, this is where the producer comes in, protecting the director and editor from a lot of extraneous noise. Getting to a *locked picture* can take months. Change the dramatic thrust of a scene and everything else may be thrown off and then must be changed accordingly. It's not usually as simple as a tuck here and a shift there. The producer must find a way to keep all parties happy, engaged, and off of each other's backs.

MEANWHILE . . .

In addition to keeping peace in the editing room, the producer is busy during postproduction. Picture editing is only one part of post. There are visual effects to be dealt with, and sound design. There are several good books on the entire process, and you should at least be familiar with the general workflow—what happens when—so that you aren't overwhelmed by the technical aspects. Your best bet as a first-time filmmaker is to do some basic research, and then to build a team who can guide you through the process.

You must have someone who is knowledgeable enough to serve as a *Post Supervisor* (a Production Manager for postproduction). This person understands post scheduling, oversees expenditures, knows the vendors and personnel (effects houses, sound editors, composers) who will be willing to work within your budget. Often an experienced Post Supervisor can pull in favors and help you attract very accomplished people to your project. At the very least, a good Supervisor can save the production thousands of dollars in missteps. Another wise investment might be a *Music Supervisor*. A good Music Supervisor can steer you to wonderful composers and amazing musicians, and can help with great deals on rights and clearances, ultimately adding immeasurably to the value of your production.

Post on even a very small film can take six months. On an effects-laden epic it can take more than a year. The producer and the production company or studio has a raft of people helping out with all this. While it's all going on—depending on whether it's an independent with distribution, an independent film looking for distribution, or a studio project—the producer will also be dealing with marketing and distribution. It's not unusual for non-industry people to be confused about why it takes a movie so long to come out, especially if they've been hearing about it for months. The prep, shoot, and edit are only a fraction of the process. Add a year of development at the front end and maybe a year of post, sales, and distribution concerns at the backend. This is why you have to really want to be a filmmaker more than you want to do anything else. It's a long haul. Once the film is shot, you're only half way there.

Paul Seydor

Paul Seydor came to editing after being a professor of literature at the University of Southern California, where he completed *Peckinpah: The Western Films* (1980, University of Illinois Press). He did his first editing for Roger Spottiswoode, one of Peckinpah's editors turned director, with whom he worked on *The Best of Times, Time Flies When You're Alive, Turner and Hooch,* and *The Last Innocent Man.* A little later he began a longstanding collaboration with Ron Shelton that eventually included *White Men Can't Jump, Cobb, Tin Cup, Play It to the Bone, Dark Blue,* and *Hollywood Homicide.* In the last several years he has edited a string of hit movies that include *Guess Who, Barbershop 2: Back in Business, Because I Said So, This Christmas,* and *Obsessed.*

What do you think first-time filmmakers should understand about interactions with the studio and/or production company during postproduction, loyalty (if that's the right word) to the director, and how much to push a decision that you are sure is right and when to let it go?

This is one of those questions that invites either an impossibly long answer or an equally impossible short one. The politics as such of postproduction are no different from the politics of preproduction and production with one huge exception: the film is now shot, "in the can" as it were, and here is where the full amateurishness of everybody who doesn't make films comes into play, i.e., everyone thinks he or she is an editor, and since the film is already shot, seems also to feel entitled to toy or otherwise tamper with it to their heart's content.

To a large extent what happens here depends on several factors. The largest single one is of course the power of the director. If he's (so I'm not ponderous, please assume I mean "he or she" here) got a good track record with a number of solid and/or critical hits behind him, then it will be relatively smooth sailing, as few people will want to challenge him too much. A great deal also depends upon preview scores: if they're high, no problem, if they're not, well, then it can get very contentious.

Paul Seydor—cont'd

Of course, if the director is relatively unknown, then all bets are off as to how he and the film will be treated. Assuming the film has come out more or less as everyone had hoped, then things will proceed relatively well until the previews, and then it's anybody's guess. Much depends upon the good will of the studio executives, but in today's world, this is nonexistent: never at any time over the last nearly 30 years that I've been in the business have I seen less respect, more outright contempt for artists, artistic vision, artistry, for anything associated with the creative side of the business. Much also depends on the strength of the producer and his or her willingness to fight for the director and for the film. Some producers abandon the director entirely, others try to mediate, others remain fiercely loyal.

Loyalty remains a problematic and dangerous area. I am always loyal to my director, even when I don't agree with all his or her decisions. But this can get you into trouble. For example, on [a film that we can't name here] I had to endure the indignity of the studio bringing in a "fix-it" editor. I wasn't fired though the studio would gladly have fired me if they could have. The new editor did his work, but because the film was edited right to begin with, the studio couldn't even finish watching the version he turned in. Most of the time, in this scenario, what happens is that the editor is fired, even though everybody knows his work is good. Why? Because the executives—and often the producer—want to isolate the director. By this point in post, the principal ally the director has is the editor. The editor is easier to fire than the director, whom they'd really like to fire, but as the director's the hardest person on a film to fire, they fire the editor and bring in an editor of their own whose loyalty is to them.

It's a nasty business. One thing I can say for certain, in fewer than five cases out of a hundred—and perhaps far fewer than that—is an editor ever let go because his work as such is not good.

The reality is that postproduction has now become so complex and complicated that postproduction supervisors or coordinators are absolutely necessary and very helpful. But the old-time politics are still pretty much as they always have been: not much of that has changed.

Chapter 23

Music

YOUR SCORE

When you make your movie, you will want a composer to create an original *score* (background and incidental music) that is specific to your plot and theme, and that works in concert with your visuals. A great score can signal danger (think about the *Jaws* theme), pull you in to the pace of a different way of life (*Witness*), sweep you away to a bygone era (*Gone with the Wind*), or pull you in to the warmth or chilliness of a story (*The Social Network*).

Music can make or break your film, but the choice of a composer is often left until late in the process, and composers are often at the end of the line where expenditures are concerned. First-time filmmakers often want to wait and see who and what the film can afford, yet your composer is a key creative team member and should be treated as such. To really understand the power that the score adds to your visuals, get hold of a DVD of your favorite movie, find a couple of scenes and turn off the sound.

The good news is that lots of exceptional composers are willing to give first-time filmmakers a price break if they like their project. They want to forge the most superior creative alliances they can. A talented filmmaker may be able to attract a composer who would seem to be beyond his or her budgetary reach. Years ago, scoring a film was an expensive affair. There was the booking of an orchestra and costly recording sessions. Times have changed. Now a composer can orchestrate your entire movie alone in the comfort of his or her home studio. What hasn't changed is the actual act of creating music. Give your composer the same kind of respect that you would want as a screenwriter or director. Composers need breathing room and time. Working with a composer might involve a learning curve for the first-time filmmaker. Try to establish a common language so that you can communicate effectively. Your idea of what you want might be more. To a composer, that could mean a variety of things: fuller, louder, more bracing. They can't give you what you want if they don't understand what you're asking for.

Be sure that you give yourself a time cushion. If you have a deadline to hit and the composer either isn't understanding the film or the work isn't being done, you have to move on. Don't settle. Don't end up with a score that doesn't raise the level of your film just because you want to be a nice guy. Be patient, but if it's not there, find someone new.

IT'S AN OLD SONG, HOW MUCH CAN IT COST?

In addition to your original score, you will most likely want to use preexisting songs and music in your film. These could be popular songs, orchestral renditions of classical music, traditional folk tunes. In order to use preexisting music, you will need to contact the *publisher* of that music and negotiate a *licensing agreement* that gives you the right to put the music in your film.

Let's look at an example from a script:

INT. Baxter High—Gym—Night
1976. Prom night. A local band plays a deafeningly bad version
of a major rock anthem. Then the band segues into an equally
loud very popular love song of the day. Couples slow-dance and snuggle.
SAMANTHA and KEVIN, crowned Queen and King, stand next to
the punch table. Kevin leans in, says something over the din,
Samantha nods, he grabs her hand and they sneak out the side door.
EXT. Baxter High—Parking Lot—Night
Sam and Kevin run to a vintage Mustang hardtop. Kevin unlocks the
door, they squeeze into the back seat. Kevin reaches over the driver's seat,
fumbles to start the ignition. The radio lights up. The ballad, the
real version, comes on. They laugh at the coincidence, whispering and
laughing and begin to make out.

This scene, while not particularly interesting, has a lot going on in terms of music. We have two megahit pop songs, performed by actors. We have one of the songs also performed by a mega-successful (and long-defunct) band. Two minutes of screen time, and you've already spent several thousands of dollars.

Let's look at the first song, the rock anthem. Who wrote it? Let's make it easy and say that the band members did. Which band members? What are the credited names? Let's say it's Page and Plant. Or Lennon and McCartney. Let's say one wrote the music and the other wrote the lyrics. Does any of that matter? All that matters is who owns the song, who owns the publishing. The band may have set up a publishing company and own their own work. Or the record company may own the publishing. Or the publishing may be split between them, or an outside buyer who has nothing to do with either the record company or the band may have at some point bought the publishing. To use the song, your first step would be to find the publisher. You can contact the record company, or you might contact ASCAP (the American Society of Composers, Authors, and Publishers) or BMI (Broadcast Music Incorporated). Usually between the three, you'll find a way to contact the publisher of the song.

You'll want the publisher to agree to a *synch* (synchronization) license. This gives you the right to use the song (music and lyrics) in synchronization with another form of media—in this case, with film or video. However, it does not give you the right to use an existing performance of the song. In other words, if we look back at our prom night scenario, you would need the synch license for the rock song. You're using the song but creating a new version of it, by hiring musicians to perform it badly. Since you're not using a preexisting recording of the song, you would not use the second type of rights, a *master use license*. The master license is between the filmmaker and the owner of the master recording—probably the record company—and it grants the right to use previously recorded material (the version of the song that is on the CD) in your movie.

Looking again at our prom night scenario, if you are just using the song as performed by the local band you need a synch license. But when the radio comes on, if you want to use the official version of the love song (the one that everyone knows and loves, which is why you're using it in the movie), you're usually going to have to negotiate your deal with a major company charging major money. By the way, if music is emanating from a radio or television on screen, it is referred to as *source music* and is almost always recorded later and inserted during postproduction, where it can be mixed into the rest of the sound track (dialogue, background noises) at the volume level desired.

Things you should know about using music in your movie:

1. These licenses are not purchases. The licenses give you rights of use, not ownership. These licenses are nonexclusive. The same song and/or performance of the song could be used in several different films.
2. A folk or traditional song may be in the public domain (and therefore the copyright has either lapsed or has never been owned by anyone), but you must not assume that just because a song is old that it's not owned, "Happy Birthday to You," for example, is not in the public domain, and if you use it, you must obtain a synch license. Conversely, if you use a hundred-year-old traditional folk song, you may not need a synch license, but if you want to use a recorded version of the song, you'll need a license covering master use. If you are using classical music in your film, you won't have to obtain synch rights, but you will have to obtain master use rights if you want to use the London Symphony Orchestra's recording of the piece.
3. There are numerous companies that license sound-alike versions of preexisting music. Usually the most expensive license is the master use license, because you're dealing with talent and record companies, and a sound-alike version of your song is one way to avoid high fees. Although you still must obtain a master use license, these companies charge much less than the real deal.

A word of caution: Listen several times before you decide to go that route. Sound-alikes that don't sound quite enough like the original can come off as a little cheesy and are sometimes more distracting than beneficial.

WHAT IF WE JUST GET FESTIVAL RIGHTS?

When you're making an independent film and hoping to sell it at a festival it may seem counterintuitive to lavish money on music licensing that could be better spent in so many other ways. So first-time filmmakers sometimes decide that rather than go for full rights, they will just obtain *festival rights,* which are much easier to get and much less expensive. So-called festival rights allow the filmmakers to get the rights to popular songs they might not otherwise be able to afford. They are licensed at a much reduced rate, but the films can *only* be screened at film festivals. That means that if the film sells, new licensing agreements must be negotiated.

The pros are obvious. A low-budget film can raise its profile with an edgy sound track. The cons are that if the film sells, a new agreement must be negotiated, and if the licensing party is aware that the film has a chance for wide distribution, that is likely to up the price of the license to above what it would have been in the first place. Also, if the festival rights agreement is not worded correctly, there is a chance that the license holders could, for whatever reason, refuse to agree to a license, in which case the filmmakers are in trouble. A distribution deal is usually offered on the film that the distributors saw, and that means with the soundtrack from the festival version, not with substitute songs. Additionally, when a distributor makes an offer for a film, it is contingent on the film being free and clear of all legal and financial entanglements. Particularly in the case of a low-budget film, a distributor doesn't want to acquire a film with issues, because the investment that will have to be made in order to solve the problems may be more money than the movie will ever return in profit. You don't want those encumbrances to hamper your ability to get your project distributed. You also don't want to use music without acquiring the proper rights. It's not worth the risk. A publisher could take legal action, and you could be prohibited from screening or selling it unless you remedy the situation.

The language in your Licensing Agreement should include the phrases "nonexclusive, irrevocable" and should be for rights that "continue in perpetuity, effective for any and all media, whether now known or devised hereafter, throughout the universe." The final part of that sentence may appear extreme: "now known or devised hereafter, throughout the universe"? But what if you'd signed a rights agreement twenty years ago? Without this extreme language you wouldn't be covered for satellite TV, Web TV, or online streaming. Now those are important outlets for your film.

There are some fairly standard versions of licensing agreements out there, and many companies have their own boilerplate agreement that is pretty non-negotiable, but I suggest that you consult with an attorney before you sign something that could be so important to your movie.

I KNOW A GUY WHO KNOWS THE BAND

There's a song you're anxious to use, and you want to use the original recording by the band who made it famous. The quote is $25,000, and you just don't have it.

You might get lucky. Do you know anyone who can get you a meeting with the manager of the band or the songwriters themselves? If you have a great clip to show, or if you're a great talker, sometimes you can personally plead your case and they'll speak with the record company, and together they'll reduce the price somewhat. Don't expect the impossible, though. Royalties and license fees are the way many musicians make their living, and record companies are not in business to help starving filmmakers. But it's worth a try. A few filmmakers I know were able to talk their way into major discounts via a personal appeal. And if you're lucky enough to have a sharp Music Supervisor on your project, he or she can sometimes work miracles.

Section IV

What Are You Doing Saturday Night?

Chapter 24

The Money, Part 2

HOW DOES A MOVIE MAKE MONEY?

One would think that there would be a straightforward answer to this. A movie makes money by earning more than it costs to make. Right? Not so simple. First, we have to define what we mean by "making money." Are we talking about showing a profit? If I raise $2 million to make a low-budget independent film, how much money does that film have to make until I start to pay money back to my investors? The film has a $2 million production budget. That means that it costs $2 million dollars to get the film from script to a finished version, ready for delivery. That $2 million has nothing to do with the cost of getting a film booked into theatres or sold to cable TV.

Let's assume I've found a distributor in the United States. The distributor is willing to pay me a very small amount money for the right to distribute my film, to get it out to theatres. It's an indie film, and this distributor is very connected with the *specialty* (independent) circuit. I think I'm in good shape. However, the way the actual costs of distribution are charged against the movie are all negotiable. The expenses of distribution include film prints, advertising, marketing, sometimes the price of supporting a film through the festival circuit, including airfare, dinners, and parties. These costs are usually in addition to the distributor's fee. It is possible that my movie could play to sold out houses every night for a couple of weeks, and my investors and I might still not make a lot of money. Or perhaps my savvy lawyer negotiated an agreement that included less upfront money for the film but more Prints and Advertising. What about my deal with the sales agent who is acting as the liaison for distributors and exhibitors in other countries? This is why you need a good attorney who knows the ropes. It could make all the difference.

Some terms that you should be familiar with:

Gross—The overall revenue generated by a film.
Points—Percentages of the profit.
Net—The gross minus expenses.

What are the expenses? They are all negotiable. Production companies are notorious for creative bookkeeping to avoid showing a profit, whether or not the money is there. They often inflate expenses because then they don't have to repay investors or profit participants. If you worked on something for no fee or a much lower fee in exchange for net points, you can wave goodbye to the thought of any money coming to you out of net profits. You want gross points, but that's not the kind of deal newcomers can often make for themselves.

THE GROSSES

Continuing on with the example of a film that is making the rounds of the specialty theatres . . . How do we know how well that film is doing? We can look at the Box Office charts in the trade papers (*The Hollywood Reporter*, *Daily Variety*). The weekly charts rank the films that are in the theatres by box office revenue. It's important to understand that on these charts, ranking number one goes to the film that is making the most money at a particular point in time. For instance, a film may be a smash hit at the box office, but if a film has been in the theatres for a couple of months, this week it may be in decline. This is not because it isn't making money but because it's passed its peak earning time. A brand new film, just released, may not ultimately make anywhere as much money as our hit, but on this particular week, it may rank higher on the box office chart.

The charts list the distributor of the films, the genre, previous ticket sales, the weekend ticket sales, the change from the previous week (negative or positive percentage numbers), the number of screenings for the week, the average revenue per screening, the number of weeks the film has been in release, and the cumulative box office (total ticket sales since the film has been released). What do all these figures mean? On a macro level, they could mean that a film had a strong opening but then ticket sales began to fizzle due to word of mouth. Or the opposite. A film opened small, at only a few theatres. It did very well and word of mouth built. Over the course of several weeks, you may find that the small opening out-grosses the big one.

Looking at the charts can tell you that a certain star will get the audiences out for a big first weekend, or that in one short week, the plan to make several new sci-fi epics should be scrapped because the public's appetite for them is not there right now. If you look at the charts with your filmmaker hat on, you might decide that the box office can guide you in how you might pitch your film at that meeting next week, or that the little indie film that was the talk of the town when it won awards at the big festivals is too eccentric for a mainstream audience. Or that the sweet comedy that seemed almost quaint when you saw it at a festival several months ago, has gained traction and is now doing respectably well around the country. This means that the filmmaking team for that project will probably be out with another film sometime soon.

DISTRIBUTION

If you make a movie and no one sees it, does your movie count? (Other than the satisfaction of having survived the process.) Sure it does, but it's preferable for your film to be seen by as many people as possible. You want your movie to play nationally and internationally. You need a *domestic distributor* and a *sales agent* to help get your film out.

At this point you may be shaking your head at the struggle of it all and wondering whether every filmmaker has to endure the endless rounds of presenting, ingratiating, and negotiating that is involved in securing distribution. The answer is mostly yes. In the world of first films, the first-time filmmaker is pretty much at the mercy of distributors.

What exactly does a distributor do? We say that a distributor purchases a film, but in actuality the distributor *licenses the rights to exploit the film* for a period of time. A license is a contract that allows the distributor to behave as if he or she owns the film. Your personal distribution deal may cover one or several avenues of distribution. This means that the distributor might make deals with exhibitors, network and cable TV, DVD companies, Internet companies, etc. One difference between you as a filmmaker working with a distributor on a per movie basis and filmmakers with big studio films is that the distribution deal on your movie is a one off—meaning that your deal is about your single film. Most major production companies that operate in the bigger budget realm have *output* deals. These are standing contracts with studios for theatrical distribution, with networks, and with subscription cable companies (premium companies such as HBO, Showtime, and Cinemax). They don't reinvent the wheel with every release. They may have sold off most of their foreign rights even before the camera rolled.

For independent filmmakers, a good distribution deal is the only way to get your film in front of an audience. A distribution deal will include not only a payment for the license of the film, but a commitment for prints and advertising. P&A is often more important for the filmmaker than an upfront fee. If your deal doesn't include very much for P&A, your film can quickly vanish from the public view. Let's say that there is some interest in your film after a successful festival run. Your distributor calls or is receiving calls from exhibitors and bookers, but there aren't enough prints available to go around, and the distributor hasn't contractually committed to a decent P&A budget. The momentum dies. Or you win prize after prize at the festivals, but there's no money for advertising, so no one knows about it until it's too late. Interest in films flares up and can die very quickly. You need to know that your distributor is paying attention and spending the money on making people aware of your work.

A sales agent is a middleman. Unlike a distributor who owns the film for a period of time, a sales agent is a hired hand who represents the film for a fee and a commission. The job of a sales agent is to get your film sold to *foreign territories*. These territories could be countries or groups of countries, and the idea is to license your film to as many of them as possible.

The following section describes the avenues of distribution for a film.

Theatrical Exhibition

Exhibition is the business of screening films in movie theatres to a paying audience. Theatre owners and the corporations that own multiplex theatre chains are *exhibitors*. It doesn't take a genius to walk into a theatre, see those enormous cartons of popcorn, candy, and soda sold at inflated prices to see that the money in mass exhibition is in the popcorn. An exhibitor may be a passionate fan of the art of cinema, determined to screen the best of the best, but the bottom line is they've got to sell snacks to survive. This is the way it works: Exhibitors negotiate with distributors for the right to screen a film. The deal covers the share of ticket sales earnings that will be paid to the distributor, and the share that the exhibitors retain. The exhibitor has expenses, including the maintenance of the theatre, employees, advertising, etc. Because of the expenses, the exhibitor doesn't make much money on the film itself unless it is held over for several weeks and does great business. The exhibitor makes the money on the concession stands. Those overpriced boxes of candy and treats keep those theatres going.

Specialty chains change up the game a bit by providing amenities that enhance the overall movie-going environment. They offer upgraded sound systems, plush seating, restaurant-caliber food, etc. Their idea is to do as much as possible to differentiate the event of sitting in a darkened theatre with being surrounded by kids texting and chatting at the multiplex, and also with a solitary evening at the computer, watching a film being streamed. The customer base for these chains are adults, discerning film lovers who are looking for a viewing environment that is as sophisticated as they are. These chains screen the best of the independent films, and they make a larger share of their money through ticket sales. They recognize and cater to their niche, grownups who are willing to spend more money for a quality evening out and who expect to be viewing a certain type of film—probably not the Hollywood blockbuster.

What does this mean for you? In the case of the big theatre chains, it means that they care most about volume ticket sales, general interest films, and that standby—teen comedies. Teenagers see a lot of movies and eat a lot of popcorn. Your intense indie drama or mature comedy may get a theatrical release if you've got name actors, or if it has received enough press and word of mouth to justify for the multiplex bookers to take a chance, but it's going to be tough. It's not impossible, but you'll have to have amazing reviews, an impressive festival pedigree, and a demonstrated following. What about a limited theatrical release, or the specialty and independent theatre circuit? You're chances are better, but those specialty houses are extremely selective. The specialty chains that are thriving in our current economy have found their niche audiences, and their challenge is to keep them loyal, therefore they are even more careful about maintaining their brand in terms of the type and quality of the films they choose to exhibit.

Television

Your distributor may be able to license the rights to show your film on network or cable television as part of a package or bundle. Network licensing deals are usually in place for a specific period of time and for a specific number of *runs* (screenings). Licensing the typical independent film to a network is a bit rare, as the major networks tend to show movies that were initially in wide theatrical release. But cable is a real opportunity for the first-time filmmaker with a good festival track record. With cable, there are many more runs involved. Your movie may screen several times a day over a period of several months. You may not make a lot of money, but your film will be viewed by a diverse audience—possibly your niche audience—and there is the opportunity to earn a bit of cash through residuals.

Home Video and Online Distribution

Although DVD profits are way down, you can still find a very small audience in the rental and retail sales market. However, the DVD audience is shrinking as consumers want to view their entertainment using their own personal digital devices, rather than renting. This could be a promising route for first-time filmmakers—the equivalent of the now shrunken direct to video market of the 1980s and 90s. Digital streaming and downloads are here to stay, and with the advent of "the cloud" it seems that the studios are figuring out a way to effectively monetize the net. The major distributors are all jumping on the bandwagon.

As of this writing, deals are being made to stagger film releases so that studios and distributors can best profit from digital delivery. Studios now look at social networking as a way to market and distribute films, contriving a way to get us back to the shared experience we seem to be losing by watching films at home on our iPads. It may go something like this: a film in the theatre profits from ticket sales. To view that new, popular film in the comfort of their own home while it is actually screening in the theatres, consumers may pay a premium. If the same consumer is willing to wait to see a film through a subscription-type operation like Netflix, it may take a few months but it will be less expensive. It's too early to know exactly how this will work, but it seems to open possibilities for the first-time filmmaker, as the actual distribution process can be less expensive.

Caution: *You may have your heart set on theatrical distribution, but most independent films are not offered theatrical deals. I have a friend who made a wonderful film and got into major festivals but was not offered theatrical distribution. She was offered a great cable and home video deal, but she was determined to hold out for theatrical. Months passed. Still no deal. Finally she went back to the people who were offering the cable and home video* *deal, but they were no longer interested. You must be realistic. Go for the gold, but realize that if you get any good distribution at all you are winning.*

Yes, you can try to self-distribute through the internet, and you can rent theatres and take your film on tour (this is called *four-walling* the film), promoting it as you go, hoping to garner enough notice and a big enough fan base to attract the attention of a distributor, but you're a filmmaker. Do you really want to be in the distribution business?

Chapter 25

Will Anybody Ever See My Movie?

SELLING YOUR MOVIE

You've made your movie. The next step is to get an audience. It used to be that a film was produced, shown to marketing pros, and then it was their job to figure out how to get those all-essential butts in the theatre seats. Now marketing experts are often brought into the process before a film is green-lit, and the green-light decision is influenced by whether or not they think there is a large enough audience to be found. And if you're trying to get a movie that's already been made out to the public, both marketing and distribution executives are heavily involved in the decision as to whether a company should acquire a film that is screened at a festival or film market.

Your Marketing Campaign

An effective *marketing campaign* (overall plan) requires a thoughtful analysis of exactly what your movie is, who your potential audience is, and how to make them aware of your film. Depending on the size of the marketing budget, a marketing plan usually involves a mix of advertising and publicity. Advertising possibilities include commercials, billboards, posters, print, and radio ads. You pay for advertising. It's expensive, so it better be worth the money. It's not enough to hear the name of the film so that people recognize it. Advertising is intended to push your audience into making the decision: "This is my kind of movie. I'm going to see it."

The publicity component of the marketing/promotional plan is a little more subtle. The articles you see about the production or the director months before the film is released? The stars being interviewed on late-night TV or guest hosting the show or presenting an award on the Oscars? Viral Internet activity? That's publicity. You don't pay for publicity directly. You choose aspects of the project that will appeal to your potential audience, and find a way to make that information alluring enough so that when you dangle it in front of them they take the bait and are motivated to see your movie. There is also sometimes merchandising, though usually not for small independent films. This would include action figures, tie-ins with stores and fast food restaurants, and specific types of contests. If utilized appropriately, merchandising can be an amazingly useful promotional tool for the right movie.

A great marketing and promotion campaign takes perception, creativity, and contacts and combines them with the skillful use of paid advertising. An effective campaign will heighten awareness of a tiny film, generate better box office returns, and can sometimes transform good word of mouth into major financial returns.

Marketing for film should work hand-in-hand with distribution. If distribution is about getting a film out there, marketing is about how to attract the right type of audience so that once the film is out, people want to see it. The first thing a marketing executive will do is decide how the film should be *positioned*. They look at the film and decide how it should be identified to the public: first, is it a family drama, a raunchy teen comedy, a thriller? Who is the potential audience? You want everyone to see your film, but who are the prime targets? What is the age range, ethnicity, socioeconomic make-up of your group? When are they most likely to go see it? Is there another film coming out at the same time of your planned release, and will that film drain your potential audience?

Your marketing person employs his or her experience and instincts in addition to research. If the film is not yet made and is in the planning stages, a marketing person can give you advice on cast—advice that is not about who you should cast for the most artistic film, but about who will make your project more promotable. A marketing specialist will use research to help make a decision about the look of your *one sheet* (advertising poster). There may be research regarding your *trailer*. Does it speak to your anticipated audience? Does it make them want to see more? If the scenes in the trailer are shifted and another, secondary actor is featured, does that help or hurt in terms of drawing your audience? Marketing experts use the results of research to help focus a promotional campaign.

Test Screenings

When you're dealing with a studio film or a film financed and/or expected to be distributed by a major distributor, the marketing department often runs a series of research *test screenings* while the project is still in postproduction to find out how an audience in your target demographic responds. Do they care about the protagonist? Do they understand the movie? How do they feel as they leave? If they love it and would recommend it to their friends, that's outstanding. If they "like it but want to think about it," that tells you something else. It may even call for some editorial changes.

There are companies who work with studios to organize the testing process. If you are a frequent mall shopper in Southern California, you can occasionally spot the clean-cut friendly employees of research companies, scoping out their possible *test audience*. They usually approach a specific demographic. It could be moms with kids in tow, or teenagers, or young couples of specific ethnicities. They ask their targets a few questions, then hand them an invitation to a screening. The screenings are usually in theatres located in an area that corresponds to the test audience. The theatres may be in outlying suburbs for the middle-class family audience, or city centers for more sophisticated, diverse urban testing. The spotters give out lots of invitations, because they know that in spite of what they may say at that moment in the mall, only a fraction of their targets will show up to see the movie.

The company doing the research rents a theatre, and the evening of the test screening, the producer, sometimes the director, and the post, marketing, and distribution people from the production company, come in after the lights go down and stand in the back. They watch and listen to the audience's reaction. Is there a joke that doesn't get the expected laugh? Or worse, is there something not meant to be funny that does get a laugh? At what point is the audience becoming restless? When the movie is over, is the audience invigorated or just glad to go? Usually the audience is asked to fill out survey cards. The results are collected, tabulated, and analyzed. Sometimes the film is altered as a result. Test screenings can be excruciating. The filmmakers are on the defensive. It's their work but it's sometimes a rough and unfinished version, and a bad or indifferent audience can shake them up. But for studio films, it's now pretty much part of the post/marketing routine.

Test screenings can be expensive and are usually not affordable when you're working with lower-budget independent films, but there are other screenings that may be part of your marketing process. There are invitational *preview screenings* for selected members of the press, when it's determined that the right review can make a real difference in finding the film an audience. There are *festival screenings* that can help the film find a buyer.

Being Your Own Publicist

Is there anything you personally can do to help the marketing and PR process along? Definitely. As your movie is being shot, you can be sure that you have good, clear, still photos of several of the scenes. You can have photos and bios of your cast and key creative crew. When a studio picture is being made, there is a publicist and a photographer assigned to assemble all of the above, in addition to managing publicity, electronic press kits, and media interviews with the director and cast. Once the shooting is over, all of these materials are handed back to the marketing department, who may use it to publicize the film. If you're making a small independent film, you don't have the budget for a publicist or a photographer, but you can certainly put together these same materials, to be used once you're going out to film festivals or trying to find a distributor.

Producer's Reps and Sales Agents

As a first-time filmmaker, you may want to employ a marketing consultant and/or a *Producer's representative* and a *sales agent* to help you obtain distribution. A producer's rep usually works for a fee plus a negotiated percentage of the deal that he or she is able to obtain for the film. A marketing consultant usually works for fee. A sales agent represents your film internationally (outside North America).

Hiring on a Producer's Rep and a marketing consultant can be a smart strategy if you get the right people at the right price. Do your research. Who has worked with films of the same type as yours, and what have been the results? On what basis will these consultants be paid? A flat fee? A flat plus a percentage of a sale? What about expenses? What expenses exactly, and how will they be accounted for? Does the fee cover a specific period of time? You don't want a marketing person to sign on and charge you money that you probably don't have, only to shrug and say, "Sorry. I tried." You want a results-based deal. Maybe your film has gotten into a major film festival. You may want to hire someone on for a few weeks before the festival screening to help get buyers and agents into the theatre, and to stay on for a period of time after the festival to help with follow up.

You'll want to have a serious discussion with these people, and you'll want them to be realistic. Don't spend money on anyone, no matter how prominent a name they may have, who doesn't really believe in your film. This means they should love it, even while they are realistic about its potential to compete in the marketplace. They may let you know that due to the subject matter, the cast, or the timing, you probably won't get a buyer for a theatrical release, but you probably will get a cable deal. Listen to them. If they love your film, they'll help push it to the next level, but they are not magicians. They can't force someone to *pick up* (purchase or distribute) a film. What they can do is bring the right buyers to the table and get the film a realistic shot at some kind of deal. If you are hiring a marketing person who has lukewarm feelings about your film, how much passion is this person going to direct towards the effort of getting it seen and sold? On a studio film, these people earn a lot of money, and even then, if they're not excited about a project, you can see it in the marketing effort. Lots of money may be spent, but the marketing campaign is flat and does not inspire. On an independent, they're giving you a price break, so it's more important than ever that if they're representing your film, they're not doing it just for the nominal paycheck.

Even if you have a producer's rep, it important that you involve a marketing person and that he or she has the contacts and clout to get the film in front of the people who have the power to acquire projects. You'll want to know how much time this person is going to spend with you and your film at the festival. I have a friend who hired a producers rep to help him get distribution for one of his films. It came out that this guy was representing more than one film at the same time, at the same festivals and to the same distributors. This meant that he was being paid by competing filmmakers. They were each paying a lower rate, but they were also sharing this person's divided attention. Each meeting this guy had with distributors was about more than one film, not just my friend's film. My friend's film, which had received critical acclaim, was a harder sell. Seeing the producer's rep in action, it became clear that the film was not getting the push that it could have. This was in part because the rep liked the film but didn't love it, liked the filmmaker but didn't love him, and in all fairness because he wasn't really a marketing guy. He didn't think about ways to *brand* or position the film. There were no stars, the subject matter wasn't controversial. It was just an excellent, well-made independent film. When people saw it, they liked it, and it eventually got a foreign sales deal and a cable deal. But the filmmaker managed to get these through his sales agent, not through the rep. A great marketing person with passion might have been able to make a big difference there.

Dawn Taubin

Dawn Taubin is one of the most highly regarded female executives in entertainment marketing. During her six-year tenure as President of Marketing for Warner Bros. Pictures the studio reached the $1 billion mark at the domestic box office every year. Among the films marketed under her leadership are the *Harry Potter* series, which has become the highest grossing film franchise in history, as well as *The Matrix* trilogy, the *Ocean's* series, *300*, *I am Legend*, *Batman Begins*, as well as the Academy Award–winning films *The Departed*, *Happy Feet*, and *Million Dollar Baby*. Taubin was responsible for all aspects of the marketing, including creative advertising, media buying, market research, Internet marketing, publicity, and promotion. After a 19-year career in marketing at Warner Bros., Taubin recently started her own company, Cinema Vision. Her clients have included DreamWorks, Sony Pictures, Relativity, and Rhino Records.

These days, how involved are the filmmakers in the marketing process?

I think that the filmmakers, producers, and directors have increasingly more power and more say in the marketing process. On the studio level, you're dealing with people who have generally made a couple of movies before so they come in and I think have a huge say. Actors have a contractual say, your top directors have a contractual say, your top producers have a contractual say, and everybody else just thinks they should have it. [[Whether or not it's contractual] doesn't stop them from having a point of view or having an opinion. And there's nothing wrong with opinions, but they're not always based on any kind of understanding of what marketing is really about. So [as a marketer] you're trying to educate and at the same time prevail with a point of view while listening to all your constituents. The rub comes when you have to take into account, whether it's contractual or not, all of these people's opinions and [continue to] hold on to your point of view. Because then if the movie fails they say, "Well, you didn't have a point of view with the marketing."

Continued

Dawn Taubin—cont'd

It's further complicated by the financing structure that goes on with movies right now. Sometimes, you can have a movie that has five producers on it. The Academy may only recognize three, but you've got whoever funded the movie and the partner and their partner, and whoever developed the script and who they bought it for and the producer who's aligned with the director, and now you have seven producers that want to meet with you over every single issue, and that complicates things a little bit more. At a marketing meeting sometimes you see camps, because then the production people at the studio weigh in and they want to be involved in the marketing as well. So now you have the marketing camp and the production camp and the filmmaking camp, and my job was just to keep everybody on the same page and to try to navigate them towards a point of view and do what's best for the movie.

What would be the difference in the way a marketing campaign would work if a marketer is on from the very beginning, which might be the case on a studio film, versus coming on once a film is already finished, as would be the case when a distributor has picked the film up at a festival?

If you're starting from the script stage and you develop your strategy on how you want to market the film, often during the production phase you can start to implement that strategy. For example, if you felt it was a movie that you wanted to get some early awareness of, you could invite *Entertainment Tonight* to the set, you could have the *New York Times* and the *LA Times* come to the set and do feature stories. Maybe you'd ask them to hold their stories until the time of release, but at least they could visit the set, talk to the filmmakers, and create some more interesting feature pieces that could come out at the time of the movie's release.

Every movie in production generally has a unit photographer who's covering the making of the movie, and that still photography is crucially important when you come down to marketing a movie. If you are there during production you can make sure that they're getting what you need—that the images that you think are important for advertising are being covered. You can realize as you're looking at that photography that you are going to have to do a special shoot with a special photographer for your poster. A lot of times you will do a special shoot while they're in production, because maybe the actors have a different physical look, maybe their hair is different, maybe the makeup is different, and it's very hard after a movie wraps to go back and get actors to get in character again.

You can shoot behind-the-scenes footage. You can hire a crew that comes in and shoots the making of the movie. Then you'll have those assets for the time of release, and those assets are great for doling out to broadcast outlets or using in advertising, or cutting together for trailers or a behind-the-scenes featurette. All of that can get done during production, which sort of lays the groundwork for your later campaign.

Also during production or between production and your release date, you can take advantage of opportunities that might present themselves—maybe it's taking advantage of an event like Show West [an event for film exhibitors] that's talking

Dawn Taubin—cont'd

about movies or promoting movies. Maybe they'll show a movie or show clips from all their upcoming movies.

If the movie has already been shot and the distributor picks it up at a film festival, you have to rely on whatever the filmmakers are able to give you. One would hope that a photographer was on the set and there is photography, but a lot of times there isn't as much material, or nobody from a marketing perspective is looking at the material that's being shot, so you don't have the option of controlling the marketing assets. It doesn't mean that's insurmountable—you can still go back and try to do a photo shoot, it's just harde. Actors go on to other projects in other parts of the country, and they might be harder to pull back together again. It's largely about assets. You have to start from scratch building awareness with publicity, and you might not have any of those long-range positioning pieces. Again none of this is insurmountable, you just start from another place. You have to start from the minute that you get the film, identifying when your release date is and then building your marketing campaign from the beginning.

First-time filmmakers who go the festival route hope they'll get distribution, and then they're working with a marketing person. They have no idea how to do that. What advice can you give them about how to work with the marketing team?

I think that first thing is, trust that the marketing team knows what they're doing. There's a general inclination, because they might not completely understand every aspect of it, for filmmakers to come in suspicious. That doesn't start a good relationship. Come in trusting that they're there for a reason, and they know what they're doing, and that you can learn a lot from them. That's a great place to start. I don't think that filmmakers should go away and just let the marketing team do the job. It is a collaborative effort. The filmmakers have lived with the movie for a long time. It might have been something they wanted to make for years. They should understand that dialogue between a marketer and a filmmaker can lead to the marketer learning something.

[As a marketer] you look at a movie and ask yourself, Who's the audience for this movie? What's the way to reach that audience? And what are the different prisms I should look through in answering those questions? A dialogue with a filmmaker can help you get there. It's not always obvious. Not every movie is, "It's a sci-fi story starring such and such that does this." Sometimes it's a longer process to get to exactly how you want to position that movie, and I think that dialogue is an important one. I think that filmmakers can also be extremely helpful when it comes to dealing with talent. They have had a relationship with the actors and actresses in the movie for a long time and can be helpful when the marketing team needs to accomplish things. Whether it's something for Advertising, having the actors come to a photo shoot, or Publicity needing them to make appearances, any of that—the filmmakers can be very helpful in that process.

It's a really important relationship. It should be based on [the idea] that we all are here for the same reason, and that's to make this movie as successful as we possibly can.

Russell Schwartz

Russell Schwartz started his career running movie theatres on the art house circuit in the late 1970s in New York. He went on to become President of Marketing at Island Alive, releasing such classics as *She's Gotta Have It, Kiss of the Spider Woman, The Trip to Bountiful,* and *Mona Lisa.* In the 1980s he was Executive Vice President at Miramax. A few of the ground-breaking independent films that he was involved with include *My Left Foot, The Cook, the Thief, His Wife, and Her Lover,* and *Sex, Lies, and Videotape.* From 1992 to 2000, he was President of Gramercy Pictures and was responsible for the release of *Four Weddings and a Funeral, Fargo, The Big Lebowski,* and *Dazed and Confused* among many others. From 2001, he was President of Domestic Theatrical Marketing at New Line Cinema for more than six years. During that time, New Line released *The Lord of the Rings* trilogy, *Rush Hour 2* and *3, Wedding Crashers, About Schmidt, Elf, Hairspray,* and many others. Russell now heads his own company, Pandemic Marketing, which provides strategic marketing, theatrical distribution, and ancillary placement solutions and execution for the motion picture industry.

When you say that you were involved with these movies, exactly what does that mean?

I was involved with the theatrical marketing for all those movies. At Island Alive, I started off as the Vice President of marketing and ended up as President. While there I worked with new and emerging directors like Spike Lee, Jim Jarmusch, and Neil Jordan. When I went to Miramax in 1989, I held the title of Executive Vice President, but the job was really to run all the company's marketing. In the early 1990s I was approached by PolyGram, at that time a huge record company, and they had decided to enter the film business.

It was a very interesting time, because PolyGram was based on the classic record company structure where there were independent record labels creating content that went through a centralized distribution system. In the typical film studio set-up, there is a vertical structure where all production decisions emanate down from a head of production. With the Polygam model there was a horizontal feed of production companies that resulted in a much more diverse slate than you would normally find inside a studio. My company was called Gramercy Pictures, and Gramercy was marketing and distribution, and involved in some acquisitions. Primarily, I was a friendly "adversary" to the four production companies, because I was always pushing them in terms of the marketing side. These are all very furiously independent companies, and back in the early 1990s it was more about making your movies, and it was my job to figure out the audience. That's changed now. What was so good about it [then] was that they all had distinct personalities, so you weren't getting a product feed from a specific mindset. There was a lot of success. I'd say the predominant success came out of Working Title—*Fargo,* all the Coen brothers movies, *Four Weddings and a Funeral* came out of that.

Russell Schwartz—cont'd

What would be the reasons that you'd vote thumbs up, and what would be the reasons you'd vote thumbs down, particularly now?

I think back then, filmmakers, particularly independent filmmakers, were much more involved with the fight to make the movies that they really believed in. Defining the audience for those movies was less of an issue for those filmmakers back then than it is now, because they thought that pretty much every movie was going to work. It's not that they weren't aware that if you're going to make a romantic comedy, you'd better work with Hugh Grant and Richard Curtis should have that screenplay and it has got to have an audience that responds to it. People were certainly aware of that, and there was a testing research process that was going on then, but it wasn't embraced as much then as it is now because [now] everybody really realizes that making the movie is probably half the project for a producer.

Now you are as much of a producer of marketing and distribution as you are a producer of the film. There are two halves, and everything that goes into the first half is a specific skill set, but then there's a whole other skill set that goes into the second half. You've got to be able to talk the talk to the people who are taking your baby and putting it out into the world. You'd better have some say in that. You'd better be sure that whatever you are making, you are able to convince people why they would want to take it out to the world for you. You have to be as versed in the whole postproduction marketing world as you are in the preproduction, development, and production world. It's essential. I believe that [when I was] at New Line, the dialogue was much more heated and more focused at a much earlier point. We would have dialogue with production executives who would come in with a script and say, read this, nothing is green lit, give us your opinions, here is why we should make it. Here's the audience, here's the budget, we think we can do this, here are the comps of other movies similar to it. We would read the script, come up with our own interpretation of the script, and sometimes I'd go back to them and say, No, you're completely wrong about that audience, this is what the audience should be for it. Or, I think you're crazy, that audience would never come into this movie. Or in the case of an international audience . . .

And that's more like what is happening now, that international model?

It is. [The concern with an international audience] even goes further now, because international is such an integral part of a box office—it's 65 percent international now, versus 35 percent domestic.

If a young filmmaker comes to you now, and they have a script that you think is a terrific script, and they say, We have this script and an indie cast, known but not huge . . . and they want you to consult, what would you tell them? Let's say it's a $5 million movie.

If it's a $5 million movie, then the chances of getting any interest from a distribution company are probably pretty small, unless it is a director who is of real interest to any of the smaller companies. At that level [$5 million], the director still is probably the most important person, because he becomes the talent magnet.

Continued

Russell Schwartz—cont'd

It's not that likely that Brad Pitt would be in a $5 million movie, but if Darren Aronofsky wants to make an art film, he'll get Brad Pitt to be in it.

So, if you have a strong director, that could create interest from some of the smaller companies, even though the choices are very, very few these days. At the end of the day, you're going to probably end up trying to finance the picture yourself through any number of ways—through a Netflix deal, through an equity investment, all the different ways that are available right now. It's a long haul. It's not easy doing a $5 million movie.

It seems to me that these days, doing a tiny movie, even a million-dollar movie, is probably easier at this point.

You're right, because anything in that range [$5 million dollars] is too expensive to do it yourself or raise it through your friends or family. And it's too cheap to attract the kind of talent you need. At $1 million, you are raising the money yourself, you are doing it with pretty much an unknown cast, and those movies are your training for the business. There is always the *Paranormal Activity* story. No one should ever count on that it's ever going to happen to them, but it is a way to get going. In cases like that, the million-dollar movie can lead you to a [second] $15 million movie. Even *Paranormal* was sitting around for [a while] before someone picked it up. [At $1 million] the talent isn't there to ring anybody's bells and say, I can sell this movie, this person has this kind of a following. The director is probably not well-known enough to elicit a distribution interest. You are really going to [have to screen at] a festival to see what you can come up with, which in itself is very dangerous.

At the same time it's usually about the only alternative that you have. A festival allows people to see the movie. Wonderful things can come out of it. Some talent can be discovered in the movie, some performances become acknowledged by the critics, and all of a sudden that propels the movie. There is something about it stylistically, some critic may take the movie and write something up about it. But of course you [may] have your five minutes of fame and then you're over because, there are three hundred movies showing in a ten-day period and you get one minute there. If it doesn't click immediately, no matter how much you do to prep—you can create your website, get your press kit together, or hire a publicity firm, hire a consultant, get an agent—you get that one minute.

It's clear what a publicity firm would do, but if you hired a consultant and an agent, what would they do for the movie?

Many filmmakers who go to film festivals usually try to align themselves with one of the traditional agencies, Paradigm, CAA, ICM, to handle their film, and they try to sell it internationally and domestically or to television, and they become your agent. Not every movie will be taken on by the agencies, though, and pretty much every movie is taken on by a publicity firm because they understand what their job is, which is to create awareness. An agency will only take your movie if they really think they can make money on it. They're not going to take your movie if they don't think they can sell it. That happens. In many, many cases, they can't sell it but at least they go out and they try.

Russell Schwartz—cont'd

What do they get if they sell it? Is there a standard deal?

Usually 10 percent of the sale price. The good thing about having an agency or a lawyer or a person who is a consulting person is they know the business, they can talk the talk, they know who to go to, they can negotiate on your behalf, and they can do all the kinds of stuff that you expect someone who's representing your interest to do. Certainly a lawyer or an agent is essential—or it's essential to have some kind of a producer's rep who understands what this business is because they have the relationships. You're not going to be able to get the attention of the acquisitions guy from Focus unless he knows the person who's contacting him. You [the filmmaker] need help. You cannot go into a film festival and expect to be discovered on Main Street in Park City or on Yonge Street in Toronto. It doesn't happen. Because nobody has the time, and the press doesn't have the time. They're always running from one screening to another. They're always more interested in the films that have some kind of awareness going in—the cast member or concept, mostly the director—that's where they're putting their attention. You have a million-dollar movie, you need somebody to tell this press person or this distributor, you've got to look at this.

So you do this, and if they love the movie, what happens then? What should the filmmaker know about the next step?

The dream scenario then is that if your agent or representative is savvy enough, he will then try to start juggling the interest, and the best thing you could possibly have is two or three companies vying for your movie. Then your representation starts trying to get the best possible deal, which is first and foremost driven by a minimum guarantee in advance to buy the rights of the picture or domestic rights, or for international rights.

If you have a number of people who are interested in the movie, the deal should not be made on how much money is being paid. Even filmmakers are getting savvy now and saying, "If you pay me a million dollars for my movie and it cost me $2 million, I'm half way out. But if you're not going to do the proper job for my movie—I know what should be done with it—then I'd rather sell it to the person who'll give me $200,000 but has a real clue or an angle or a philosophy or a sales plan about how to push the movie out there."

Companies that are more DVD-driven, more like Anchor Bay, or more television driven like IFC, or even like Magnolia primarily, their business model is all about feeding their ancillary world, their television world, their cable television world, their HDNet world, or their home video world. Smaller companies who are more theatrically driven usually come up with interesting plans. But at the same time, you're not availing yourself with the resources that some of these other companies might have. If you want the marketing clout that some of the bigger, independent companies [like Focus or Sony Classics] have, you could be better off giving them the picture for a small amount of money as long as they give you a decent commitment on how much they're going to spend on prints and advertising.

Let's take the other scenario. The film doesn't sell at the festival.

We're talking Sundance, right? There are other festivals, Toronto, Cannes, South by Southwest. There is of course the issue of festival fatigue, if the movie starts going

Continued

Russell Schwartz—cont'd

to too many festivals and doesn't get picked up, nothing is going to happen. Which is where 85 to 90 percent of the movies end up, but we'll come back to that. If it doesn't sell on the first couple of days, you wake up and realize that everybody doesn't love your passion project as much as you thought they would. But there is still an afterlife to the festivals, which is becoming more and more the norm rather than the exception, where you hear that movies get picked up a week later, two weeks later, four weeks later, six weeks later, eight weeks after the festival is over. What that means is the buyers had interest, but they don't want to get into any kind of a bidding war. So the movie isn't so important to them that they must have it. They're laying back and waiting for the prices to come down, waiting for everybody to get more rational, and then a lot of movies are sold at a much lower price. From the euphoria of the sell to the reality of the release is a big difference.

For the 85 to 90 percent of the movies that don't find homes, that's where the real reality sets in, and what do producers do about that? A lot of producers will go out and raise another million or $2 million to give their film a theatrical shot so they can try to make ancillary deals, because theatrical box office is still very important for creating awareness.

They're distributing themselves?

No, there are companies that will take your movie for a fee. You come up with the P&A. They'll take anywhere from 8 percent to 10 percent after they release your picture for you. Some companies will do it for a flat fee—$200,000, or $50,000—"Let's put it in a number of theaters." That is where most independent festival movies end up.

Has anything that you can think of broken out that way? It seems like a long shot.

It's a very long shot, because the bottom line is there's a reason why a lot of these movies did not get picked up initially. When you go through six or eight or ten companies and your picture doesn't get picked up, there's probably a reason. There's always a surprise [success], but it's not a happy place you want to be.

What's happening now is that people are starting to take that idea and creating more of a hybrid distribution model, where you go into your production knowing that you may be releasing it yourself, and you prepare for that. You start seeding your film and all your online stuff, your social media place. You get your communities going. You have your conversation with television people early on. Maybe Netflix wants to make it a premier picture, maybe HBO wants to take it. There are so many options now, that to go those traditional theatrical routes is not always the best way to go.

People find that at festivals, HBO will buy a movie, will then partner with somebody and go theatrically, or they'll just go ahead and put it right on cable. It's perfectly fine, nothing wrong with it. There are buyers everywhere. It may not be how you envisioned it, but it doesn't mean your premier is not going to be as big. As a producer, you're there to return the investment to your investors. You're not there to get the glory of having a movie released. You are a business person first and foremost. That is your job. If you don't return as much as you can to your investors, you're not going to get a chance to make another movie.

Pat Quinn

Pat Quinn started as an agent at ICM, where she became Head of the West Coast theatre office. Within two years, she became a television packaging agent, packaging TV shows. After five years at ICM, she then moved over to Warner Bros. Television as Vice President of Comedy Series Development for two years, and followed that by a career as an agent at Metropolitan, Innovative, and Paradigm. Her clients have received Tony, Emmy, and Academy Awards. Pat was involved in the fundraising and financing of the early stages of Sundance (when it was still the U.S. Film Festival), helping with the development of their programs, including the film festival and the Sundance Film Institute. Four years ago she started her own company (Quinn Media Management) and is now an international television consultant. She represents UK and Irish production companies' formats and sells them to U.S. networks. Her other clients include two leading broadcasters in Europe, who she advises on content acquisitions.

One thing that's not going to happen is you're not going to be able to raise a million dollars on a full-length film script that has any resemblance to the film you did at film school. The film school model can be a little deceptive, because there is no distributor saying, who are the stars? What is the content? How is it going to do internationally? There's no one really vetting it. What you're doing at school is you're getting an incredible experience of working with equipment, working with the team, seeing if you have any leadership qualities at all, seeing how you are at casting. You're not dealing with big crews, you're not dealing with a distributor—and you know what, you don't have to make a profit!

The tricky thing is with your million-dollar movie is that you have to [find] a genre that has some track record in the marketplace. Those are horror, some "spiritual" movies, and thrillers. I think something like a *Napoleon Dynamite*, the quirky little weird movie, could do well. Teen comedy. Something that's also not going to suffer from the smallness of your budget.

It would be a fabulous opportunity if the first-time filmmaker went to AFM (the American Film Market) and just walked around and looked at the posters and also studied the grosses on those movies. You have to do that because the process of raising the money—even with the benevolent investor—is, is this going to make any money? is this going to make any money?

First-time filmmakers should go around and they should meet with distributors. Distributors are willing to meet with them. When I'm in line at AFM, I'm behind people on laptops showing those distributors [their plan]. It's a real wake-up call, because the distributors are going to tell you whether they can sell that genre in their territories, whether they think there's any commercial value, how flooded the market is or isn't with that, and they're also going to tell you, if you give them a list of actors you're going after, they're going to tell you, yes, no, yes, no, yes, no. It's going to be clear as day, and this can be a painful experience. Going later [after the movie is made] to the distributors ... then they're just going to say no, I'm not going to distribute the movie. Why didn't you come to me and tell me you had [actor's name]? I would have told you not to go with them, they're poison in the market.

Continued

Pat Quinn—cont'd

If you approach the fundraising as an investment, someone is going to wonder how they're going to get their money back. It is just like selling a car or selling a house. They're going to want comparables. And they're not going to want fantasy comparables, they're going to want real comparables with the same budget, a similar genre, a similar production method (live action or animation), and secondarily, cast and director. That's tough, because often in the $1 million, $2 million [budget range], most of them don't make their money back.

I worked for a distributor in Germany, and she could not have been more polite. People would come to her who had this movie, "It's about this, it's about that," [and she'd say,] "I can't sell that." Now, most of them [will act like the meeting] didn't happen. "That didn't happen. I'm moving on with my passion and my dream. I'm doing [my movie] no matter what." These people just don't get it, or [they feel] this is too depressing, or that they don't need to worry about it, or "I'm going to enter into Telluride and Sundance and Toronto and I'm going to win. . . ."

FILLING THE SEATS: THE FUTURE OF THE MOVIE THEATRE BUSINESS

Ted Mundorff

Ted Mundorff started his career in high school—he worked as an hourly usher for General Cinema Corporation. After college, he went to work at Paramount Pictures in an entry-level position, and a few years later, he left and started his career as a film buyer at Cinemette Corporation of America, where he was responsible for negotiating and/or selecting the motion pictures that played in the movie theatres he represented. In 2003, Ted accepted a position with Landmark Theatres and a few years later became the CEO of the company. Landmark currently has 1,400 employees, 61 theatres, and 297 screens. They are the largest exhibitor of specialized product in the United States—and possibly the largest exhibitor of specialized product in the world.

How would you define specialized product?

I would define it as independent product, which includes foreign-language film, documentaries, and smaller independent titles. We also play larger independent titles from the major studios, and we select studio films that fit our niche—our niche being an older [demographic] than you'd find at your normal megaplex. That demographic is actually looking for quite a bit of a different experience than the megaplex provides, more of an adult experience, and that's what we do. We are in the top 18 of the top 20 markets in the United States, and we are continuing to look to expand and grow the company, as we have since 2004.

Ted Mundorff—cont'd

Is the role of movie theatres changing? Who sees their movies at the theatre and who watches their films on other media or formats? What are you doing now with your theatres to make seeing a film at a theatre a different experience?

There are a number of questions there. Number one, we are very bullish on the business, and we are bullish due to the facts. The fact is that this year we are currently 9 percent up over our previous year. Last year was a tremendous year, and yet we [still] are 9 percent up. The fact is that the commercial fare, the movies coming out of the studios, I think the public has gotten tired of them. I think as the culture of America has gotten older, the theatre-goers are supporting theatres like Landmark.

The major exhibitors have changed. They've entered into the independent specialty business. They are trying to grab a piece of that pie, because they've seen that that has been a growth area at least since 2004. Everybody was crying back in 2007, 2008 that it was "the end of the independent film," and "independent film doesn't do any business." Companies went under, and for a moment in time, we didn't have the amount of distribution companies and film providers that we'd had in the previous years. But as everyone was crying about the end of independent film, we [Landmark] were very confident that [that] wasn't the case. If anything, the value of Landmark has soared because the independent film, in fact, has survived. Is it a smart way to spend two hours of your time, [seeing an independent film,] instead of watching [a major star] do the same part over and over? I think people have spoken with their pocketbooks.

There is a loss of income for studios and for companies in the DVD market. Everybody is worried about monetizing the internet, everybody is trying to come up with new ways to see movies, and yet people are still apparently wanting to see a lot of independent films in theatres.

It's still a $10.5 billion business. It's still a healthy business. The way people are seeing movies is changing. It doesn't mean that anything is unhealthy; possibly I won't invest in a DVD company today, but the *VOD* world, the video-on-demand world that we hear so much about, what that does is it provides people with the opportunity to see a movie. There is a period of time when even if people want to go to movies—when they have children, etc.—they can no longer go. The VOD world, the on-demand world, the Netflix world, keeps the movies in front of those people. Those people still are connected to seeing movies, so when they return to the marketplace, they are current—instead of feeling, I haven't seen a movie in 20 years. Because if you haven't seen a movie in 20 years, you're not going to go see a movie.

I think that most people, I don't care what age they are, would prefer to see a movie in a theatre. That doesn't mean that someone isn't also going to see a movie somewhere else. When VHS came out, [it was thought that]it was the end of the world for the theatrical exhibition. The reality was just the opposite. The reality is that it gave people movies on demand. Instant access to film history. When I grew up, the only way I could see older films was *Saturday Night at the Movies* on TV. You didn't have a lot of access beyond that. There were some rep [repertory] theaters, but usually they were grungy and awful and that probably wasn't what you

Continued

Ted Mundorff—cont'd

were going to do. So you only had a limited amount of films that you would ever be exposed to in your life. It was like the 25 songs they play on the radio all the time. What happened with VHS was, it expanded that playlist, and that playlist educated people and created a pop culture of film. We see that every Friday and every Sunday when you turn on CBS, ABC, NBC, and they're reporting box office like it's a baseball score. That is a product of VHS. It's a product that continues into DVD, and it continues into the world of Netflix.

My assumption is that people reading this book will be either people in film school or people just out of film school or just getting started, and they usually gravitate towards independent films ...

Because studios are not going to fund them for their first movie.

A lot of them will make movies and never get distributed, but some of them will get limited distribution. And they really want to see their films in theatres. What is some advice you have for them?

There has been a stigma for almost 30 years now, of straight to video movies. I think that stigma will change. I think five years from now there may not be that stigma. I think there will be [straight to video] films as there were films made for television. At one time, those were below theatrical standards. Not today, with HBO in the world. They've done a tremendous job, and many of their productions and series are better than the theatrical. I think that will change, and that's an important thing. There will be movies that will play better as straight to video, just as there are movies that play better on television.

I think there will be different avenues that one can go. They're starting out with an independent film. They'll be saying, "During this part of my career, I had three films and I went in the Netflix direction, or it was released through Cinedigm ..." There will be different ways to see the movies. There will be fewer movie theatres, but people will still gather in community to go see a movie. That isn't going to change. There's not a filmmaker who doesn't want that moment ...Who doesn't want that moment on the opening night of the film, where the theatre gets dark before it hits the screen, and you can't replace that moment. It's a great moment for the filmmaker, and it's also a great moment for the person going to the movie, because it's an opportunity. The darkness comes, it wipes out everything, and you get to start fresh. It doesn't matter if the last movie you saw was terrible, it's a fresh start, and there's really nothing in the world like that.

This book is about the business aspects of filmmaking that people who want to make movies should know, but they don't think of themselves as business people ...

We're all business people.

... ***so my last question is just, how do the exhibitors make money? People say it's all about popcorn.***

Everyone loves to say that. Everyone loves to say it's about popcorn, but if we don't drive bodies into the theatres, there's no popcorn sales. The fact is, in the specialized world, we do not survive off of popcorn, because our demographic doesn't have three kids in tow, buying out the store. The answer is to put butts on seats.

Ted Mundorff—cont'd

It's important to maintain that relationship with your customers and provide them with an experience that makes them want to come back to you. To provide them [with this experience] from the physical side of it and from the customer service side of it. It's also important as far as your product mix, what you're putting in the theaters. Landmark's brand, using Landmark as an example . . . today, the brand is an adult experience, an adult environment. Not texting in the theatre, not [having cell phones] on, not having conversations on cell phones during movies. It is generally about our customers, and it's about our staff. We're very, very engaged with our customers. Companies that recognize their niche and serve it well will survive.

Chapter 26

Festivals

Once upon a time, there were only a handful of film festivals. There was the ultraglamorous Cannes Film Festival, there were Venice, Berlin, and Karlovy Vary (in the Czech Republic). There were smaller, more niche festivals, and journalists, critics, filmmakers, and fans knew all about them. But to Hollywood and the general population, film festivals were not such a big deal. Then, in the late 1970s, came the Toronto International Film Festival, and very soon after that, Sundance.

Sundance began its life as the very small U.S. Film Festival and became the Sundance we've all heard of in the early 1980s, soon after it was taken over by Robert Redford. As Sundance became a success, lots of other festivals cropped up, and many small, specialty festivals became bigger. It became evident that there were many filmmakers who were willing to submit their work for exhibition, and many film fans who were happy to spend their holidays seeing movies. Festivals were good business. They attracted both locals and tourists and gave new economic life to resort and vacation areas in the off-season.

WHICH FESTIVALS REALLY MATTER?

There are hundreds of festivals all over the world, and the make-up of the attendees at each festival is different. There are several really charming festivals that cater to film lovers who are looking for a long weekend of movie viewing and guest celebrities, and these are always a lot of fun. People are there because they love watching films and want to see not only the latest efforts of their favorite filmmakers but also to discover the work of the next wave—the up-and-coming film students, the emerging darlings of the independent world.

There are also *niche* festivals. The people who choose the films for these festivals select them on the basis of how effectively the creative work speaks to a specific constituency. There are family film festivals and gay film festivals. There are festivals that show only *shorts* (films under 40 minutes in length), documentary festivals, sci-fi and horror festivals.

Most relevant to you as a young or first-time filmmaker, there are the industry festivals. These festivals attract people in the business: studio executives, marketing and distribution pros, agents, filmmakers, the national and international press. By Hollywood standards these are Cannes, Toronto, Sundance, Telluride (in Colorado), South by Southwest (in Austin, Texas), the AFI Fest (in Los Angeles) of the American Film Institute, Tribeca (in New York), the New York Film Festival, and Comic-Con in San Diego. This is not to say that the other festivals are not terrific, and that a string of acceptances into them will not help you, but there is a substantial name value attached to getting in to one of the major festivals. Whatever the perception of your movie is before, "Official Selection of the Sundance Film Festival" has a seductive ring. People in the business will be a little more willing to pay attention.

WHY DO FESTIVALS MATTER, AND HOW DO THEY WORK?

The point of a festival is to get your work shown, and in the case of the industry festivals, to get your movie shown to people who might write about the film, sell or buy the film, and help you to advance your career. There is a lot of cachet to having a film at one of these festivals, as they serve as showcases for what is commonly assumed to be the best, most original new films and filmmakers. The eyes of the industry are on the selected films and filmmakers. Many films are purchased for distribution at or as a result of screening at these festivals. If your film is screened *in competition*, a distinguished *jury* of critics and filmmakers will view, discuss, and judge your work. It is an honor to be the recipient of an award at any festival, but to be awarded "Best" at one of the industry festivals will lead to major buzz about you and your movie.

Some festivals are part of actual film markets (Cannes, Toronto). Some festivals take place at the same time as a major market (AFI Fest and the American Film Market, or AFM). And some are stand alone. and the market aspect of the festival is just the hustling of various buyers and sellers trying to move and acquire the various projects. The markets are trade events, almost film bazaars. Even if a film is not accepted into a festival competition, it can screen at the market and take advantage of the huge gathering of potential buyers. Sales agents and distributors buy space at the markets in order to collar those representing international territories. They have marketing material, a room to screen the film, and they are often successful in licensing or selling foreign rights on the basis of the cast or the film's genre.

HOW DOES YOUR FILM GET INTO A FESTIVAL?

Each festival has a different submission process and different criteria, and many charge a different fee to submit. You must read the application/submission form carefully. You can find listings of film festivals online. There are hundreds of them, so again, you should do your homework. A small submission fee is legit, but paying the festival to screen your film is a scam. You must look beyond the festival website. What press has the festival received in the past? Have you heard of any film that opened or closed the festival? Have you heard of anyone on the panels, if there are some? Being an "Official Selection" of a questionable festival will not work to your advantage.

It's important to recognize that not all films are the right type for all festivals. No festival screens only one kind of film, but people in the festival world tell me that festivals have distinct personalities. Sundance seems to go for American films with an indie feel, and that the films are often off-beat but with heart. Toronto is a blend of commercial and independent and seems to cover a broad spectrum. Cannes is truly an international festival and tries to program films from as many countries as possible. Back in the United States, Telluride trends towards drama that deals with serious subjects—political issues, environmental issues. A friend of mine said of the programmers at Telluride, "They don't like to laugh." South by Southwest leans towards quirky, individualistic films. By all means give these festivals a try, but don't discount the several nicely run, legitimate, smaller festivals. Although they are not packed with people in the industry, they have good credentials, and some of the shorts festivals are Academy qualifiers. Collecting awards or even being accepted to a multitude of festivals works for you, because it helps draw interest and press to you and your project.

Helpful hint: There is an online festival submission service called *Without A Box* that has become an important participant on the festival circuit. Without A Box enables filmmakers to submit their film to several festivals at once, streamlining the process considerably and ultimately saving the filmmaker money—which is obviously useful for first-time filmmakers.

There are a several ways for an independent film to become an *official selection* (invited to screen) at a festival. There is the ordinary submission process. You get on the website, read the directions and the rules, pay a submission fee, and send in your film. Your film is usually previewed by a group of volunteers, and recommended or not recommended. The volunteers watch hundreds of films. Although they are supposed to watch the films in their entirety, several volunteers told me confidentially that after the first half hour, if they're not engaged they go on to the next. If recommended by the volunteers, the film makes its way up the evaluative chain to the screeners, and then hopefully it continues its upward climb until it gets to the final authority—the *programmers*. The programmers give the final nod or thumbs down. They also piece together the slate of films that are selected to screen, deciding at what time the films will screen and in which theatre. The placement of a film can be important. It sends a signal about the programmers' expectations for the film.

If it's a large venue and scheduled for primetime, Friday or Saturday evening, clearly the programmer is a fan. The level of competition at the most major festival—Sundance—is as fierce as you might guess. According to the Sundance Film Festival website (www.sundance.org/festival), in 2010, 9000 films were submitted and 200 were chosen. The odds are a bit daunting, but every year people submit and are accepted through this process.

Does it help to know somebody in order to be invited to screen at one of the industry festivals? If the right person knows the right person, possibly a little more attention will be paid. Sometimes a powerful executive will make a call because they feel strongly about a project. Or a producer's rep with a project might whisper in the ear of a programmer friend. But by and large, the process of selection is objective.

If your film is accepted, you will usually receive notification six weeks to a few months in advance of the actual event. Upon this notification (after guzzling that bottle of champagne) your producer and director should immediately begin to plan their festival strategy. This strategy depends upon how much money you have or can cobble together. You might

1. Hire a producer's rep if you don't already have one.
2. Hire a marketing or PR consultant.
3. Inform your lead actors of the acceptance. Inquire about their availability during the days or week of the festival, in case your promotional strategy involves bringing them along with you (publicity photos and post-screening Q&A sessions.)
4. Reach out to everyone and anyone you might know with any power in the business, to let them know that you got in, in case they know distributors or agents who might be interested in seeing the film, and try to set up as many meetings as possible for the hours and days after the screening.
5. Try to parlay your newly minted buzz into meetings with people who might not have been willing to meet with you before to talk about projects you'd like to do in the future.

Whatever the perception of your movie was before, once you've gotten into a major festival, it becomes more valuable. "Official Selection of Sundance" or "Telluride" or "South by Southwest" has a nice ring to it. People in the business may be more willing to pay attention.

Industry festivals combine premieres, screenings, panels, and parties. Premieres are usually star-studded events and often open or close the festival. These are new films distributed by studios and established production companies, and they are not part of any competition. So your film is not competing with Scorsese's latest, even though they are both showing at the festival. These projects are being exhibited to generate accolades from the press and positive word of mouth from the festival-goers

Most of the festival activity is centered around the screenings. The screenings are usually divided into themed sections, such as "American Stories," "New Voices," etc. The audience has a printed program with the show times of each film and a thumbnail description, the names of the lead cast, and usually a tiny publicity photo from the film. In the back of the program there is usually a single-paragraph bio of the director of each film. The casual audience members use the program to decide which screenings to attend.

The professionals who come to do business have done most of their research before they fly in and pretty much have a list: there are the films they haven't seen but have heard about through pre-festival contacts and promotion; there are the films they've seen but they want to see again to finalize their decision as to whether to get involved; and finally there are the wild cards—films they know nothing about but there is something intriguing about the director, the cast, or the synopses. They are also curious about the results of the juried screenings. Which film wins Best, which wins the Audience Award? Every once in a while there is a surprise groundswell of affection for a jewel of a film that no one expected. There is the excitement of the discovery of new, unexpected talent. Sometimes there is the thrill of a bidding war. And there is the media coverage of all of it.

This glimmer of possibility is why young filmmakers are determined to play the odds and submit their projects, and it's why the people whose job it is to find the next great film make the pilgrimage to these festivals year after year. You just never know.

HOW TO WORK A FESTIVAL

Your film has been accepted into a prestigious festival. How do you make the most of the opportunity? How do you get it seen? Or you've made a short film, maybe a student film, and you've been selected to screen at one of the important festivals. What do you do? How do you use it to get you and your film additional opportunities?

As discussed, you should start doing your advance work weeks before the festival to approach people about seeing your film. If you're a director and you've made a feature, you may try to be in contact with potential agents or managers. Sometimes they'll promise to attend the screening at the festival; sometimes they'll ignore your call. Once they see the film, they may want to hop on board and help you get the right kind of audience in, and the right kind of attention. If they have any clout and they love your film, they'll want to be sure that the journalists who count are there to review it. It's possible, too, that they'll want to wait to see what kind of reviews your film receives before they decide if they want to sign you on. If there's a very positive reaction, they may want to sign you before anyone else does. If you get a nice but not outstanding reception, they may want to leave the theatre without saying hello. All you can do is try to get the buzz going.

Caution: *Don't screen your film for groups before the festival, especially if it's for a festival like Sundance. You want to use the momentum of the festival to generate some excitement, and too many advance screenings can age the film in people's minds.*

Be sure that your promotional materials are as professional and compelling as possible, and that they are readily available. Your promotional material should include: cast bios, credits, and headshots (color and black and white); bios of the director and producer (no more than a paragraph); and a plot logline: "Two brothers are rivals for the same woman—their mother." (Only kidding—please don't make that movie.) You should also have a short plot synopsis and a few still photographs from the film. And you should be sure that you've included the name and number of the person representing your film, or your name and number (a cell where you can be reached at the Festival, not a home number where your voicemail will pick up and you'll get the message a week later.)

You must have a way to get your film into the hands of people who can do something for you. I personally believe that means never giving anyone at a festival a copy of your film. People are handed all sorts of cards and DVDs at festivals. Once they are packing to leave, many of the DVDs end up in the hotel wastebasket and they can't remember why they took your card, so they throw that in a pile and never look at it again. Work smarter. When you meet someone who likes your movie or is interested in you, ask for her card and ask if you can call to set up a brief appointment once you are back in L.A. If she says yes, then a few days after the screening or the third workday after the festival (the first couple of days back, everyone is too busy playing catch up with the calls and work they've missed), call or send her an email. Remind her who you are and which film was yours, and ask if she has a few minutes to meet to give you some advice. If you can't get to her directly, ask her assistant if he or she (the assistant) has time to meet.

Learn to pick people's brains. Don't be defensive, although it's hard not to be. Listen to what people say about your work, both the good and the bad. If several people have the same problem, you may want to consider making some changes. Realize that you may not find a buyer or distributor at a festival, but that doesn't mean the festival was a wasted effort. If your film does well, you become someone to watch, and people in the industry are always on the lookout for new talent. They may not take out their checkbook or sign you on, but now they're aware of you, and that can only be to your benefit.

If you've got a short (usually these are student films) in a festival and someone likes it and asks you what you want to do next, don't just say, "I want to do a feature." Have a few pitches ready. Short films don't have much of a non-festival life, so the person is asking you because he thinks you might have an interesting feature planned. Be prepared. If he loves your short, maybe your third idea will be a feature-length adaptation of the short plus two other ideas. *Be aware that many excellent short films excel in part because that particular format works for that story. If you want to have a career as a filmmaker, it should never appear that you have only one story to tell.*

Derek Horne

A Festival Veteran

Derek Horne has worked both sides of the festival fence. He's worked at many festivals, including Sundance where he worked and volunteered for six years. He's programmed for festivals coast to coast, from Newport, R.I. to Newport Beach, Calif., and in between at Anaheim, Avalon, Sarasota, and Shorts

Derek Horne—cont'd

International in New York. He can also identify with what filmmakers are going through when they submit their films. He's worked at Chapman University for eight years as the film coordinator, where part of his responsibility is submitting student films to festivals and promoting them.

Let's say you're a starving filmmaker. You've made your first feature and you get into an important festival. If you don't have much money, how can you make the festival work best for you? What should you do while you're at the festival, and how should you follow up after the film is screened?

You want to strategize on how to get a big audience for your film. The goal is to get a distribution deal or garner positive press or word of mouth. In the weeks leading up to the festival, you should decide how you want to package the film and market it, and what you want on the poster and the postcard to catch people's attention. You want to try to get as many industry people there at your screening. Tickets are limited, and as a guest of the festival you're given some complimentary tickets, but probably not as many as you will need. So it's best to purchase your own ticket packages, to have extra tickets to give to your friends and other industry people that you want to invite. This would also be a good time to talk to a sales agent, who can help you negotiate potential distribution deals. You don't necessarily want to take the first distribution offer that comes along, unless it's a really good one. A lot of filmmakers will jump at the chance of having the prestige associated with being bought by a [known] distributor. But you should look at that company's track history and question if it will work hard for your film.

What about contacting people you know will be going to the festival to let them know about your film so that they will actually go to see your film? Or how about screening it for them before the Festival?

You definitely contact them to let them know you're screening. If they don't come to your screening, you can host a screening for them afterwards, but make sure it's soon after, before the hype wears off. As soon as the programming list is released, filmmaker's voicemails will start getting filled up with distributors who probably want to see an advance copy of the film, which the filmmaker should not send [it can dilute the impact of a premiere]. Many films use a festival as their launching pad and for publicity. Even if your film doesn't attract huge crowds at the festival, you can still use the festival acceptance as a way to rev up your overall marketing efforts and convince other festivals to program your film.

Say we've got a filmmaking team that has gotten into Sundance. They've done whatever pre-marketing they can, they hire a publicist, and they have a sales agent, but they don't have distribution. It's now the week before their screening.

They usually should arrive in Utah the day before their screening. The week before the screening, they should already be solidifying many of their appointments, since they have hopefully received a flood of emails from people who want to meet with them. They should be setting up as many meetings as possible. When they get to Sundance, they should start hanging up their posters and flyers. They should take a trip to the press office and drop off their press packets. (Most filmmakers are moving away from paper press packets. Now everyone has got a thumb drive.)

Continued

Derek Horne—cont'd

It's smart to have a website built up, a very nice eye-catching website that draws people to them, not only as an artist who makes great films but as someone who knows how to do an amazing publicity campaign, because the new method of publicity and building the audience is online. You definitely need three or four different versions of your synopsis. A one-sentence logline, a two- or three-sentence short synopsis, and a medium synopsis that is probably four paragraphs long. You could also include a long page-and-a-half synopsis, which tells in detail what happens in the film and which is for those journalists who didn't have time to see your film.

You should also have photos. Not just the cast headshots; those are usually included on the page with the bios. I am talking about the still images that come from within the film, not behind the scenes. It should be a photo that looks like it is a scene from a film, like a screen grab. A lot of those photos will not only go into the festival's souvenir catalog to promote your film, but hopefully they will make it into a news story that will feature a picture that will make people want to see your film. Choose photos that are intriguing, that catch people's attention, and that tell something about the story. You also want to include a page of cast and crew credits which list in perfect detail without typos, everyone's name, their character name, or their position on the film.

Now you're at the festival. You go to your screenings, attend your Q&A sessions, and try to say things that are smart and that will help you get a distribution deal. Don't mention the budget. Maybe give people interesting stories that a journalist in the room might think, "Ah, I want to know more and write an article about that." Give them an angle. And I don't think it is stupid to advise filmmakers to try and come off as a nice, likeable person.

Then you've got to drag yourself to the cocktail receptions even if you are really exhausted. Work the room as fast as you can and give out business cards. I am most comfortable working the room at a film festival because you have a topic in common, so it's easier to strike up a conversation with people and ask if they've seen any good films. That is the best conversation starter. It is intimidating to go to a party by yourself. So if you're a director, make sure you have your producer with you. At the very least take a friend, anyone, just to avoid standing around awkwardly with nothing to say or do.

Hopefully you will have your schedule filled up by official events that the festival has invited you to, special exclusive events just for the filmmakers, like the Sundance Film Festival brunch with Robert Redford. You may not have a lot of time in your schedule to go to any insignificant events, so try to pick the ones where you know other industry people will be.

If we're talking about Sundance, there is an Industry Office, so you could hang around there and try to meet distributors. At festivals like Cannes or the international short film market at Clermont-Ferrand in France, which is the largest short film festival in the world, they have either guide books that include people's photos, or they have something like a bulletin board on the wall or online where they post everyone's photos. Once you know what somebody looks like, you can try to spot them at the festival events.

Derek Horne—cont'd

What if there is a distributor that you really feel would be a good match for your movie and you know they're going to be at the festival where you're screening?

You would do the same thing a distribution company does with its slate of films. Send out emails before the festival saying, "Hey, we are playing at Sundance, and we'd love to invite you to our screening, and we are available any time for a meeting. Here's our cell phone number and here's our office."

Something I should mention that is an increasingly frustrating element of all this, is how bad press can stifle the process of getting a distribution deal. I'm not talking about the films that are really bad and that deserve the bad press. I am talking about the films that are extremely entertaining and the audience loves, but that the film critic pans for whatever personal reason or agenda. I really wish distributors and other festival programmers would continue to approach films objectively, even after reading a review, and perhaps get second opinions from the audience. But I think that some distributors get lazy and put all of their stock in the critics' opinion. I wish the distributors would remember that many critics are not interested in reviewing films for their entertainment value but are only interested in validating them as an art form that matches their own idiosyncratic criteria and taste.

What are the important places to get good reviews?

Indiewire, Variety, Hollywood Reporter, the *New York Times, LA Times, Film Threat,* Internet blogs. It's important to try to get a high score on Metacritic and Rotten Tomatoes, which are compendiums of a lot of different reviews.

For those of you who already have a film, if you're ready to start the festival route, Derek has his "Top 10 Get Discovered" Festivals list.

These U.S.-based festivals offer filmmakers the opportunity to meet industry movers and shakers, score distribution or development deals, or get discovered by other festival programmers:

1. Sundance Film Festival (Utah) www.sundance.org
2. Tribeca Film Festival (New York) www.tribecafilm.com
3. South by Southwest (Texas) www.sxsw.com
4. Los Angeles Film Festival (California) www.lafilmfest.com
5. AFI Fest (California) www.afi.com
6. Austin Film Festival (Texas) www.austinfilmfestival.com
7. Florida Film Festival (Florida) www.floridafilmfestival.com
8. Hamptons International Film Festival (New York) www.hamptonsfilmfest.org
9. Santa Barbara International Film Festival (California) www.sbfilmfestival.org
10. Seattle International Film Festival (Washington) www.siff.net

And for Short Films only:

- Palm Springs International ShortFest (California) www.psfilmfest.org
- L.A. Comedy Shorts Film Festival (California) www.lacomedyshorts.com

Filmmakers should also know about Derek's additional list, *"Festival Gems with Great Hospitality."*

Continued

Derek Horne—cont'd

These U.S.-based festivals provide both feature and short film directors with lodging and sometimes free airfare and are just plain fun:

1. Ashland Independent Film Festival (Oregon) www.ashlandfilm.org
2. Bend Film Festival (Oregon) www.bendfilm.org
3. Cucalorus Film Festival (North Carolina) www.cucalorus.org
4. Nantucket Film Festival (Massachusetts) www.nantucketfilmfestival.org
5. Port Townsend Film Festival (Washington) www.ptfilmfest.com
6. Sedona International Film Festival (Arizona) www.sedonafilmfestival.com
7. Starz Denver Film Festival (Colorado) www.denverfilm.org
8. Stony Brook Film Festival (New York) www.stonybrookfilmfestival.com
9. Waterfront Film Festival (Michigan) www.waterfrontfilm.org
10. Williamstown Film Festival (Massachusetts) www.williamstownfilmfest.com

And for Short Films only:

- Aspen Shortsfest (Colorado) www.aspenfilm.org
- DC Shorts Film Festival (D.C.) www.dcshorts.com

Final question: For recent grads who have only made short films, how would you suggest they work their shorts so that they meet people who might help them to get financing to make a feature?

There are those shorts that are basically a short demo of what the feature film will be, and then there are shorts that the filmmaker doesn't plan to make into a feature but it's a great example of what they can do. There's nothing wrong with using the success of your short film as a conversation starter and saying, "Hey, I won the Palme d'Or in Cannes." After winning an award like that, I think anybody would be curious to see what your next work will be. And that's always the burning question—what your next work will be.

Chapter 27

The Glory

REVIEWS

In these days of instant information via texting and postings, print reviews matter less than they used to. Newspaper circulation is down, and by the time a magazine comes out, everyone pretty much knows whether or not they plan to see the movie. Are they irrelevant? No. A great review in a major paper can help focus attention on a small film. By revealing a bit about the plot, the genre, and the cast, a reviewer gives the wavering reader a little insight and can help propel him or her to get in the car or walk downtown and spend money on this film rather than another.

Raves can attract an unexpected audience by hitting a broad demographic. A series of great reviews can be a boon to filmmakers who can't afford to buy advertising or who must be very selective about the ads they do buy. There are television shows where films are reviewed, and great reviews can shine a spotlight on a film to an audience who might otherwise not know anything about it. When people hear and read the same thing over and over again, it can pick up some steam with "I heard that was a great movie" credibility. Reviews can also be useful in marketing. Quotes from important sources can be part of an overall promotional campaign.

Reviews alone don't have the power they used to pre-internet, but as part of a campaign, good press can help a lot. Online reviews, whether they are formal critiques to be found at specific websites, casual postings, or tweets, all matter. Online comments reach a fairly specific demographic and are circulated to a huge audience. If the demographic is your target group and the buzz isn't good, it can hurt. If the buzz is great, you can create demand. Marketing people spend buckets of time and money on online campaigns, using the internet as a way to raise interest and keep the burners hot, building an audience for the film while it is still in prep, production, and post, so that a crowd is anxiously awaiting the film. They want their promotional materials to be so exciting or intriguing, funny or raunchy, or just plain controversial that the targeted online audience will forward it on, creating a viral demand for information about the movie—and eventual box office for the movie.

Caution! Be sure to use only genuine review quotes, and be sure that the quotes are from people who count for something. Several years ago there was a minor scandal when it was revealed that the marketing department of a production company manufactured a person—supposedly a critic—who wrote positive reviews for several of the production company's films. The reviews appeared in blogs, were quoted, and so on. There was quite a backlash when it was discovered that it was all faked, and extremely embarrassing for the company.

PRIZES

Festival prizes are good. Big festival awards—the Grand Prize, the Audience Award—are even better. A succession of Audience Awards helps convince a distributor or sales agent that it's important to get the film out, that there is an audience waiting. No prize is bad. However, much to the shock of several filmmakers I've met, sometimes a movie is a critic's darling, but it is just not commercial. What you want from a festival is a solid distribution deal if you don't have one, and great word of mouth.

The Big Ones

There are several awards that every filmmaker should be aware of. There are the *Spirit Awards*, put on by Film Independent, the nonprofit organization that supports the work of independent filmmakers through screenings, workshops, and educational programs. The Spirit Awards ceremony, which takes place before the Academy Awards, is a more casual event than the Oscars. The ceremony takes place in a tent on a beach in Santa Monica, and although it has a red carpet, its share of major stars, and is now televised, it is considered to be looser and more fun. Members of Film Independent vote on the winners, and in addition to the usual "Best Actor, Best Actress, Best Director, Best Screenplay," etc. awards, the categories include "Best First Screenplay," "Best First Feature," the "John Casavettes Award," awarded to the best feature made for under $500,000, and the "Someone to Watch" award, given to an up-and-coming filmmaker deserving of special recognition.

There are the *Golden Globes*, put on by the Hollywood Foreign Press Association. These awards are voted on by journalists living in the United States, who write about Hollywood for the international media. There are only about one hundred members of the HFPA, but the awards are highly publicized and televised, presented at a gala event, and often predictors of the Academy Awards, so everyone pays attention to the Golden Globes.

Finally, there are the *Oscars*, the *Academy Awards*. The voters are members of the Academy of Motion Pictures Arts and Sciences. For the most part, members nominate practitioners of their own craft—Costume Designers nominate for Best Costume, for instance—and all members may nominate for Best Picture. The rules for features are complicated and precise, including the length and the release date of the film. The rules are listed on the Academy website.

A tip: at this stage in your career, the rules you may be most interested in are those for the Student Academy Awards, the Nicholl Fellowship (for screenplays), and the Best Short Subject. These may be more relevant for you for the next few years.

Awards tend to be political. Someone who has had a long and illustrious career may be voted for a Best award in part because the voters think it's time. Sometimes the actual best person or film won't win an award because the creator of the film is not liked by the Hollywood or independent community. Sometimes people may vote for someone because they broke out of whatever they usually do and took a risk that paid off. Awards are no guarantee of success. Many of the Grand Prize winners at Sundance made very little money once they were released to the regular theatre-going public.

A Student Academy Award is a wonderful thing to have on your resume, and it will get you meetings and some money, but it won't ensure success in your career. It's about what you do next—and you should always have a "next." When someone asks, "What've you got?" you should have several ideas, a couple of scripts, and a great pitch for all of them.

Chapter 28

Other Little (and Not So Little) Things That You Should Know

LOYALTY IN BUSINESS

The way you choose to deal with people affects your success in even the most practical aspects of the business. If you are going to go into production on a film, you will be working with lots of specialty vendors. There are rental houses for grip and electric equipment; specialty houses for cranes, dollies, inventive camera rigs; insert car rentals for moving vehicle shots; camera houses, film stock companies, and film labs; sound houses and post facilities; props, set dressing, and costume houses; and sound stages. Each of these vendors can be your best friends, helping a project with amazing discounts, or they can charge "book rates," the published and usually very expensive rental rates—no discounts, no special deals. How generously you are treated by vendors is usually determined by two factors:

1. How busy they are—you will not get the best deals when the town is frantically active with TV pilot season (the time, typically mid-to-late January through March, when networks and production companies are in production with the programs they hope will be picked up for the fall lineup);
2. how pleasant and professional you are to deal with.

Really. If they like you and they have the equipment available, a vendor will come through. If you are organized, appreciative, careful with whatever it is you've rented, do what you say you're going to do when you say you're going to do it, vendors will make all sorts of allowances for you. They'll help get you what you need when you have no money because they're interested in working with you as you rise up the ladder and work on bigger and bigger projects. They want to cement that relationship. Vendors have been known to give first-time filmmakers longer rentals at lower fees because they liked the filmmaker's approach and respectful manner. They can be sources of advice and can help you figure out what you really need for your shoot, rather than what you might have thought would help you get that tricky underwater shot.

If you're not professional and pleasant to deal with, they will let you fend for yourself, often to the detriment of the project and your budget.

Make Your Movie: What You Need to Know About the Business and Politics of Filmmaking.

How to Work with Vendors

1. Have a fairly solid schedule and budget. Nothing irritates a vendor more than being asked for props, set dressing, or equipment availability and negotiating a price, then receiving a call that circumstances have changed, then receiving yet another call—oops, it has changed again. Vendors quote rates based on availability and timing, and especially if they're giving you a break, you don't want to be so much trouble that they regret it. You should get an initial price quote in writing, but if your dates or circumstances change and you notify the vendor, don't be shocked if the price quote changes as well.
2. Designate the expert on your crew in each area. They should be the contacts about everything except money. (Your producer, production manager, or production coordinator are the ones who deal with the money).

   The first step is to be sure that people speaking to the vendors know what they're talking about. Usually someone in the camera department, Best Boy Grip, and Best Boy Electric decide on the equipment needs for their departments, based on the locations. Production Designers, Prop Masters, and Set Decorators decide on the best places to find what they need. Often each department will have strong feelings about which vendor is the best or the worst to use, due to past experience. It is best to send out a bid list of what is needed to three different companies. If the rental house the crew members prefer comes in with close to the best number, it's wise to go with them. If you insist that they go with the absolute cheapest alternative, you are likely to pay for it in other ways—bad feelings, complaints about the quality of the rentals, and a general "you wanted us to use this stuff, now it's your problem to solve" if things are not up to snuff.

   Once you've settled upon a rental house, the person who is in charge of the money should set up an account and work with the contact at the facility. He or she should specify in writing the system of approval for changes to the items or package rented, including who can approve changing the length of the rental period, who can approve add-ons, and who has authority regarding any kind of payment.
3. If you are handling the money and negotiations start with, "We're a very low-budget independent," not with "We have x dollars," be sure that the price you are being quoted includes everything and that there will be no surprises.

   If you're dealing with Art or Costume department rentals, the people in those departments are responsible for doing the negotiating, and they will come back and tell you what they've worked out and how it fits into their budget.
4. Once the order for equipment or set dressing is finalized, a date and time for the pick up and load in of the equipment should be set.
5. Be sure that the vendor has your Proof of Insurance Certificate well in advance of the pick up.

6. Arrange for a truck to be at the loading area, and be sure that the heads of each department knows when and where to be for the pick up. Again, Art and Costume department members usually handle this themselves and just make the production office aware of the arrangements.

   Equipment load-ins take several hours, sometimes more than a day, and involve not only the vendor's employees doing a physical check out of the equipment, but your crew physically checking whatever is rented to be sure that both lists—their list and your crew members' list—are in synch and that the rentals are in good shape. If something is defective, missing, or damaged, this is the time when your crew should speak up. The minute they leave the rental house, any loss and damage is on you and your budget.

   The same procedure should work in reverse once you've wrapped production. The people who have handled the equipment all along should be the ones who physically return it and stay until it's examined and checked in by the vendor. Your crew members should return to the production office with a checklist of all returned equipment and information about anything that may result in loss and damage charges down the line.

   Once everything is reviewed, any deposits you left with the vendor should be returned to you fairly promptly—certainly within a couple of weeks.
7. Thank the vendors who helped you. In writing. Budget for wrap presents. They don't have to be big—a couple of bottles of wine or a gift basket. If there are crew T-shirts or souvenirs, send them a few. Invite the people who helped you to a screening. Remember that they don't owe you any sort of discount, they are doing you a favor.
8. The next time you have the opportunity to rent goods or equipment, remember who helped you and try to give them the business. You may not get the same deal. Circumstances change. Also, you may have a bigger budget the second or third time around. Don't lowball the vendors who helped you. When you have a little more money, pay a little more.

In your career in production you will be working at many budgetary levels. If you are generous when you can be and professional and grateful when you can't be, vendors will go out of their way to make you a friend.

Chapter 29

Remember What Mom Taught You

ETHICS AND PERSONAL LOYALTY

We started this conversation by addressing your passion. It's easy to let yourself be swept away by that passion and be convinced that doing the right thing is old-fashioned. We hear stories about what an S.O.B. so-and-so is, and how so-and-so goes through assistants and staff like a shredder through old papers. It can lead you to believe that being the nice guy or girl is not the way to go. You'd be wrong. It's a people business, and many agreements move ahead without contracts precisely because there is an assumed level of trust between players. Your word must be worth something. Don't agree to take anything on but then decide you're too busy to do it right. Play by the rules but know those rules better than anyone else and play as intelligently and as passionately as you can without resorting to bad behavior. You may not end up with everything you want in the exact timeframe that you want it, but if you're good *and* good to be around, you'll advance.

The minute you have moved up in any way, help someone else, maybe the new intern, assistant, or PA. If you see them doing something wrong, pull them aside and politely and quietly give them some help. And keep the fact that you did it confidential. If you're working on a film and there's a chance to "feather" your expenses, even if it seems like a trivial matter (extra gas mileage money, for example), and even if you can rationalize it because everybody does it and you're being paid so little—forget it. If you cheat, that's who you become in everyone's mind, no matter how low the stakes.

This doesn't mean you can't be absolutely determined to get your movie made or rise up in the ranks. It means that there is a honorable way to conduct yourself and a dishonorable way, and sometimes it will be easier to shift towards the shady side. Once you make a very bad judgment call, it is almost impossible to recover.

And don't discuss anyone else's bad luck or personal business. You may not know the whole story, and even if you do know all the dirt, how does it serve anyone to spread mean-spirited news?

Cautionary Tale: A crowd of production people were having dinner on location. The name of a legendary Line Producer came up. The accountant on the film, who was a major gossip, casually dropped, "He's a great guy. He's not working as much as he used to, though, 'cause of his drug issues." Maybe it was true. Possibly it wasn't. Either way, that little comment reverberated around a full room of colleagues who from that moment on, had it in their minds that this guy was now an incompetent addict. It's almost guaranteed that no one will remember where they heard it, but they heard it and it would stay with them and affect their perception of this person they didn't know, hadn't worked with, and chances are they would repeat it and it would circulate around the industry. Even if the guy really had a problem, whose business was it? Certainly not the business of a bunch of people hanging around, drinking their gin and tonics, and chatting about the local scenery, none of whom were entertaining thoughts of hiring him. Not to even mention the damage done to this person if it wasn't true.

Another Cautionary Tale: An extraordinarily nice man who has helped several people I know in the Industry came down with a rare ailment that effected his sense of balance. He became a bit unsteady on his feet. Word got around that he had a drinking problem. This person didn't drink at all. When he and his doctors finally figured out what was wrong with him and he recovered, someone in the business who didn't know him very well commented that she was glad he'd got his drinking under control.

Gossip is not harmless, and a lot of it goes around. Learn to disengage without being self-righteous. Don't contribute. Next time, all that incorrect—or even accurate information that is no one's business—could be about you.

Anyone who has ever seen a juicy movie about the shark-like behavior in Hollywood will say with authority that there is no loyalty. There are angry and bitter veterans of the industry who might say the same thing, but there are all kinds of exceptions. There are hugely successful men and women in the industry who have not only maintained their artistic and personal integrity but who have demonstrated loyalty to those who have helped them along the way—whether by serving as the liaison to a deal that will enable a green light for a project, or going out of their way to recommend and even push their employment when they need a job, or by being an available advisor whether or not they were feverishly busy with their own work.

One of my mentors in the business received an anxious telephone message from me when I was supervising my first production. I had no idea he was away on vacation, and I was amazed when he called me back the next day on a ship-to-shore phone. When I thanked him about a million times for responding to my call he only said, "You sounded worried."

On the other hand, you must be a realist. A friend of mine had been extremely loyal to his assistant, hiring him on every film, insisting on this person as part of his deal. Several people had spoken to him negatively about the low quality of the assistant's work, but my friend didn't want to hear it. It got so that he even lost a job on a major film that would have given him a longer than six months run at the top of his pay rate, because the powers that be wanted him to hire a different assistant and he refused. His intentions were stellar, his loyalty unquestionable. But he was refusing to see the truth.

This assistant just wasn't very good at his job. He was lazy, had a bad attitude, didn't take care of loose ends, and in fact was hurting my friend's reputation in the business. After several months of hearing the same thing over and over again, he hired the assistant one last time. This time he really watched, and he finally saw. He had a talk with the assistant, who listened to the criticism then stomped off. The second time he had to speak with the assistant, the assistant accused my friend of being disloyal. Finally, my friend got the picture. He said, "What about your loyalty to me? Hiring you is hurting me!" The assistant argued, shouted, and eventually my friend let him go. It was a difficult decision. He was firing someone he'd thought of as a friend. Years later, remembering the whole thing, he said, "After that, I worked with a new person who was great at the job, worked his butt off, and got along with everyone. It was an incredible relief, and I realized how tense I had been, always on the defensive on my assistant's behalf. I thought I was being a good guy, but I was actually being a sucker."

Loyalty doesn't mean accepting substandard work or behavior or covering up for someone who has done something dishonest, and you should not expect anyone to cover up for you because you're a buddy. That's career—and personal—suicide.

REFERENCES

A reference is a recommendation—or not. Common sense should tell you that you should ask first if the person you are listing would feel comfortable with you giving his or her name and number or email. If they seem hesitant, go on to the next possibility. You should be sure that your references know you and your work well, and that they will give you a glowing review.

If someone asks you to be his or her reference, think it over. Better to say you're not really comfortable with it than to give either a false positive (the people who are asking you about this person are relying on the fact that you'll tell them the truth) or to be the person who shoots down someone's chances.

If, on the other hand, someone calls you for a reference not because you're a listed referee but because it's known that you've worked together on the same project, you must handle the request with tact and honesty. If you feel the person was great, say so. If you feel the requester would be better off not hiring the person, don't gossip, don't chat, and don't do a character assassination. A simple, "It didn't really work out," or "I wouldn't do it again," is fine. Don't tell stories. The person asking will get the idea. And realize that in some cases a reference that keeps someone from being hired, "He was dishonest," "She was incompetent," "He had a substance issue," is *actionable* (grounds for a lawsuit.) Whatever anyone tells you, *nothing*—not references or production news, not business news, or salaries—absolutely *nothing* is confidential.

SOONER OR LATER YOU WILL HAVE TO FIRE SOMEBODY

Unfortunately, the day will come when someone, for whatever reason, just does not work out. You'll do everything you can, explain whatever can be explained, give second chances, and it's still not going to happen the way it should. On a production, time is compressed. You hire someone quickly, based on history with the person, recommendations, or because he or she was in the right place at the right time and you had the gut instinct that this person could handle it. Now you've found that you were wrong. Things aren't going to get any better.

Before you let someone go, there are several things you should remember:

You are communicating to this person in a very primal way that he has failed. Even if the person is aware of the situation and agrees that he is in over his head, it will feel awful. Don't fire someone without a warning. Don't fire anyone in front of a group of people, no matter how angry you are. Don't berate someone while you are firing them. Once the decision has been made to let someone go, do it privately. If he's done something really bad or dishonest, be sure that someone else is in the room with the two of you—someone senior to both of you. Make it quick and final. If the person hasn't done anything terrible but just isn't good at the job, maybe you can arrange for some kind of severance. You can reassure the person that you will not give him a bad reference if someone calls. You can always say that he is a good person, it just wasn't the right job for him, and stick to that. Your words will echo over and over in this person's head for days, weeks, maybe years. Make it as painless as you can.

SOONER OR LATER YOU WILL GET FIRED

Being fired is devastating. If you are the least bit insecure you will take it personally. At the same time, there are very few people in the Industry—and even fewer on the production side—who have not been fired at least once in their career. Why is this?

Everyone is under pressure to achieve, whether it's to excel at a studio or production company, to work well on set during shooting or in post. Pressure brings out the worst in most people. When something goes wrong or doesn't turn out as planned, it is easier to look for someone to blame than to be philosophical and say, "Oh well, next time . . ." Sometimes errors *are* someone's fault, and there is the fear that the errors will be repeated. Or sometimes a person will just get on someone's nerves, and the tightly wound person with the power doesn't want to deal with that burden. My favorite reason that people get fired in the film business is because someone else, the previously unavailable person that an executive or a director originally wanted to hire, suddenly becomes available, and so due to no fault of their own it's out with the old and in with the new.

During preproduction and production everyone is in a hurry. There is not much time for learning on the job. When a mistake is made, the guillotine can fall quickly. People are frequently fired on films, and sometimes for reasons that seem petty and unreasonable. If you screwed up, you can learn from it and never again do whatever it was you did. If you didn't screw up and it was a personality thing, all you can do is figure out if how to recognize and avoid working for the same kind of person again. If you are fired a few times, it's probably not that you were the helpless victim. You've got to figure out what you keep doing wrong.

SOME FINAL CAUTIONARY TALES

Dennis, a production assistant, did things very slowly. The production coordinator would send him out for a run, and it would take forever. He'd be asked to pick up lunch down the street, and he'd be gone for hours. He was a talker. Everyone else would be working, and Dennis would be talking. He was spoken to after week one, and it was clear that he thought he was doing a terrific job. He was fired at the end of week two. He was not a bad guy. He just didn't get it.

Jessie was a production office secretary who spent more time hanging with her new boyfriend, who was the Director of Photography, than she did taking care of the intricate travel arrangements that are part of doing a film on location. She messed up a few airport pick-ups, booked someone who was contractually flying first-class in coach, and generally didn't pay attention. Jessie was not technically fired, because the producer and director didn't want to upset the DP, but an office PA was elevated to her job, and she was relegated to answering the phone. The entire production office staff, previously her prime source of employment, was so irritated with her they didn't work with her again.

A production accountant, for whatever reason, kept falling behind in his cost reports. That meant that the daily decisions the Line Producer and UPM made were based on old information. The accountant worked "normal" hours—from about 8:00 am until about 7:00 pm—and he didn't stay late a few days to catch up. He was tired. He was overwhelmed. He was a nice guy who was used to working on smaller films, and he just wasn't ready for a big project.

A Production Manager acted superior and officious to the shooting crew, as if he were the CEO and they were, as they put it, "the cleaning service." He was snippy to them, clearly saw most of them as manual labor, didn't care much about the overlong hours, the cold, wet weather, or the unappetizing catering. The crew seethed quietly. They waited for their moment. The crew was comprised of union veterans. They were all aware that this was a low-budget film. Many of them had made the concession of lowering their pay rates when they were hired. It was slow in town, and they needed the work. They were beginning to regret it. To their way of thinking, the film might have had no money, but appreciation and respect didn't cost a thing.

At the end of the third consecutive very long day, the UPM made a decision that betrayed his lack of knowledge of union rules. Had they liked this guy, the Key Grip, who served as spokesman for the crew, would have informed him that he was making a decision that would cost the film over $20,000 and gain the production only one hour in lost shooting time. But they didn't like him, and so he said nothing. Someone in the production office heard what was going on and was concerned enough to call the Production Manager and mention the mistake. The UPM said, "I've been doing this a long time. I know the rules." He stuck to his guns.

The next day, a late model Mercedes came careening in to the parking area and a furious production executive came slamming out. He grabbed the Production Manager, pulled him into a trailer, and for the next 15 minutes all the crew heard was the sound of one angry voice. As the executive stormed off the set, he turned for one final salvo, "This would never have happened if they'd liked you," he said.

Who knows how the executive knew that? But there are no secrets, and for one more uncomfortable week of shooting until the wrap, it was a tense and awkward set. The UPM never worked on a film for the production company again.

On the corporate side there are too many easy examples of "don'ts":

There are the executives who treat their assistants in an ugly way. Years later the assistant moves on and up, and soon the assistant is an executive and now is his or her former boss's boss. This is not an unusual situation. It's also not unusual for the former assistant to get even.

An executive has an affair with his assistant, gives her all sorts of privileges, then breaks up with her. The daily presence of the assistant now makes the executive uneasy. He fires her. She sues the studio. The studio makes a settlement. The executive is considered too valuable to dump at the time, but then there are a couple of bad calls and he's toast. The unfortunate part of the story is that the assistant can't get a job in the Industry because she's now known as someone who sued a studio—and potential employers think, "who wants that kind of grief?"

Not a pretty picture. Yes, people who work closely together in a business that sometimes blurs the boundaries between professional and social activities have a tendency to bond. And sharing long, late hours, and high drama can be exciting and sexy. And the industry is full of intelligent, attractive people. But try not to fool around in your own backyard. If you do, at least refrain from "breaking rank." It's not as big a deal when an assistant is dating an assistant or if a middle management type is dating another mid-level exec. It's when two people cross that line and one has much more power than the other that first gossip, then resentment, and finally lawsuits often happen. Sadly, as most film people are romantics who want to believe in the happily ever after, these things usually end badly.

Chapter 30

Now What?

IT'S OK TO LEAVE . . .

Something has happened at work. You stepped away for a minute to use the bathroom, and voice mail picked up a call from someone your boss has been waiting to hear from, and when you give him the message he says, "Where *were* you?"—as if he doesn't know that for the past four years you've been virtually chained to your desk unless you're making arrangements for his dry cleaning or interviewing prospective nannies for his kids while his wife is at her yoga class.

Or someone has done something really unseemly and crass, but this time you can't seem to get past it, and a little voice is whispering in your ear, "Do I really want to do this any more?"

You attend your tenth high school reunion and see that your friends are doing well, buying houses, settling down, and you're thinking of your tiny one bedroom with no parking in the not-so-great neighborhood, or the house you're sharing with four other assistants or struggling directors, and something clicks. You've had it. You feel as if you're still living like a student, and for what? A movie. Just a movie.

Some day when you least expect it, when you've done everything you're supposed to be doing, paid your dues, and are carefully ascending the ladder in your chosen area of the industry, you will have a moment when you're ready to walk away. You're working your butt off, you never see your girlfriend or boyfriend or family, you can't believe that you were so thrilled when the AD whom you don't even like tells you that you did an amazing job that you called long distance and repeated the compliment to your mom—who doesn't even know what an AD does and gave you back a dutiful, "That's nice, dear." You're thinking, what am I doing?

Pretty much everyone goes through it. For some, it's a passing thought to be shrugged off or laughed at, and then it's back to work and back to feeling lucky that you're doing what you're doing rather than selling real estate or working in a corporate setting making widgets instead of movies. Some people are adrenaline junkies, and it's all about the drama and the risk-taking. For others it's knowing that each time you take on a project it will be different, and though your job may make you tear your hair out, you're not bored. When the lights in the theater dim and you're looking at your work, however critical or miniscule your contribution to the finished film, you know that you have something to do with what's up there.

You're helping to tell a story, and if you're a lover of stories there is nothing quite as exciting. You may start out by crying or kicking the wall because the business is so frustrating, so ego-driven, and can be so cruel, but then eventually for the sake of your sanity and your walls, you shake your head and learn to laugh.

Or you leave.

Sometimes it's just not worth it. I have two friends who left the film business not because they weren't successful but because they were, and once they were doing exactly what they'd dreamed of, they realized that they weren't happy.

One of them told me that she was tired of working until 10:00 pm, going home, and getting up at 6:00 am just to be back at work. "I had business breakfasts, business lunches, business drinks, and business dinners. I love to read, but the only books I read were those we were looking at possibly buying. I was spending time with all these so-called friends in the business I really didn't like, and I had no time to see my real friends. It was just business, business, movies, movies. That's all I heard and talked about. It was just too much. I had a mini-meltdown and realized, I have to get out." So she left the business and moved out of town. She's very happy. Does she miss it? "When I go out and see a film that I really love, I get a pang. It's like, I could have made that movie. But I have no regrets. I like my life."

My other friend who left the business is a bit more conflicted. "I'm glad I left. I'm much healthier now. I was not built for the movie business. I was a nervous wreck all the time. I was a freelancer, and it was always, What if the phone doesn't ring? What if I never work again? I do miss the creativity and the camaraderie of being on set. What I do now [working at an internet company] can be creative, but it's not the same. But it is better for me."

If you decide to leave the business, you will take with you skills you might not have otherwise acquired. You'll understand the process of networking and getting yourself where the opportunities can be found. If you've worked at a production company or at an agency, you'll be able to communicate with and work efficiently and effectively with a wide variety of people. If you've worked on set, you'll understand organizational hierarchy and be able to look around, size up a situation, and act appropriately. These are basic business survival skills, and they will help you wherever you go, whatever you decide to do.

AND IT'S OK TO LEAVE ... THEN COME BACK

If you miss it, you can always come back. You'll be seasoned, wiser, and no worse for the time you've been away. I've met several filmmakers who decided to take a break. Invariably when they've returned, they've found a way to view the ins and outs of the movie industry with more perspective. Some of them took a slight left turn. One went from production to development. Another moved from narrative theatrical films to documentaries. One of them went from working in development to writing and has sold his first script. Their leaves of absence helped them to get distance, to think and review, and to better understand the game. Now they're back again and ready to play.

Chapter 31

Out Takes

FINAL WORDS OF ADVICE FROM PEOPLE WHO HAVE BEEN THERE, DONE THAT

Pat Quinn, Quinn Media Management

You're at your job all day with the person who works you into the ground and makes you get their dry cleaning and makes you cry; and you really become friends with all the other assistants, with all the other assistants who are going to go on and get these incredible jobs. Go to industry events, and like any other business, get to know the names. Study the business, read *Variety* and *The Hollywood Reporter* every day. An assistant should be able to demonstrate to their boss that they're going to be out there ahead of them every day. You have to do more than what's expected. That person has to feel like they can trust you, that you're going to stay as late as they want you to stay—which will be probably when you're not getting paid overtime—and that you completely have their back and that you anticipate things.

You're an assistant at an agency, you're going into a meeting, and it's a meeting of all the assistants, and one of the agents wants to hear what you read for the weekend. You go in unprepared. You have to go in *over*prepared. You should go in with typed up notes. You should be more prepared than anybody in the room. These jobs are detail-oriented. If you don't write every single thing down, if you don't have every single thing documented, if a call came in from a buyer or a call comes in from a producer and you forget to put it down or forget what the message is but your boss finds out, by the end of the day you will be gone.

I can tell you the easy ones [mistakes assistants make]: showing up late, being slovenly, acting like you don't care, being checked out, saying you haven't done something, giving any kind of an excuse even if it's completely legitimate. If have to pick up a relative at the airport, that kind of excuse is the worst. They'll just want somebody who never has to go to the airport. You have to be a ninja-like Zen master—that's all they should feel coming from you. No personal calls. Everything has to be like, "we are the ninjas together." That's how it has to be.

Priscilla Elliott, Art Director

People people people. The business is small. Your paths will cross with the same people more often than you can imagine. You never know where someone is going to end up. People hire people who are talented and work hard, but they also hire people they want to work with . . . Best to learn as fast as you can when to speak up and when to be quiet and listen. Everyone in the film business is at least partly crazy. Embrace it.

Always speak your ideas, your concerns, but try to keep in mind the relative importance of what you are working on in terms of what is happening throughout the department. Don't be self-involved with your inspiration. Express it, but try to wait for the proper window. You will be listened to if you pay attention and hold your tongue until the proper moment. Don't cry wolf, but also don't give up. Keep thinking.

Michael Shoob, Director

If you're just starting out, you've got to be game for just about anything. You've got to be game for working hard, staying late, working long hours if you have to. You need to have a "can do" attitude. I don't want to hear excuses—why you had to be late—once maybe, but not again. You need to be prepared, and you need to be willing to do what is given to you.

Listen and be aware that you probably don't know as much as you think you do. Think of it this way: the man or woman you're working for used to be you. They were young and eager and thought they knew everything. And now they have wised up a little and know how little they actually knew back then. So, one thing that's going to irritate the hell out of them is to see you doing the exact same thing—acting cocky about what you know.

Everyone, no matter where they rank on the entertainment business food chain, must be treated with respect and courtesy. That's very important to me, because you are a reflection of me and my company. It's also something that will benefit you down the line—because, trust me, people will remember you and how you treated them when you run into them on another project or at another production company years later.

Don't be afraid to show your passion, but be aware of the temperature of the room and don't be needlessly argumentative. Your present job is an audition for your future jobs, and your reputation is always on the line.

Don't let rejection deter you.

Christopher Cronyn, Producer, UPM

Everyone loves an optimist, and you can be seduced into becoming one. But you're paid to be a realist.

Your Resume

If you are looking for a job or an internship at a production company or studio . . .

Production companies and film studios receive hundreds of resumes each week. Sometimes they are geared towards a specific position, and sometimes they are general, as in "please keep me in mind if there is anything appropriate." Even if you have direct contact with someone at a company or studio and you are encouraged to send them your resume, the resumes are almost always forwarded to the Human Resources (*HR*) department. Some will be filed for future reference, and some will be dealt with more proactively. If you have a relationship with a person who has some clout at the studio or company, it is likely that HR will call around to see if anyone needs someone in their office. This is a sign that those all-important connections are at work again.

Think of your resume as an introduction. The objective of a resume is to get you a meeting. Once you're in the meeting, it's up to you. Here are some tips for your resume that might help:

- Don't use anything but white paper and black ink.
- Use an easy to read, sans-serif font. No tiny fonts—11- or 12-point is good.
- Don't get fancy with logos, company names, trademarks, and quotes.
- Your resume should be simple, and it should be only one page.
- These days, your resume will most often be an email version rather than a hard copy, so once your resume is done, email it to a friend to be sure that your formatting holds.

Your name, phone number, and email address should be centered and in bold at the top of the page. You don't have to include your address, but if the area code for your cell phone is not local to Los Angeles (or New York, if you're looking for work in New York) you should definitely include your local L.A. or New York address. They won't call you if they think you live in Indiana.

If you are a currently enrolled student looking for an internship, your education should be the first entry on your resume, because your education is your current job. If you've graduated from college or graduate school, the education section should be the last entry on the page. Don't include your high school. It's assumed that if you went to college, you managed to graduate from high school.

Although there is some general debate about this, I would not advise you to include an objective. Your objective is to get whatever job you can find. If your objective is more specific than that, it can narrow the field of possibilities before you even get a meeting. If your objective is a vague "to learn/advance/gain experience, etc.," it's generic and boring, so why bother? Just be sure that you're ready with a good answer when you are called in for an interview and they ask you what you eventually would like to do. It is acceptable to say something like, "I love film [production/the business side/finding materials], and I'm trying to find a position where I can learn as much as possible about X"—whatever this particular job involves.

If you're looking for an entry-level position, it's great if you've had an internship with a known company. That way the first job-related item anyone sees is a recognizable industry name. This is another reason why internships are important. If you haven't had an internship, don't despair. If you've been a student all your life and haven't had any actual work experience, the key is to communicate what you know how to do. Don't list classes you've taken. No one cares about that. But if you've had any type of on-campus job, or were a TA (teaching assistant) in a department at school, or if you were the coordinator of a fraternity or a big campus event, that counts. And if you're reading this while you're still in school—get busy! It's important for you to seem enterprising. No one really cares about your GPA, although if you've been on the Dean's List or Honor Roll or received any kind of academic honors it can be mentioned, but only for about a year after you've graduated. If you've been out of school more than a year, nothing about school matters other than the fact that you have the degree.

Something to remember is not to use full sentences on your resume. Bullet points make it easier for someone looking at the resume to understand what you know and what you've done. A straightforward font and bullet points make your resume easy to read.

If you have actual production experience, be sure to list the name of the project in all caps or italics or quotation marks, so that it stands out.

Don't list hobbies. Do list languages, and definitely list your computer skills.

Finally, if you are answering an ad or posting for a particular job, companies receive thousands of resumes, and they often rely on *key words* to whittle down the pile. Be sure to echo the words and phrases used in the actual posting when you create your resume. When the posting says, "Looking for someone who is meticulous and a team player," your resume should reflect that by using phrases like "detail-oriented" and "organized groups." If the posting says, "Looking for someone creative," then your resume should have phrases like "conceived and produced," "created and assembled."

One last tip: in Western countries, we read from left to right. We are accustomed to finding the most pertinent information towards the left side of the page. Your most important information (any industry company or person's name) should be the first words, in bold, that anyone sees.

Take a look at the resumes on the next few pages. You can use them as models for your own resume.

RESUME FOR AN INTERNSHIP

Jen O'Brien
1234 Sunset Place
Los Angeles, CA 90025
(323)555-1212
jeno@XXXX.com

EDUCATION 2012	University of Santa Clarita, CA Program: BFA, Film Production Minor: Economics Expected graduation 2014 Honor Roll 2010, 2011
WORK EXPERIENCE	University Book Shop, Clerk
2011	Responsibilities: • Scheduled student workers • Reconciled cash receipt • Processed book orders for seventy classes • Tracked sales and assembled sales reports Spring Fling Coordinator • Coordinated University's 150th Anniversary celebration • Events raised $125,000 for scholarships and international programs • Worked with Events Office to recruit and organize volunteers at six campuswide galas • Worked on Public Relations Committee, helped to create posters; interfaced with vendors, photographers, and local print, radio and cable media.
2010, Summer	Clark Insurance, Springfield, MO Receptionist • Handled busy phones, greeted customers
SKILLS	Office Software: Microsoft Office, Photoshop, Adobe Production software: XXX editing software; xxx script software
LANGUAGES	Conversational Spanish

What will someone learn about Jen from this resume? That she worked while she was in school, which is always a good sign to employers. She also held some kind of front office position, which indicates that she is personable and that she is current on office software. Finally, a potential internship host can see that she has organizational skills, has at least a rudimentary sense of the media, and that she is reliable, since she was trusted to schedule work shifts and handle cash receipts. Jen looks like a pretty good bet for an internship.

If Jen is not looking for an internship but an entry-level job, all she would do is update her year of graduation and move the Education section after the Languages section at the end.

If Jen gets an industry internship, graduates, and is looking for an entry-level position, she will make the internship the first entry, as in the resume in the next section.

RESUME FOR AN ENTRY-LEVEL POSITION

Jen O'Brien
1234 Sunset Place
Los Angeles, CA 90025
(323)555-1212
jeno@XXXX.com

WORK EXPERIENCE

2012 — H&H Productions, Los Angeles, CA
Intern, Development Department

Responsibilities:
- Script coverage
- Updating agency lists
- Attending and taking notes at Creative meetings
- General Office tasks—phones, filing

2011 — University Book Shop, Clerk
Responsibilities:
- Scheduled student workers
- Reconciled cash receipts
- Processed book orders for seventy class sections
- Assembled sales reports for store manager

Spring Fling Coordinator
- Coordinated University's 150th Anniversary celebration.
- Events raised $125,000 for scholarships and international programs.
- Worked with Events Office to recruit and organize volunteers at six campus-wide galas.

- Worked on Public Relations Committee, helped to create posters; interfaced with vendors, photographers, and local print, radio and local cable media.

2010 Summer — Clark Insurance, Springfield, MO
Receptionist

- Handled busy phones, greeted customers

SKILLS — Office Software: Microsoft Office, Photoshop, Adobe
Production software: XXX editing software; xxx script software

LANGUAGES — Conversational Spanish

EDUCATION
2014 — University of Santa Clarita, CA
BFA, Film Production, Minor: Economics
Honor Roll 2010, 2011

RESUME FOR A PRODUCTION POSITION

One final type of resume that you'll want to know how to do is the production resume. This resume would work for you if you want to be on set as a PA or an entry-level production position, and it's where you would present your actual physical production knowledge.

Jen O'Brien
1234 Sunset Place Los Angeles, CA 90025
(323)555-1212
jeno@XXXX.com

FILM EXPERIENCE
2012 — H&H Productions, Los Angeles, CA
Intern, Development Department

Responsibilities included:

- Script coverage
- Updating agency lists
- Attending and taking notes at Creative meetings
- General office tasks-working executives desk, filing contracts

STUDENT FILM EXPERIENCE

Director, Producer

- Produced and directed three short films. Scheduled, budgeted, assembled shooting crew; was responsible for Location Agreements, shooting permits.

ADDITIONAL PROFESSIONAL EXPERIENCE

2011 University Book Shop, Clerk

- Scheduled student workers, reconciled cash receipts
- Processed book orders for seventy class sections
- Assembled sales reports for store manager

Spring Fling Coordinator

- Coordinated University's 150th Anniversary celebration.
- Events raised $125,000 for scholarships and international programs. Worked with Events Office to recruit and organize volunteers at six campus-wide galas.
- Worked on Public Relations Committee, helped to create posters; interfaced with vendors, photographers, and local print, radio and local cable media.

2010 Clark Insurance, Springfield, MO
Summer Receptionist

SKILLS Microsoft Office, Photoshop, xx Production Software,
xx editing software, Xscript software, XXcamera

LANGUAGES Conversational Spanish

EDUCATION

2014 University of Santa Clarita, CA
BFA, Film Production, Minor: Economics

As you accumulate production credits, everything moves down and you will soon be able to drop the Receptionist and Spring Fling experience, as you won't need them. When you add production credits to your resume they should appear as:

2013 *SAND DOGS*, [Name of studio or production company]
Key Set PA

UPM: Name of UPM
First Assistant Director: Name of First AD
Second Assistant Director: Name of Second AD

If you were an Art Department PA, you would use the same format but list the names of the Production Designer, the Art Director, and the Art Department Coordinator, if there was one.

If you were an assistant to the Director of the Producer, you would include:

2013 *SAND DOGS*, [Name of studio or production company],
Assistant to Producer, [Name of Producer]
Responsibilities included:

Then go on to bullet point your responsibilities as you did in earlier versions of the resume.

Remember that the entire point of a resume is to get you a meeting, so any names, companies, or projects that your potential next employer will immediately recognize, or any names that he or she can immediately call for a reference, give you that much more credibility.

Index

Note: Page numbers followed by '*b*' indicate boxes.

D

T

U